The Work of Sir Gilbert Scott

The Work
of
Sir Gilbert Scott

David Cole

The Architectural Press · London

First Published in 1980 by the
Architectural Press Limited London

ISBN: 0 85139 723 9

Printed in Great Britain by Biddles Ltd,
Martyr Road, Guildford, Surrey from
composition by Alacrity Phototype-
setters, Banwell Castle, Weston-super-
Mare, Avon

Contents

1	Parson's Son, 1811-35	1
2	Scott and Moffatt, 1835-44	8
3	Church Architect, 1844-51	35
4	Success, 1851-56	54
5	Man of Business, 1856-59	69
6	Restorer, 1859-64	88
7	Public Figure, 1864-72	126
8	*Viri Probi Architecti Peritissimi*, 1872-78	158

Epilogue 182

Notes 185

Appendix 1   Sources 201

Appendix 2   Architectural Works 205

Appendix 3   General specification of works required
to be done in the Proposed Restoration of
Barnstaple Church 229

Appendix 4   Assistants and Pupils 232

Appendix 5   Clerks of Works 236

Index 237

Acknowledgments

This book can only give a partial survey of the immense industry of Sir Gilbert Scott's office. Perhaps a complete and documented account is in the future. But if the present work makes Scott better known, this will be a small achievement. Meanwhile, the assistance of very many over the years is most gratefully acknowledged. My wife Olive has drawn all the plans. Battersea District Library has faced the strangest requests with no surprise. The London Library, Guildhall Library, the British Library, the Public Record Office, and libraries at Bath, Brighton, Bromley, Dover, Guildford, Kensington, and Tunbridge Wells have all been helpful. The material at the Royal Institute of British Architects has of course been quite invaluable. So has the National Monuments Record. The interest taken in Scott by the Victoria and Albert Museum is quite heartening.

Anna Dickens helped with the workhouses. Julian Litten is a fellow labourer in the same field. Jean Curtis, Beryl Freeman and Mary Nethercote have typed many drafts over the years. The following have all given assistance in various ways at some time: Rev. P. Ashley Brown, the County Archivist, Buckinghamshire, the late Canon B. F. L. Clarke (whom one remembers with particular gratitude), Clwyd County Planning Office, Les Connell, Dr Roger Dixon, Rev. D. Eastman, East Sussex County Council, Patsy Fagan, Peter Ferriday, Jim Franks, Dr Mark Girouard, Rev. Harold Godwin, the County Archivist, Hereford and Worcester, Elizabeth Hoare, Professor Patrick Horsbrugh, Katherine Jervis, Paul Joyce, J. K. Knight, Rev. Canon Geoffrey Lawn, Col. A. H. Maude, Allan Miles, Frank Noble, V. W. Oubridge, Rev. A. C. P. Payne, Rev. L. F. Peltor, C. J. Pickford, Sir Nikolaus Pevsner, A. Price, R. M. Robbins, Silvia Robinson, A. Sartin, the late C. M. O. Scott, Richard Scott, Harold Smith, Sir John Summerson, W. H. Smith and Son Ltd., Michael Snodin, Gavin Stamp, Dr. Phoebe Stanton, Stratton and Holborow, Eric Tansley, the late Lt.-Com. Frank Theodore, Dr. Paul Thompson, Ian Toplis, Michael Trinick, Sir Ralph Verney, C. R. St. Q. Wall, Joan Walley, Walton Hall Hotel, Marcus Whiffen, and J. F. White.

List of Plates

1 Sir Gilbert Scott in 1869, aged 58
2 House for Henry Rumsey, Chesham 1834
3 Fishmongers' Hall, City of London
4 Tavistock Poor Law Institution, 1838
5 Guildford Union Workhouse, 1838
6 Dunmow Poor Law Institution, 1838
7 Windsor Poor Law Institution
8 Amersham Poor Law Institution, 1838
9 Clifton Pauper Lunatic Asylum, York, 1845
10 Weston Turville Rectory, about 1838
11 St Blazey, restored 1839
12 Martyrs' Memorial, Oxford, 1841-3
13 St Nicholas, Lincoln, 1839-40
14 Holy Trinity, Shaftesbury, 1842
15 Holy Trinity, Shaftesbury — interior
16 Turnham Green, 1841-3
17 Chudleigh Kingston, 1841-2
18 St Giles, Camberwell, exterior of old church burned in 1841
19 St Giles, Camberwell, interior of old church
20 St Giles, Camberwell, 1842-4
21 St Giles, Camberwell
22 Woking, St John Baptist, 1842
23 Zeals, 1845-6
24 Abergwili, 1843
25 Abergwili, interior
26 Chesterfield, restored 1842-3
27 St Mary, Stafford, view in 1806 before restoration
28 St Mary, Stafford, as restored 1842-5
29 St Mary, Stafford
30 Wasperton, altered 1843
31 St Nicholas, Hamburg, 1845-80
32 Barnet, Christ Church parsonage, about 1845
33 Newfoundland Cathedral, 1847 on
34 Alderney, 1850, a contemporary view

35 Bradfield, restored 1847-8
36 Bradfield
37 Harrow. Church restored 1846-9: chapel, 1855-6:
   Vaughan Library, 1861-3
38 Aylesbury, restored 1850 on
39 Ely Cathedral
40 Ely Cathedral
41 Ely Cathedral
42 Ely Cathedral
43 Westminster Abbey, reredos, 1867
44 Westminster Abbey
45 Westminster Abbey
46 Resurrection, Longton
47 Trefnant, 1855
48 Trefnant
49 All Souls, Halifax, 1856-9
50 All Souls, Halifax
51 Camden Chapel, Camberwell, altered 1854
52 Eastnor, restored 1852
53 Newark, restored 1852-5
54 Hampton Lucy, addition, about.1857
55 Shinfield, restored 1855-6
56 Shinfield
57 St George, Doncaster, old church
58 St George, Doncaster, 1853-8
59 Hereford Cathedral, screen, 1862
60 Lichfield Cathedral, interior, restored 1855 on
61 Hamburg Town Hall, competition entry, 1855
62 Halifax, Akroydon, 1851
63 Harrow, Vaughan Library, 1861-3
64 Kelham Hall 1858-62
65 Kelham Hall
66 Kelham Hall
67 Walton Hall 1858-62
68 Westminster, Government Offices, 1862
69 Leafield, 1858-60
70 Oxford, Exeter College Chapel, 1857-9
71 Oxford, Exeter College Chapel
72 Albourne, restored 1859
73 Englefield, restored 1859

74 St Alban, Wood Street, London, altered 1855-6
75 Salisbury Cathedral
76 Salisbury Cathedral
77 Chester Cathedral
78 Chester Cathedral
79 Chester Cathedral
80 Chichester Cathedral
81 Chichester Cathedral
82 Ripon Cathedral
83 Pershore Abbey
84 Brecon Priory
85 St David's Cathedral
86 St David's Cathedral
87 Worcester Cathedral
88 Stoke Talmage, restored 1861
89 St Hilary, restored 1861-2
90 Hawkhurst, 1859-61
91 Hawkhurst
92 Hawkhurst
93 Muswellbrook, 1863-9
94 Muswellbrook
95 Edvin Loach, 1859
96 Sherbourne, 1862-4
97 Sherbourne
98 Sherbourne
99 Leith, 1862-6
100 Leith parsonage, about 1862
101 Kensington, Albert Memorial, 1864-71
102 Leeds Infirmary, 1864-7
103 Preston Town Hall, 1862-7
104 Godstone, restored about 1872
105 St John, Leeds
106 Sarratt, restored 1866
107 Fleet Marston, restored 1868-9
108 Buckingham, restored 1860-7
109 Norton, restored about 1868
110 Latimer, addition 1867
111 Westminster Abbey, Chapter House
112 Westminster Abbey and Chapter House prior to 1864
113 Westminster Abbey, Chapter House

114 St Asaph Cathedral
115 Lincoln Cathedral
116 St Leonard, Ludlow, 1870-1
117 Mirfield, 1869-71
118 Kensington, St Mary Abbots, 1870-2
119 St Mary's Homes, Godstone
120 Savernake hospital, 1871-2
121 Brill's Baths, Brighton, about 1874
122 St Pancras Station, 1866-76
123 St Pancras Station
124 St Pancras Station
125 Holborn, Law Courts, design 1867
126 Dundee, Albert Institute, 1865-9
127 Glasgow University, 1867
128 Berlin, Parliament House
129 All Saints, Gloucester, 1875
130 Bombay University, hall, 1876
131 Edinburgh Cathedral, 1874-80
132 London, Lincoln's Inn Buildings 1875
133 Clarkson Monument, Wisbech, 1879
134 Exeter Cathedral
135 Rochester Cathedral
136 Tewkesbury Abbey
137 Tewkesbury Abbey
138 Oxford, New College Chapel, altered about 1877

1
Parson's Son,
1811-35

At the time of his death in 1878 Sir Gilbert Scott was widely regarded as the most successful architect of the 19th century. His Foreign Office, St Pancras Station, and Albert Memorial, which last earned him his knighthood, stand among the towering monuments of Victorian architecture, and over 800 other buildings were designed or altered by his hand. He restored many of the most important mediaeval buildings of England and did much to enhance public consciousness of old English architecture. Yet Scott, who did as much as any man to shape the face of Victorian England, has not received the serious consideration he richly deserves.

Scott claimed descent from John Baliol, King of Scotland, but more recent generations were of humbler stock. His great-grandfather, John Scott (1701-77) of Bratoft, Lincolnshire, was a grazier and had thirteen children; Thomas the tenth, born in 1747, was the grandfather of the architect.

Thomas Scott, after brief apprenticeship to a surgeon apothecary, and nine years of misery working for his father, by perseverance took holy orders and became curate of Stoke Goldington and Weston Underwood in Buckinghamshire.[1] He taught himself Hebrew, and devoted himself to a study of the Scriptures. After other curacies he moved in 1785 to London, becoming joint-chaplain at the Lock Hospital, a refuge for women with venereal disease. Two years later he began to prepare a commentary, 'The Bible, with Explanatory Notes', which eventually ran to 174 serial numbers, published from 1788-92. With the bankruptcy of his publisher, Scott lost all his money, and only much later were his affairs ordered, bringing him £2000. Meanwhile, as a result of his youthful privations, he suffered ill health, taking in 1802 the living of Aston Sandford in Buckinghamshire, where he died in 1821. By his first wife Jane Kell he had seven children: three surviving sons all went to university and took holy orders; one daughter married a clergyman.[2]

He was influential in the Church Missionary Society, and was connected with the 'Clapham Sect', a body of wealthy Evangelicals including Henry Thornton, John Venn, William Wilberforce, James Stephen, and J. W. Cunningham, for fifty years the militant incumbent at Harrow. They lived around the then rural Clapham Common, insisting upon the doctrine of salvation by faith and attracting the ire of most clergy, who considered their proselytising zeal and uncompromising beliefs bad form. Gilbert Scott remembered his grandfather as a formidable, learned, and upright gentleman retaining archaic dress, and greatly respected as 'The Commentator'.[3]

John, the eldest son, began a Scott family dynasty as vicar of St Mary, Hull. Benjamin, the youngest, died in 1830 as vicar of Bidford on Avon, Warwickshire.

Gilbert Scott's father, another Thomas, was born at Weston Underwood in 1780. He attended Queen's College, Cambridge, and became in 1805 curate at Emberton, near Olney. He married in 1806 the Antigua-born Euphemia Lynch, the niece of the rector of Bledlow, Nathaniel Gilbert. The Gilberts had strong Wesleyan connections and numbered among their forbears Sir Humphrey Gilbert, the half-brother of Sir Walter Raleigh. Euphemia, reared in London, was disappointed by the simplicity of her marriage, and feared her father-in-law. She brought up her children with a thorough regard for propriety and nicety.

Gilbert Scott remembered his father as 'in his way very much a man of the world.... He was the farthest possible from being a sanctimonious man, and, although he made religion his primary object and guide he did not bring it to the front or parade it in the least degree so as to give offence to others. He was a peculiarly gentlemanly man, ready and well fitted for any society, and as much at home with men of rank as with his equals or inferiors. He was also a man of especially popular manners, thoroughly genial, merry, and courteous in all companies and to all comers .... I often witnessed, with admiring wonder, my father's gentlemanly address when he met with persons of a higher station, so superior to what we young villagers could ever hope to attain to.'[4]

In 1806 Thomas became perpetual curate of Gawcott, two miles from Buckingham. He fathered thirteen children, of whom three or four died in infancy. The details of the family are not entirely certain. Thomas, the eldest, won a classical scholarship at university and entered the Church, eventually succeeding his father, in plurality, as rector of Wappenham. John, the third child, went to Cambridge, becoming successively rector of Tydd St Giles and of Wisbech, and an honorary canon of Ely Cathedral. George Gilbert, the future architect, born in 1811, was the fourth child.

One son, Nathaniel Gilbert, died at the age of sixteen. The seventh son, William Langston, also took holy orders and the ninth child, Euphemia, married her cousin John Henry Oldrid, later vicar of Alford and Boston in Lincolnshire. Samuel, the eleventh child, practised medicine in Brighton until his death in 1865. The youngest son, Melville Horne, born in 1827, won a scholarship to Caius College, Cambridge, entered the Church and became archdeacon of Stafford and canon of Lichfield.[5]

Thus George Gilbert Scott grew up surrounded by Evangelical clerics, in an atmosphere of well-bred, but impoverished, gentility in a village full of eccentric natives, inviting comparison with the Shinfield of Miss Mitford's contemporary *Our Village*. He never attended school, and felt himself uneducated. His father was too preoccupied with young men intent on taking orders to have much time for him. He later wrote: 'Though I have reason to be most thankful for my success in life, the defects of my education have been like a millstone about my neck, and have made me almost dread superior society.'[6]

Scott received much training from a drawing master, a Mr Jones from Buckingham, apparently a thoroughly competent teacher who, as a protégé of the family at Stowe, had studied at the Royal Academy. Stowe itself, four miles away, a treasury of work by the best classical architects of the 18th century, the Scotts occasionally visited. Scott studied the Gothic village churches at Maids Moreton, Tingewick, Chetwode, and especially Hillesden, a Perpendicular church of 1493, where he would meet Jones for a lesson. In 1824 Scott made a trip to London which included Westminster Abbey.

His great interest in these old churches suggested to his father, himself responsible for the design of Gawcott church and parsonage, that he should become an architect. In 1826, at fourteen, he went for a year to his uncle Samuel King at Latimer, receiving instruction mainly in mathematics, including mechanics and trigonometry, but also in Classical architecture, based upon Chambers and on Stuart and Revett.[7] King, 'an excellent astronomer, and perhaps the best amateur ornamental turner in the Kingdom, a glass painter, brassfounder, and a devotee of natural science in many forms',[8] had a knowledge of historical architecture, and gave Scott his own sketchbook, the first in a series of over 120.

Meanwhile, enquiries were pursued for an architect of religious habits with whom Scott could serve the customary four years as an articled pupil. This proved difficult until 'the travelling agent to the Bible Society' recommended James Edmeston, Senior, to whom Scott was articled about 1827, living with his master at Homerton and working at his office in Bishopsgate Street.

Edmeston was at that time aged thirty-five, of a religious bent, a Dissenter, and possessed of a good library, some culture and possibly also a private income. His practice embraced, to Scott's dismay, houses at Hackney, but to Edmeston the cost of Gothic architecture was prohibitive. He had tried it once at a dissenting chapel at Leytonstone, but 'the very cementing of the exterior had amounted to a sum which he named with obvious dismay'.[9]

There were compensations. Edmeston was an agreeable companion, 'a most superior man in everything but his own professional work, viewed in its artistic aspect'.[10] Scott learned much, read books, mostly on Classical architecture, and drew in the evenings. He used Nicholson's pattern book[11], taught himself perspective, and attended at Furnival's Inn the classes of the well-known drawing master and architectural draughtsman George Maddox, where he met with a variety of young men. Scott found Maddox 'a man of real ability with a wonderful power of drawing', though he was 'an infidel, and his conversation on such subjects was truly appalling'.[12]

Scott met many other architectural pupils during his time with Edmeston. About 1829 a builder who had taken a contract under Edmeston induced him to receive his son, the seventeen-year old William Bonython Moffatt, an intelligent but uneducated native of Cornwall, who had been trained as a joiner. Scott helped to instruct him in drawing, and persuaded him to take lessons with Maddox.

In addition to other slack periods there were long Christmas and summer holidays. At both times of the year there were opportunities to travel and to sketch. The young Gilbert thought it unexceptional, in June 1830, to walk to Gawcott by way of St Albans, Cambridge, Ely, Northampton and Geddington, where he sketched the Eleanor Crosses, a total journey of well over 150 miles: his sketchbook of the tour still exists.[13] Shorter periods of holiday were spent sketching around London: the Old Palace at Westminster had not yet been burned, nor the Houses of Parliament erected. Old London Bridge still stood: the mediaeval Southwark Cathedral largely remained.

In March 1831, Scott's four years' articles expired, and he returned to his uncle King at Latimer for a month. In April he sketched details of the great cruciform friary at Kings Langley, whose foundations were then being dug up.[14] His cousin Caroline Oldrid, to whom he had become attracted, was at Latimer, but Scott had to leave the Chiltern spring to return to a cold and snowy Gawcott, remembering his mother's warning against 'sentiments', for he knew it might be years before he could support a wife. After a brief stay with his eldest brother, he set out for Hull to stay with his uncle John Scott, and for the first time saw and sketched Gothic churches at Peterborough, York, Selby, and Beverley.

Scott returned to London in the autumn, concerned to shape his career. Many introductions to architects and others led only to good advice: so having met Samuel Morton Peto, apparently at Maddox's, he took an unpaid position with Grissell and Peto, a leading contracting firm, in order to have the run of their establishment. He was posted to the Hungerford Market,[15] then under construction, a thoroughly modern and fireproof building of iron, granite, York stone, and tiles in cement, perhaps the best work of its designer, Charles Fowler. This was a marked contrast with Edmeston's practice, and Scott eagerly assisted in measuring, copying extracts from specifications, and took ample opportunity to admire Fowler's working drawings.[16] After a time Scott's interest in pricing began to irk Peto, and he needed to earn money, so in 1832 he took a position as the only assistant to Henry Roberts.

The twenty-eight years old Roberts, a 'gentlemanly, religious, precise, and quiet man'[17] of independent means, had worked for some years for Sir Robert Smirke, the most successful architect of the early 19th century, whose output consisted largely of well-constructed but dull and often unscholarly buildings. Roberts had imbibed Smirke's modes of construction and method of making working drawings, and had recently won the appointment as architect to the new Livery Hall of the Fishmongers' Company, a class of building peculiar to the City of London, for a site adjacent to the then new London Bridge. Scott prepared all the working drawings, superintended the work, and helped measure the extras and omissions until early 1834, when Roberts appointed him as clerk of works to, probably, the Collegiate School at Camberwell, an arrangement Scott described as 'much more beneficial to myself than to the building'[18] which indeed lasted only some twenty-five years.

During this time Scott made some steps into the world. He listened to Parliamentary debates in St Stephen's Hall, hearing the eloquence of Peel or 'the quaint absurdities of old Cobbett'.[19] In 1832 he exhibited a 'West View of Louth Church, Lincolnshire' at the Royal Academy,[20] his first of some forty-eight submissions, and attended a course of Sir John Soane's lectures there. His first competition entry, in the Gothic style, was probably that for the King Edward VI Grammar School in Birmingham, lost to the entry of Charles Barry.

His father, now not in good health, received preferment in 1833 to the living of Wappenham, eleven miles north of Gawcott. The rectory was in an extreme state of dilapidation, and Thomas Scott sent for his son to undertake a survey.[21] The upshot was that the widow of the previous incumbent had to pay £1500 to Thomas Scott on account of the rectory's disrepair, and as a new building was needed, Gilbert Scott supplied 'a very ugly design, founded on one of Mr Roberts' plans',[22] which the builder altered for the worse, though it survives as a good Georgian-type house in red-brick. Also, Henry Rumsey commissioned him to design a house in Chesham to be built by local tradesmen, and Scott named Moffatt, who had left Edmeston before the expiration of his articles, as the clerk of works, which task he carried out efficiently but tactlessly. These two houses were Gilbert Scott's first works.

At the end of his time with Roberts, about September 1834, Scott took an extended holiday which included a sketching tour, after which he intended to set up in practice. About Christmas, however, he received a letter from his architect friend Sampson Kempthorne[23] urging him to take the vacant chambers next his in Carlton Chambers, Regent Street, and offering employment in assisting with union workhouses.

1834 brought Edwin Chadwick's Poor Law Amendment Act, which reversed previous policy and removed paupers into institutions rather than providing outdoor relief. A need for many more poor law institutions or workhouses to serve the 'unions', or groups of parishes formed for the purpose, became evident. Kempthorne came from Gloucester, and his father was a friend of a Poor Law Commissioner.[24] He was accordingly given the task of preparing designs for workhouses to be recommended to the boards of guardians of the unions for adoption. Scott, who had accepted Kempthorne's offer of work, thought those prepared 'of the meanest possible character, and very defective in other particulars'.[25]

Scott had worked there for less than two months when news came that his father had died, aged fifty-four. He was the eldest of six children remaining without a settled career. He acted upon his resolution to enter practice, left Kempthorne, wrote to influential friends of his father's to solicit patronage, and touted for the appointment of architect to workhouses in the area where his father had been known, with some success. Several small works and four workhouses came his way.

2
Scott and Moffatt, 1835-44

At the age of twenty-four, Scott had set up in practice, at a time when competition between persons calling themselves 'architect' was intense and clients, from ignorance or malice, were ready to exploit the situation. Many of the resultant cheap buildings of this decade, some of them Scott's, survive. Scott worked hard to establish himself.

'For weeks I almost lived on horseback, canvassing newly formed unions. Then alternated periods of close, hard work in my little office at Carlton Chambers, with coach journeys, chiefly at night, followed by meetings of guardians, searching out of materials, and hurrying from union to union.'[1] He employed one clerk and Moffatt, invited to help with his early working drawings, did so 'with the utmost diligence and efficiency'.[2] When work on the four Northamptonshire unions began, Moffatt moved temporarily out as site architect: he had also made the acquaintance of a magistrate, who got him appointed as architect to Amesbury workhouse in Wiltshire, and these drawings were done in Scott's office. Moffatt proposed a working arrangement based upon their seeking work in different areas and doing the drawings in Scott's office, foreshadowing their formal partnership from 1838-45.

Accordingly Moffatt with Scott's assistance cultivated Devon and Cornwall; Scott retained his personal practice and sought commissions in the East Midlands. The work was arduous and the few existing railways were of little help; most journeys had to be made by coach. Nevertheless, the two young men enjoyed the ceaseless excursions, the broken rest, and the odd hours. They produced over fifty workhouses during 1835-45.

Official figures[3] released ten years later show the progress of the Poor Law Institution programme:

TABLE 1

	No. built	Accom.	Cost	Cost per head	Cost per Poor Law Institution
1836	127	36,056	£659,154	£18.28	£5190
1837	86	21,132	£403,342	£19.09	£4690
1838	92	20,862	£404,179	£19.37	£4393
1839	18	4425	£87,917	£19.87	£4884
	323	82,475	£1,554,592	—	—

(the last two columns and the totals are computed)

Almost all the work was concentrated into the years 1836-39. Scott and Moffatt's contribution was about fifteen per cent of the total. The customary fee was 5% of the cost of the work: perhaps they did not always get this, though they were paid £473 19s in the first two months of 1839 alone.[4] There is a dearth of material about these buildings, and Scott's early records were destroyed.[5]

The early buildings were often based upon Kempthorne's standard plans, and everything was intentionally unattractive as the official intention was strongly to discourage the pauper from claiming relief.

The typical plan, modelled on Bentham's 'panopticon' prison system, enabled the master to survey from a central position all the courts of the building and the entrances to the work sheds. Accommodation for able-bodied paupers, the infirm, the aged, harmless lunatics and imbeciles, mothers and infants, the sick, children, and vagrants was provided in a block, cruciform or Y-shaped, cheap to build and to supervise. This was contrary to the suggestions of the Commissioners in 1834, that four main sorts of accommodation should be provided separately for able-bodied men, children, the aged and infirm, and able-bodied women. Even where the planning provided this separation, it was usual to make one building of the whole. In practice, it was found advisable to segregate vagrants, to isolate contagious diseases, and to separate the schools and the 'receiving wards' from the main body. Thus many of the workhouses underwent considerable alteration within a few years: Windsor, one of Scott's more luxurious buildings, was about to undergo alterations to the infirmary less than six years after its erection.

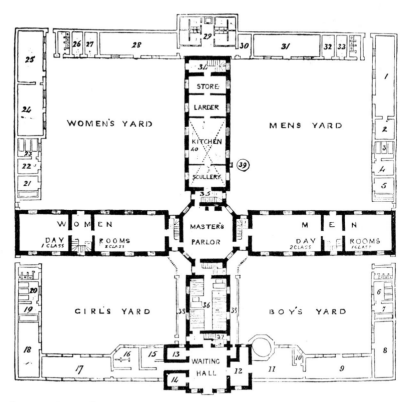

Sampson Kempthorne's X plan for a workhouse for 300 paupers

Perspective view of Kempthorne's workhouse

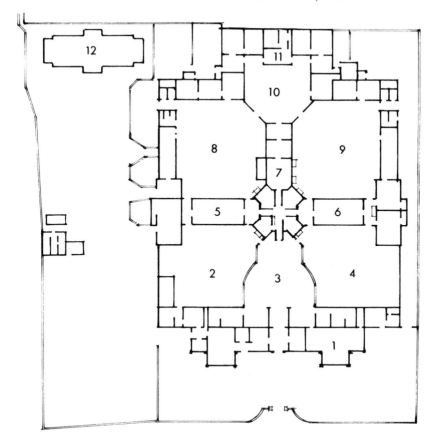

1. Chapel
2. Girls' Yard
3. Front Garden
4. Boys' Yard
5. Womens' Dining Room
6. Mens' Dining Room
7. Kitchen
8. Womens' Yard
9. Mens' Yard
10. Yard
11. Surgery
12. Fever Hospital

Scott's workhouse plan, as used at probably a majority of his buildings. This is
Bideford

Because the basic plans were inadequate, there was much informed
criticism; competitions were introduced in response and in order to
damp nepotism. In fact these competitions gave much scope for
lobbying and chicanery. In Scott's words, they

... were conducted on principles quite peculiar to themselves. They were open in every sense, and each of the competitors was at liberty to take any step he thought good. They used first to go to town and call on the clerk, the chairman, and any of the guardians who were supposed to have any ideas of their own, and after the designs were sent in, no harm was thought of repeating those calls as often as the competitor pleased, and advocating the merits, each man of his own arrangement. On the day on which the designs were to be examined the competitors were usually waiting in the ante-room, and were called in one by one to give personal explanations, and the decision was often announced then and there to the assembled candidates.

Moffatt was most successful in this kind of fighting, having an instinctive perception of which men to aim at pleasing, and of how to meet their views and to address himself successfully to their particular temperaments. The pains he took in improving the arrangements were enormous, communicating constantly with the most experienced governors of workhouses, and gathering ideas wherever he went. He was always on the move. We went every week to Peele's coffee house to see the country papers, and to find advertisements of pending competitions. Moffatt then ran down to the place to get up information. On his return, we set to work, with violence, to make the design, and to prepare the competition drawings, often working all night as well as all day. He would then start off by the mail, travel all night, meet the Board of Guardians, and perhaps win the competition, and return during the next night to set to work on another design. I have known him travel four nights running, and to work hard throughout the intervening days, a habit facilitated by his power of sleeping whenever he chose. He used to say that he snored so loud on the box of the mail as to keep the inside passengers awake. He was the best arranger of a plan, the hardest worker, and the best hand at advocating the merits of what he had to propose, I ever met with: I think that he thoroughly deserved his success, though it naturally won him a host of enemies and traducers.[6]

At Derby, a workhouse was required, and pressure was exerted on behalf of a local firm, Lee and Dewsbury. A competition was instituted to destroy a counter lobby raised by friends of Scott and Moffatt, after which the winners were Lee and Dewsbury, with Scott and Moffatt second. Indignant pseudonymous letters in *The Builder* maintained that the winning drawings had been sealed with a prearranged device.

The individual workhouses came in two styles: Classic, like Tiverton, Devon, and Tudor, as at Dunmow, Essex. Tiverton is solidly constructed of stone with a slate roof. There is a single storey entrance block with a high pedimented gateway, whilst the main building has a four-storey central octagon crowned with a wooden turret, with pediments on four faces, linking two three-storey wings. The appearance is rather that of a cotton mill. Dunmow is a rich example of Tudor dress which dominates one end of the town. It seems an ornamental pile was demanded, with lots of diapered brickwork and gables, and a little ogee turret. The detail is perhaps derived from Blore's houses,[7] but the arrangement is similar to that of Tiverton.[8]

For Scott, the end of the workhouse period coincided with his assumption of the responsibilities of a married man. He found time to meet his cousin Caroline Oldrid once again during the summer of 1835, and they became engaged. After waiting three years, they were married at Boston on 5 June 1838. The day before Scott sketched Sleaford church from his inn, noting in the margin, 'the happiest day in all the year (the day I was married)'.[9]

After a short tour the couple returned to London, soon settling in a comfortable Georgian house at 20 (later 31) Spring Gardens,[10] leased from John Britton, the antiquary and topographical publisher, who soon wrote to Scott objecting to a notice indicating his profession which had been placed outside. As neighbours they had barristers, doctors, and Sir Josiah Guest the ironmaster. The office moved there from Regent Street, to remain until Scott's death.

Scott's first two sons, both future architects, were born while the family lived at Spring Gardens: George Gilbert, Junior, in 1839; and John Oldrid in 1841.[11] After John's birth, Caroline suffered, or claimed, endemic ill-health, and chose to remain at home rather than accompany her husband on his travels about the country.

Besides the Poor Law Institutions, Scott and Moffatt entered a number of competitions for other institutional buildings. In that for Liverpool College, in 1840, they came second to Harvey Lonsdale Elmes: fortunately, for the client committee then appointed a local surveyor to prepare working drawings on the cheap, with unsatisfactory results. Their entry for 'public baths and washhouses for the labouring poor' in 1845 was also unsuccessful.

Moffatt is credited with an entry[12] in the competition of 1840 for the new Royal Exchange in the City, won by William Tite in somewhat discreditable circumstances. If these drawings are indeed from Moffatt's hand, they stamp him as a fine draughtsman in ink and wash.

In 1841 the partners competed successfully for Dr Andrew Reed's Infant Orphan Asylum in Wanstead, Essex. Moffatt designed the plans, and Scott the elevations in Elizabethan style, to be faced with

Sneaton limestone from North Yorkshire. This was the largest, most expensive, and most prestigious building they had undertaken, and the foundation stone was laid by the Prince Consort himself. Success went to Moffatt's head: he carried out the works ably but 'contrived thoroughly to alienate his employers'.[13] The building was exhibited at the Royal Academy in 1842, finished in 1843, and opened by Queen Victoria's uncle, Leopold, King of the Belgians. The result is fine and substantial.[14]

In 1842, the Berkshire County Gaol at Reading, an even larger work and Scott's only prison, was begun.[15] Difficulties over cost, by no means unusual in the practice at this time, arose, for even though a costing surveyor was employed, time permitted only rough estimates. The Inspector of Prisons was positive of the likely cost, but first required alterations to the designs, then persuaded the magistrates to contract for a schedule of prices rather than a tender figure. The work was done, and measured at the end of 1844, but was found to have cost £40,000, a sum equal to the cost of eight workhouses. This did not help Scott and Moffatt: as late as 1848 a letter explaining away the overcost appeared in *The Builder*.[16]

The finished building is in bright red brick with blue diaper and Bath stone dressings, in the presumed style of a 15th century castle, battlemented and slit-windowed, showing around the entrance signs of its workhouse lineage, with square-headed Tudor-type windows. But this was the invariable style for Victorian prisons.

There followed three pauper lunatic asylums, the last of this class of work with which Scott was associated. The Shropshire Asylum at Shelton, Shrewsbury was built in 1843; the Somerset Asylum near Wells was won in competition early in 1845; the North Riding Lunatic Asylum at Clifton, York was offered for tender early in the same year. All were in the accepted Elizabethan style.[17] Clifton is particularly attractive: the sandstone building has a central three-storey block with two plain gables, a small dark entrance, and an ornamental cupola, a constantly recurring composition.

At the same time, a wider practice was being built up. There were commissions from, or through the influence of, friends and relatives, and the Poor Law Guardians themselves were often men of substance, with influence in the church. There were also competitions, initially of some importance.

St Blazey, Cornwall, is in Moffatt country and near the St Austell workhouse. If indeed the partners restored this church in 1839, it is the first church restoration in which Scott had a hand. The church is of the 15th century, of granite, with chancel, a nave of five bays, an embattled west tower, and aisles (the north added by Scott and Moffatt in imitation of that on the south). The old south porch entrance was evidently re-used as the west door of the tower.[18]

A number of domestic buildings date from this period. Another house at Wappenham (1835) and the rectory at Weston Turville (1838) are attributed to Scott; both are Classic in style. There is the vicarage at Dinton (1836). The parsonages at Blakesley, Northamptonshire (1839) and Clifton Hampden, Oxfordshire (1843-46), the rectory at Teffont Evias, Wiltshire (1842) and almshouses at Whitby (1842) — the Seamen's Houses, were in a late Elizabethan or early Jacobean style similar to that of the later workhouses.[19]

If the attribution and the date 1844 are correct, Pitt House, Chudleigh Knighton is the first and the smallest of Scott's country houses, a pseudo-Jacobean design in stone with semi-circular bays under curved gables at each end crowned with battlements, with a smaller version of the motif at the entrance bay.

The influence of friends of Scott's father led directly to an invitation in 1840 to compete for a monument to be erected in St Giles, Oxford, based on the Waltham Eleanor Cross, to commemorate the Marian Protestant martyrs Cranmer, Latimer and Ridley, who had been burned in Broad Street. The catholic architect Augustus Welby Pugin wrote an intemperate pamphlet condemning the proposal and stigmatised the martyrs as 'vile blasphemous imposters pretending inspiration while setting forth false doctrines' and the subscribers for the monument as 'foul revilers, tyrants, usurpers, extortioners and liars'.[20] The controversy rocked Oxford, but at the time passed over Scott's head.

He referred to his sketches of all the Eleanor Crosses and produced a very competent version, with diminishing tiers of blind windows and niches on a hexagonal base raised on steps, if anything more elegant than the prototype, and of a quality of detail, copying that of the late 13th and early 14th centuries, unusually good for this period. Scott remarked rather obtusely in later years that he fancied it was better than anyone except Pugin would have produced. Scott related:

An amusing incident occurred at, I believe, my first interview with the committee.

I found them in disagreement as to the best stone for the monument. The commissioners for selecting stone for the Houses of Parliament, had not long before made their report in favour of the purely mythic stone of Bolsover Moor. One party favoured this imaginary stone, for its warm colour; another, the white variety of magnesian limestone from Roche Abbey, on account of its fine grain. I ventured on the suggestion, that by visiting the district, it might be possible to find a stone uniting these qualities, when Dr Buckland snubbed me with great scorn, saying that such a suggestion might have been made in years gone by, when little was known of the geological productions of the country, but that now, when every variety of stone was so well-known, it was hopeless to look out for new ones. I happened, however, though without scientific knowledge, to have nearly as practical an acquaintance with stone quarries as Dr Buckland . . . . I therefore started off with Moffatt for the magnesio-calcareous district. The first quarry we went to was that at Mansfield Woodhouse, which, on the discovery of the Bolsover delusion, had been re-opened for the Houses of Parliament: this stone did not meet my wishes, being too coarse in grain, and not pure enough in colour. On describing, however, to the foreman of the quarry what I was seeking for, he . . brought us to an ancient and long-disused quarry, grown over with brushwood, and on striking off a fragment from the rock, presented to me the very stone which my imagination had pourtrayed (*sic*)! The committee at once, though at a great increase of cost, adopted it, and in their next report attributed the happy discovery to the pre-eminent geological skill of Dr Buckland.[21]

Success with the Martyrs' Memorial led directly to the restoration of the adjacent St Mary Magdalene in 1841-2. The north aisle was entirely rebuilt, at the considerable cost of £8000. Some 12th-century remains were removed, but the aisle itself, like the Memorial, is of a scholarship unmatched at the time. Much of the east wall was refaced, a window entirely renewed, and the southern buttresses and parapet renewed on the lines of the old.[22]

Scott's first new church, at Flaunden, a 'poor barn for my uncle King'[23] was built in 1838, largely at the expense of Samuel King, the vicar, in replacement of a small church of Greek cross plan inconveniently situated two miles from the village. The new church stemmed directly from the family evangelical tradition and contained many features anathema to the 'informed' high church taste of ten years later. The lack of any chancel, the west gallery, the plastered interior, the ceilings, the simple lancets, and the odd bits of detail like the dentil course at the top of the gallery front all qualify for Scott's favourite adjective: 'wretched'.[24]

The church's form is ungainly: the corner buttresses appear too

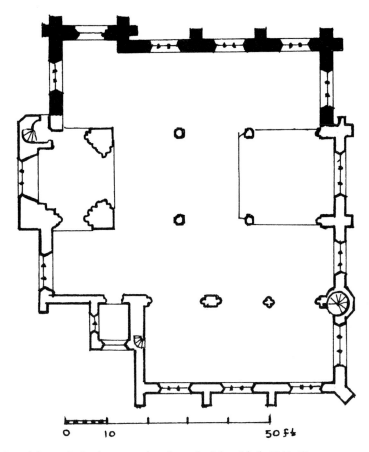

St Mary Magdalene, Oxford, restored and north aisle added, 1841-42.

small; those flanking the east window seem to have been rebuilt or added. Flint, a favourite material of Scott's, is used externally, with red brick quoins.

St James, Gloucester, erected 1837-41, was possibly a joint work by Kempthorne and Scott.

Scott's third new church, the first he won in competition, was St Nicholas, Lincoln, begun in 1839 and consecrated in November 1840, in belated replacement of its predecessor, badly damaged in the Civil War. Of stone in the Early English style, it had a nave with a south aisle, short transepts, no chancel, a south-west tower and broach spire, and galleries (removed in 1879): it cost about £2000.[25]

Six more churches[26] followed in quick succession, all designed in 1839-40. At least four other churches of this period are similar, with transepts and a short chancel, but without aisle galleries (see table 2).

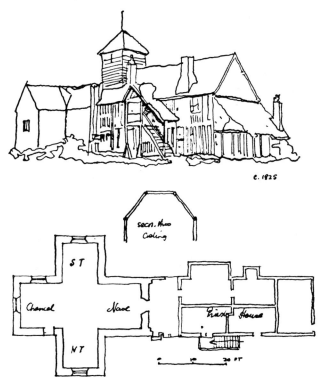

Flaunden Old Church about 1825. It was demolished when replaced by Scott's first church. This is characteristic of the state of many churches at this time.
The Builder, ii, 156

Flaunden. Plan

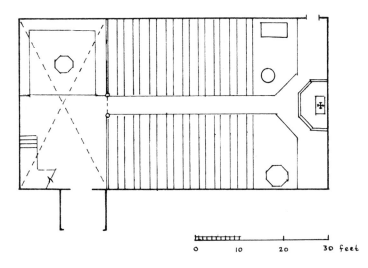

TABLE 2

Dedication	Style	Tower/Spire	Aisles	Clerestory	Cost £	Alterations	Started	Material	No. of sittings
Birmingham St Mark	EE	spire removed 1890s	-	?	-	1882: demolished	1840	-	-
Bridlington, E. Yorks Christ Church	EE	spire 1852	yes	-	2300	1854 1866	1840	stone	-
Hanwell, Middlesex St Mary	EE	spire	yes	yes	-	1897 1912	1841	flint and brick	-
Norbiton, Surrey St Peter	Norman	tower	yes	no	5189	1868 1909	1842	brick	920
Shaftesbury, Dorset Holy Trinity	EE	tower	yes	yes	3230	1908: demolished 1974	1841	stone	854
Turnham Green, Middlesex Christ Church	EE	spire	yes	no	-	1887-95	October 1841	flint	930
Chudleigh Knighton, Devon St Paul	EE	bellcote	no	-	-	1876	1841	flint	-
Frogmore, Herts Holy Trinity	Norman	bellcote	yes	yes	-	none	1841	flint	-
Hulme, Lancs Holy Trinity	EE	tower	yes	yes	-	1892, 1931: demolished 1953	1841	-	-
Penkhull, Staffs St Thomas	Dec	spire	in 1892	-	-	1958	1842	-	-

Some replaced old churches; some are new parishes. It made little difference, and Scott found it convenient to repeat himself. All had short transepts, suggested by those at Harrow and Pinner in Middlesex, a more respectably antiquarian feature than Scott appreciated. They had no proper chancels, 'all my grave idea being that this feature was obsolete', as indeed it was, with respect to the form of service normal at that time.[27] Most were Early English in style; these shared many common and simple details: windows, doorways, arcades, gallery fronts. Most or all of the first six originally had galleries, for the provision of a great deal of seating at low cost was requisite. 'Everything I did at that time fell into the wholesale form',[28] but this type of standardised design had sound mediaeval precedent and was indeed a rational application of Scott's workhouse design methods to churches.

Hulme, Norbiton, and Shaftesbury had western towers, five others broach spires. Scott's strange propensity, which he shared with Pugin, for erecting East Midlands broach spires in the most unlikely places is seen here: for instance, there was probably no spire in the county of Middlesex, brick country with no building stone, in 1840, though now there are many. Later, one finds very misplaced spires; Birmingham, Glasgow, Ambleside in the Lake District, Ryde in the Isle of Wight, even in miniature as a lantern over the crossing of 'a church in a tropical country', perhaps an early design for Lucknow Cathedral in India.

Four of the ten make use of flint as a facing to a rubble wall, another Scott eccentricity. Scott was familiar with flint in walling and used the material a great deal, but confined it to the traditional areas of the south-east.

It is not known whether any of these churches were won in competition. Chudleigh Knighton most likely came through Moffatt. There were family connections with Bridlington. Penkhull, built largely at the expense of the Rev Thomas Webb Minton of Darlington, Scott probably owed to Thomas Stevens, Assistant Poor Law Commissioner for Stafford and Derby, whom Scott had met in 1838 in Uttoxeter, probably in connection with the workhouse. They became friends and discussed the restoration of Bradfield church, for which Scott prepared drawings and a model.[29] Scott worked also on an abortive scheme for a church at Dunkirk, Kent in 1839.[30]

In Holy Trinity, Hartshill, Stoke-on-Trent, and St Giles, Camberwell one sees already the typical Victorian church. Scott designed Hartshill in mid-1841 for Herbert Minton, the encaustic tile manufacturer, a friend of Pugin.[31] It was of Early English character in red sandstone, with an aisled nave of five bays, a west tower with octagonal spire, and a square-ended chancel, the first of Scott's considered adequate by Victorian standards, built apparently at Minton's insistence. The careful details were not standard, but were taken (another mediaeval practice) from the 'mother church' of Lichfield Cathedral, which Stevens at one time habitually attended. The floors and the dado in the chancel were of rich encaustic tiles. Scott designed the school and the parsonage at the same time.

In 1872 careless workmen started a fire in the organ loft which burned most of the church. Scott restored it on the former lines, but with a slightly longer apsidal chancel, organ chamber, and south chapel.

Fires gave Scott many of his best opportunities. The old church of St Giles, Camberwell, heavily bodged over the years, was burned on 7 February 1841 and a competition, assessed by Edward Blore,[32] was held for its replacement. Scott and Moffatt won, but their competition entry differs from the church as built, a fully developed Victorian church, suitable for a free-standing site.

Scott had been involved, up to the end of 1841, with thirteen new churches, all but one in a period of less than five years, representing a minuscule proportion of the church building at this time. The pace of church building increased as arrears of maintenance began to be tackled; many churches were in a state of shameful neglect. The population had been steadily increasing since the turn of the century, and church building was further spurred by elements of conspicuous consumption, desired for status, motives of benevolence, and aims of providing local employment.

Also, a marked increase in religious fervour was manifesting itself, and many professed themselves dissatisfied with the state of the Established Church. Radical non-conformist bodies proliferated: whilst within the Church, Evangelicals sought to elevate the tone of religious sentiment and practice, at the other extreme Tractarians,[33] led by Oxford figures like Newman and Pusey, attempted to accentuate the ritual aspects of Anglican worship, with the inevitable consequence that the 'High Church' moved closer to Rome, Newman himself and others crossing the boundary to Catholicism.

The Oxford movement had a vague counterpart in an amateur, almost accidental, body in the University of Cambridge, the Cambridge Camden Society, formed in 1838 by John Mason Neale and Benjamin Webb, both undergraduates. Later called the Ecclesiological Society, it concerned itself with the ritual arrangement of churches new and old, adopting the motto *Donec templum refeceris*, and, from 1841, forcefully putting forward its views in a periodical, *The Ecclesiologist*.

Noting that most revived Gothic churches of the time were mean and unscholarly, the Society demanded that all churches should adopt the style of the late 14th century, without box pews or galleries, with a long chancel, employing 'real' materials rather than plaster, and conforming in numerous other details, mostly tending to make the buildings quite unsuitable for Anglican worship. Anyone departing from the party line was earnestly vilified.

In 1841 the *Dublin Review* published an article by Pugin, later reprinted in his book *The Present State of Christian Architecture*, setting out his account of the traditions of parish church building, and culminating in a manifesto on the design and furnishing of contemporary churches. Scott read the articles, with pronounced effect: 'Being thus morally awakened, my physical dreams followed the subject of my waking thoughts'.[34] They met that year: Pugin 'was tremendously jolly and showed too much *bonhomie* to accord with my romantic expectation. I very rarely saw him again . . .'[35]

At much the same time Scott read an article by Benjamin Webb, and wrote to him deploring Charles Barry's intention to demolish the remains of St Stephen's Chapel in his rebuilding of the Houses of Parliament, the same issue which had occasioned his meeting with Pugin. Webb proceeded to lecture Scott on church architecture in general, and on such matters as the necessity of chancels. 'I at once saw that he was right, and became a reader of *The Ecclesiologist*.'[36]

Scott dramatised this conversion until in retrospect it seemed like the light from heaven which shined round about Saul near Damascus. He immediately found that his first seven churches had been conceived on entirely erroneous principles 'As I had not awaked to the viciousness of shams, I was unconscious of the abyss into which I had fallen. These days of abject degradation only lasted for about two years or a little more, but, alas!, what a mass of horrors was perpetrated during that short interval! Often, and that within a few months of this period, have I been wicked enough to wish my works burnt down again. Yet they were but part of the base art-history of their day.'[37]

Scott wished desperately to reproduce mediaeval churches, and sought any authority on which to lean. In spite of his Evangelical background, he joined the Cambridge Camden Society in February 1842.

All this had repercussions on the progress of St Giles, Camberwell. Scott sent a lithograph for criticism to *The Ecclesiologist*, which published a notice. The competition scheme had had terracotta vaulting, plaster mouldings internally instead of carved stone, and a hexagonal apse like that of the original Turnham Green. *The Ecclesiologist* thought the design 'on the whole a magnificent one',[38] but wanted a chancel of at least three bays. The design was altered in this and other respects by late 1842, when the foundation stone was laid. The church was originally to have cost £20,000, part to have come from a parish rate, but after protest meetings Scott and Moffatt prepared a new design to seat 1500 for which they estimated, correctly, £14,500.

The central tower was Scott's first, but he felt confident enough to tackle the problem of supporting it on four corner columns without unduly restricting sight within the church, which had undone many mediaeval masons.

The reredos was undertaken by the carver who had worked on the Martyrs' Memorial.[39] There was poor wall-painting on both sides of the chancel, later plastered over. The west window included some German 13th-century glass, whereas John Ruskin, who lived in the parish, designed, with Edward Oldfield, the glass in the east window. The wooden bench ends were made with the help of a machine invented by a Mr Pratt for cutting Gothic tracery, an innovation which neither Pugin nor Ruskin, with their dreams of Godly mediaeval craftsmen at work, would have applauded.

The stonework was Kentish rag with Caen stone quoins and, in the interior, Sneaton stone from Yorkshire. Atmospheric pollution in London quickly caused the external stone to blacken and waste. Consecration took place on 21 November 1844.

Another group of churches of about this time started as simple two-celled structures, straight out of the Cambridge Camden

Society's publication, 'A few words to Church Builders' (see table 3): nave and chancel only, sometimes under the same roof, often with a south porch.

Designs for Farncombe were made as early as 1842, and tenders submitted in August 1844: the lowest was £1450, but the building was not finished until 1848 and cost £3038. It must have been redesigned, but it had always consisted of nave, chancel, and south porch. The chancel was in the Early English style with a triplet of lancets surmounted by a roundel at the east end, a motif Scott used again and again, and it was praised for having no galleries. In 1860 Scott added a north aisle and a gallery for the school children (!); in 1875 a south aisle and a new porch, and chancel aisles. As every element has its own pitched roof, the massing is muddled.

Another similar church, Wembley, opened in the summer of 1845, ended up with pitched roofs like those at Farncombe: to the original two-celled church aisles faced in flint were added in character with the original building.

Wood Green, started in 1843 as a ragstone building 77 x 23ft, with nave and chancel under one roof and a south porch, has been so radically altered that it is probable that nothing of Scott and Moffatt remains except a re-erected porch.[44] The ubiquitous Cox carved the pulpit and font.

Westwood Heath, Stoneleigh, near Coventry is praised as 'one of the first archaeologically conscientious churches in England'.[45] The parishioners raised its cost and Lord Leigh gave the site and the endowment, as was typical of the financing arrangements for such buildings.

Having joined the Ecclesiological Society, Scott at once sent off to them illustrations of nine recently designed churches.[46] *The Ecclesiologist* printed in January 1843 a reasoned review of the lot, concluding, rather strangely: 'We know that many... have been spoilt by the "improvements" of Church Building Committees or from want of funds ... [in] the only instance in which Scott has been allowed to follow his own taste he has produced a very beautiful and Catholick church. Therefore if we censure any thing we are to be considered as censuring not so much the architect, as the church committees whom he was, or thought himself, obliged to please.'[47] Scott became for a time a regular contributor of designs to the Society for their criticism.

Eleven more new churches were apparently designed before the

TABLE 3

Dedication	Style	Tower/spire	Cost £	Alterations	Started	Material	No. of sittings
Wall, Staffs St John[40]	Perp	spirelet	-	none	1839	stone	-
Farncombe, Godalming, Surrey St John the Evangelist	EE	spirelet	3038 (?)	1860-75	1846 (?)	stone	-
Freehay, Staffs St Chad	EE	bellcote	-	none	1842	-	-
Greenstead Green, Essex St James the Apostle[41]	Dec	spire	-	-	1844	-	-
Nailsea, Somerset Christ Church	EE	bellcote	-	none	1843	-	400
Woking, Surrey St John the Baptist	EE	bellcote	1450	1879-83	1842	stone	-
Wood Green, Middlesex St Michael	EE	-	1777	1864-74, 87	1843	stone	200
Westwood Heath, Warwicks St John the Baptist	Dec	bellcote	1600	1876, 1928	mid-1842	-	400
Zeals, Wilts St Martin[42]	Dec	tower spire in 1876	2000	1874-6	September 1845	stone	296
Wembley, Middlesex St John the Evangelist[43]	Dec	spirelet	-	1859, 1900-35	1846	flint	-

end of 1844: Scott employed a repertoire of details grouped in various ways, giving a considerable variety of size, style, and character (see table 4).

Swallowcliffe, unlike anything the office had thus far produced, has nave, chancel, north aisle, and tower with a corner turret; it seems all of a piece, although the stone show side, set at the curve of the road, becomes brick on the north. The style generally is Norman, but the detail is loosely handled, unlike the monotonous regularity of Norbiton.

Abergwili, Carmarthen, was one of the first of many churches erected during the bishopric of the scholarly, liberal, and energetic Connop Thirlwall of St David's, whose palace was here. The old church was replaced by one with nave and wide chancel (convenient for ordination services) under one roof, north aisles, and a tower with a broad spire: misplaced, for all the local churches have battlemented towers. The plan itself is of a North Wales type: could Scott have known this?

Halstead, a church with chancel, clerestoried nave and aisles, combined two geographical anomalies: it used flint with brick dressings, and had a south-western tower with broach spire. The tower was built too quickly, 30 ft a week, for the cement to develop strength, and early in July had reached a height of 115 ft. Warning cracks were observed, and presently the tower and spire fell, injuring three workmen. Early Victorian tall structures often fell — *The Builder* is full of accounts of collapsing factory chimneys — and the ruins were rebuilt without any particular fuss being made.

West Meon is an advanced design, with a nave with a steep pitched roof, aisles with leaded roofs, no clerestory, a good chancel, a south porch, and a west tower with a stair turret in one corner and rather heavy battlements on top. It was built alongside the old church, and may share features with its predecessor. Strangely, the exterior is of flints, carefully squared,[51] which gives the walls an odd scale. There are early examples of 'pretty' effigies terminating labels, and fine, even if derivative, gargoyles and rainwater heads.

Plans for the Great Western Railway encompassed the building of extensive repair shops at Swindon, and provision had to be made for housing the workmen. In August 1840 the Directors had proposed to devote half an acre of the Company's land there to the erection of a church, but faced considerable objections from the 'Proprietors'. Finally, George Henry Gibbs, a Director, in August

TABLE 4

Dedication	Style	Tower/spire	Cost £	Started	Material	No. of sittings
Swallowcliffe, Wilts St Peter	Norman	tower	-	1842	stone and brick	-
Abergwili, Carmarthen St David	EE	spire	-	by 1843	stone	-
Donington Wood, Salop St Matthew[48]	EE	bellcote	-	Feb 1843	stone	600
Nottingham St John the Baptist	EE	-	-	June 1843	stone	802
Halstead, Essex Holy Trinity	Dec	spire	5000	July 1843	flint	703
West Meon, Hants St John the Evangelist	Dec	tower	-	Aug 1843	flint	-
Swindon, Wilts St Mark	Dec	spire	5500	1843	stone	-
Wimbledon, Surrey St Mary[49]	Perp	tower	-	1843	flint	-
Worsley, Lancs St Mark	Dec	spire	-	June 1844	stone	-
Leeds, W. Yorks St Andrew	EE	spirelet	-	1844	-	-
Skirbeck, Lincs Holy Trinity[50]	Dec	bell gable	5058	c.1844	-	-

NEW CHURCH AT SWINDON, ON THE GREAT WESTERN RAILWAY.

St Mark, Swindon, 1845. A contemporary view
Illustrated London News, 11 October 1845

1842 bequeathed £500 towards a church and school; the Directors appealed for further contributions. In 1843-5 St Mark's church and school, costing £5500 and £800 respectively, were completed to designs of Scott and Moffatt, who won the competition ahead of, among others, William Butterfield.

The church was built in the late Decorated style, ornate and unpleasantly proportioned, with a very high clerestoried and aisled nave, no galleries, a south porch and chancel, and a 170 ft tower and spire attached to the north aisle near the west end, an unusual position at the time. St Andrew, Leeds, although Early English in style, is similar in its plan and its great height, but instead of the tower originally intended, has a very odd west spirelet, which indeed may be of a later date.

St Mark, Worsley, near Manchester is perhaps Scott's finest early church. Lord Francis Egerton, later Earl of Ellesmere, had Blore at work building Worsley Hall, but went to Scott for his new church in 1843. Work started in June 1844, Scott having been respectfully firm about the necessity of a long chancel. The church, consecrated in 1846, is Decorated, with a west tower and a spire unusually replete with crockets and gargoyles. Eventually Scott was to design the Earl's coffin and tomb. The artists of the stained glass are not recorded, but some glass may have been by Pugin.

From 1842-4 at least ten church restorations are known to have commenced (see table 5).

TABLE 5

Dedication	Started	Completed
Chesterfield, Derbys All Saints	1842	1843
Stafford, Staffs St Mary	May 1842	1844 (?)
Betley, Staffs St Margaret	1842	1842
Corringham, Essex St Mary	1843	1844
Wasperton, Warwicks St John the Baptist	1843	1843
Boston, Lincs St Botolph	early 1844	1845
Beeston, Notts St John Baptist	1844	?
Clifton Hampden, Oxon St Michael and All Angels	1844	1844
Castlechurch, Staffs St Mary	mid-1844	1851 (?)
Crosthwaite, Cumberland St Kentigern	late 1844	Aug 1845
Barnes, Surrey St Mary[54]		
Debenham, Suffolk St Mary[55]		
Hougham, Lincs All Saints	1844 (?)	

It has been our wish to introduce no feature but what has its use and no ornament which is not a part of an essential feature. to trust for effect to the correctness of our outline and the simplicity of the general forms. to adopt such forms only as have been consecrated to ecclesiastical purposes from the earliest times and such decorations only as were applied to them in the best days of Church Architecture. to prefer substantial Construction. to external decoration and Simple reality to shewy pretence –

The general outline of the whole may perhaps be better judged of by the accompanying sketch, than by the geometrical drawings but from its peculiar Character it would be infinitely better in execution than in a drawing – and it has none of those ornamented features which give so much effect to a drawing – Should our general Views on the subject with the leading Character of our design be honoured by your approval we were loth to say that it would not be our wish to adhere

Worsley, 1844-6. An extract from a report on the proposed new church.

At Chesterfield, the partners' third restoration, Scott removed the Perpendicular east window and replaced it with one with five lights and flowing Decorated tracery: the style of most of the church was fortunately that favoured by the Camdenians. Galleries were added, despite both Scott's and the incumbent's opposition. The displaced rood screen was recovered and re-erected in the north transept; the Foljambe chapel at the south-east corner of the nave was removed as it was 'right in the way of the arrangements'[56] and the screenwork was made into a reredos.[57] The reading desk and a Norman incised slab disappeared, but Scott measured the twisted timber spire and left it alone as 'giving character and quaint antiquity to the building'.[58] He had still a good deal to learn.

Stafford was probably next. Thomas Stevens had advised Scott that the rector wished to restore the church of St Mary's, which had been much damaged when the spire fell in 1594. Stevens persuaded Jesse Watts Russell of Ilam Hall to donate £5000 for the restoration on the conditions that a further £3000 was raised from the public, that Scott and Moffatt were named the architects, and that the Cambridge Camden Society approved the scheme. A contract was let on 30 May 1842.

The contract drawings show that the intention was to rebuild the buttresses and windows at the west end (unexecuted), the south porch and doorway, the east window of the north chancel aisle, and the whole wall of the south chancel aisle. A spire was intended, but never built, and, in accordance with a common obsession at this time, the church was to be reseated. Scott wrote of the project in 1866, when his restoration technique was being attacked:

the questions which arose out of it were among the most difficult; and whatever may have been its success, I can safely say that no work of restoration could have received more anxious and conscientious attention. It is a large cross church, with central tower. The nave and the tower-piers are of the twelfth, the south transept, the chancel, and its south aisle, of the thirteenth, and the north transept and north chancel aisle of the fourteenth century. These earlier parts had been altered by the addition of good Perpendicular clerestories to the nave and north transept (the former having a fine roof); the south aisle of the chancel retained its high pitch, but that on the north side was made flat, while the chancel proper, and the south transept, had very bad and late clerestories and bad roofs; and the great window of the latter, originally a very noble thirteenth century triplet, had been deprived of its piers, and its jambs united by a flat elliptical arch, filled in with Perpendicular work of a very debased kind. This and the roof, &c. of the chancel, there is reason to believe were the result of rude repairs after the fall of the spire in 1590 [*sic*]. This late work was thoroughly decayed, and the question arose whether it should be restored in its existing forms or whether the early design should be revived.

An epistolary discussion on the subject was referred to the Oxford and Cambridge societies, who gave their verdict in favour of the revival (for the chancel and south transept) of the earlier forms. In removing the decayed later work, details of the earlier design were found embedded in the walls, ..., so that there is hardly a detail of the smallest kind on which there is room for doubt as to its being an exact reproduction of the old design. This applies to the south transept, the south side of the chancel, and the east end of the chancel, and its south side. All other parts were restored as we found them; the clerestories, and roofs of the nave, the north transept, and the south chancel aisle remaining.

Such was my anxiety that everything should be exact, ... that I employed as clerk of the works (first alone, and for a time jointly with another) my late friend Edwin Gwilt, a devoted antiquary: and in the work done under him every new stone was, not only in detail but in size, a counterpart of the old, the new ashlar even being a *fac simile* joint for joint of the decayed work whose place it supplied.

At that time the importance of retaining the *ipsissimi lapides* had not become duly appreciated, and the stonework being in an advanced state of decay, it was extensively renewed; but, making allowance for this, and reserving the question referred to the two great societies (certainly an unimpeachable mode of settling them), I would boldly assert that a more careful restoration — at least so far as intention went — never was made, and it was rendered the more difficult by tremendous modern mutilation of the interior, and by the tower piers being so crushed as to necessitate their renewal.[59]

Scott was consulted as early as 1840 in connection with the Church of St Botolph, Boston, where his brother-in-law John Henry Oldrid was vicar. This is one of the largest parish churches in England, with a famous west tower. In November 1843 tenders were invited for repair work. £3831 was spent in 1844-5 on the nave, the roof[60] and on the renewal of external details. The nave roof was of 18th century timber, but was not removed, and years of white-washing were cleaned off the walls.

Nothing more was done until 1851, when a competition for the reseating of the nave was instituted. G. G. Place was appointed for this and other restoration work. Scott was named as 'consulting architect' and for some reason chose that the new east window should copy that at Carlisle Cathedral, with which he had no other connection. It is recorded that £13,421 was spent up to 1867.[61]

Clifton Hampden, Oxfordshire was another thorough restoration commissioned by the young banker Henry Hucks Gibbs, whose father had been the motive force behind St Mark's, Swindon. Scott admitted there was 'hardly anything left to restore' of the decrepit church; it was rather 'a refoundation, keeping in the main to the old plan'.[62] It now looks wholly Victorian.

In June 1844 a faculty was granted for the complete restoration of Crosthwaite church near Keswick in Cumberland, which may be considered a memorial to the poet Southey who had died the previous year. The church is much farther north than Scott's practice had previously penetrated.[63] Scott renewed the roofs, covered the walls with a thick smooth layer of plaster, repositioned the east window,[64] relaid the floor and refurnished the church. The tower was covered in roughcast. In 1845 a south porch was added, to the design which remained standard for years in Scott's practice, used, with minor variations, in all parts of the country.

Scott and Moffatt needed help to deal with their increasing workload. The greater competence in work and in estimating reflected an increase in capable staff in the office and on site at major jobs. They would of course not all necessarily be in continuous employment. In 1839 there were two clerks, Burleigh getting 10s a week and Boyce 7s. Stephen Salter was being paid for model making. It seems likely that T. J. Ricauti, from Devon, was employed: we have also the names Enright, Lea and Ensch.

In 1841 two good men came and though the partners probably dealt with all of the design work, the office could now continue despite their absence. John Burlison of Durham came to Scott in 1841 or 1843, after articles and various jobs. He was about Scott's age, a practical, reliable man, skilled in building construction and estimating, and stayed until his early death in 1868. John Drayton Wyatt, apparently unrelated to the various other Wyatts of British architecture, was engaged in 1841 as assistant draughtsman, becoming in time Scott's chief draughtsman, preparing drawings for illustration and known especially for his ability to prepare rapidly accurate detail drawings. Wyatt began his own practice in 1867 and died in 1891. He was one of the founders of the British Association of Architectural Draughtsmen, which eventually became the Architectural Association.

Scott, no Pecksniff, had several articled pupils. Benjamin Woolfield Mountfort was apparently the first, staying from 1841 until 1846. George Frederick Bodley studied and lived in his master's house like a mediaeval apprentice from 1845.[65] He began his own practice in 1854 and became one of the best architects of the century. George Henry Stokes was articled to Scott from 1843 till 1847, when he left to work with Joseph Paxton, the designer of the Crystal Palace, ultimately becoming a partner in Paxton's family and firm. Seven other pupils are known in the period 1840-7.[66]

There were also clerks of works, appointed by the employer to superintend building work and maintain standards of materials and workmanship, but generally nominated by the architect, and Scott relied on them a great deal. Over forty are known by name. They either came up after apprenticeship to a building trade, or were sent out from the office as part of a general training, or were local men with knowledge of local materials, and indeed might be in provincial practice as architects themselves, like Buckeridge of Oxford or Chick[67] of Hereford. Such local architects are sometimes recorded as joint architects on particular buildings.

In 1844 there were many changes: it was Scott's *annus mirabilis*. The family moved away from over the office at Spring Gardens; with two children under five and another on the way, they needed more room, as indeed did the office. Moffatt was living at Kennington, and drawings for the competitions for institutional buildings of all types, his special charge, were prepared at his house, which was often full of clerks slaving over drawing boards.

Scott found a fairly new house in Avenue Road, St John's Wood, to which the family went in August, a few days prior to the arrival of Albert Henry, the third son, to commence a stay of over twenty years. Scott's status as a propertied man involved him in sitting on the Grand Jury at the Old Bailey on two occasions, providing frightening glimpses of the 'other nation'.

With Scott so much at Spring Gardens or travelling around the country, Caroline was increasingly bereft of his company. Each year the family went to the seaside and Scott joined them when he was able. In 1844 he made his first visit abroad, a two-day trip to Calais, but later in the year came a reason for a more prolonged visit to the Continent. A fire in Hamburg in 1842 had destroyed, besides much else, the great Nikolai Kirche, and an international competition was instituted for its replacement. A friend of Scott's had been asked if an English architect could be persuaded to compete, and Scott decided to do so.

3
Church Architect,
1844-51

Scott determined to base his design for Hamburg Cathedral on German Gothic, of which he knew nothing. He set out on his first continental tour, with his brother John and two lawyers, Smith and Cameron, travelling across Belgium, with Scott sketching all the while. At Cologne, Scott went off alone to Altenburg, rejoining his brother at Bonn. From there they journeyed up the Rhine to Frankfurt:

we were greatly interested by the conversation of Dr Schopenhauer, an old German philosopher, who usually took his meals at the hotel at which we stayed. I think I never met a man with such grand powers of conversation; but, alas, he was a determined infidel. ... I was quite astonished at his brilliancy, and, for all his infidelity, at the noble philosophical tone of his thoughts and conversation. I meant to have sent him some books on the evidences, etc. of Christianity, but I forgot it.[1]

After Hanover, Brunswick, Magdeburg, and Hamburg John Scott returned to Cambridge; Gilbert Scott stayed to collect local information, visiting Lubeck before sailing for London. He began enthusiastically to prepare a design on shipboard, but storms arose and he became very ill. On arriving home he was forced to lay up for some days, during which time he completed the general design, and the office began work on the set of drawings due to be sent off within a month. Closely involved with these preparations was the twenty year old George Edmund Street, who had recently joined the practice and was to stay for five years.[2]

The large package of drawings, with a long report, was despatched by steamer, arriving three weeks late due to ice on the Elbe. Scott's agent managed nevertheless to get them accepted. Over forty sets of drawings were exhibited before the award was made.

Two opposing factions sprang up in the town, supporting either the Gothic or the Classic style, and pamphlets flew. Gottfried Semper's domed Greek temple won the first prize, and Scott and Moffatt achieved third place, behind Strack of Berlin. The *Kirchen-Collegium* was dissatisfied, and the matter was referred to Sulpice Boiserè and Zwirner. Zwirner, the architect to Cologne Cathedral, championed Scott's Gothic design. Scott was in Hamburg when his success was ensured, and stayed for some time to make arrangements for the work to begin.

The original scheme had a great western tower, a nave 42 ft wide with two pairs of aisles, totalling 88 ft, with an apsidal chancel flanked by a sacristy and a chapel. This was altered, first in favour of shallow transepts, then to accommodate greater transepts and two aisles. An octagonal baptistery was added to the south-west corner. The work was to be executed in the German style of the 14th century, which indeed was more akin to English architecture of the time than to French and for which Scott claimed an especial perfection, unsullied by early coarseness or later decadence. He aimed not to copy the buildings of a particular district but rather, 'to take advantage of the varied beauties exhibited by German churches of corresponding style in general . . . and to endeavour so to meet the subject as we may imagine that the ancient artists would have done, if they had possessed all the practical advantages which can now be obtained'.[3]

Construction began on 8 October 1845 and continued past the

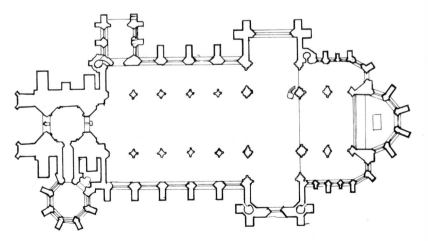

St Nicholas, Hamburg, 1845-80. Plan as built

1 Sir Gilbert Scott in 1869, aged 58. The negligence of appearance noted by
T. G. Jackson is apparent
Victoria and Albert Museum

2 16 High Street, Chesham, 1834. House for Henry Rumsey, one of Scott's earliest works, of a wholly Georgian character
By courtesy of the County Archivist, Buckingham

3 Fishmongers' Hall, City of London. Henry Roberts, 1831-3. View from south. Scott made all the drawings and superintended the work; the interior has been redecorated three times and suffered extensive war damage. National Monuments Record

4 Tavistock Poor Law Institution, 1838. View. A classic design
Margaret Tomlinson

5 Guildford Union Workhouse, 1838. Front elevation. A contemporary lithograph
George Underwood Collection, Surrey County Library.

6 Dunmow Poor Law Institution, 1838. Entrance. A late example with Tudor details and patterned brickwork — red with blue diaper and gault quoins: a contrast to the austere Kempthorne drawing

7 Windsor Poor Law Institution, 1838. View

8 Amersham Poor Law Institution, 1838. View. A characteristic use of flint and brick

9 Clifton Pauper Lunatic Asylum, York, 1845. Entrance. A substantial stone building with many later additions by J.B. and W. Atkinson and perhaps others

10 Weston Turville Rectory,
c 1838
Ian Toplis

11 St Blazey, restored 1839. Scott and Moffat's north aisle copies the remainder
of the building
L. Connell

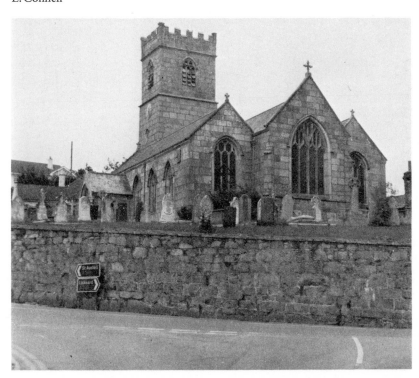

12 Martyrs' Memorial, Oxford, 1841-3. Based on Scott's early studies of the Eleanor Crosses

13 St Nicholas, Lincoln, 1839-40. View from south-east

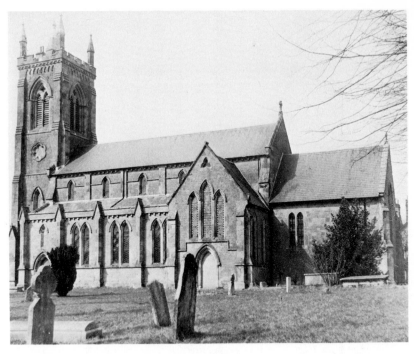

14 Holy Trinity, Shaftesbury, 1842. Demolished

15 Holy Trinity, Shaftesbury — interior. There were galleries on three sides

16   Turnham Green, 1841-3. The east end is an addition by James Brooks

17   Chudleigh Knighton, 1841-2. Small, cruciform, Early English, and possibly a Moffatt job

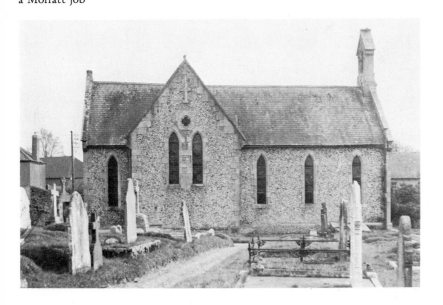

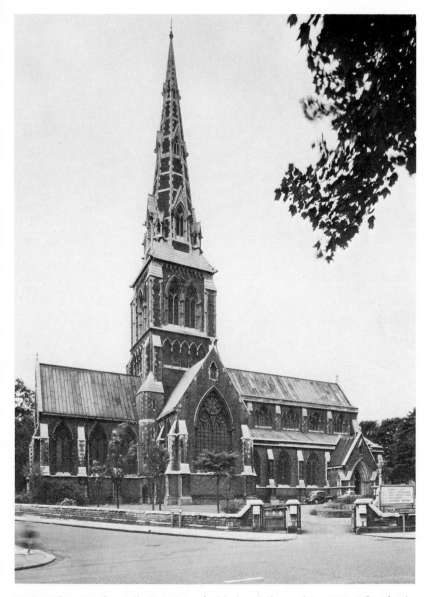

18 St Giles, Camberwell. Exterior of old church burned in 1841. The classic
porch, 'debased' windows and rendered exterior were features disliked by
The Ecclesiologist
National Monuments Record

19 St Giles, Camberwell. Interior of old church. Note the galleries, box pews,
prominent pulpit, and plaster ceilings
National Monuments Record

20 St Giles, Camberwell, 1842-4
National Monuments Record

21 St Giles, Camberwell. An early cut of the interior of the new church
Illustrated London News, 28 December 1844

22 Woking, St John Baptist, 1842. A characteristic Scott Early English east end and wooden bellcote

23 Zeals, 1845-6. Unusually, in the flowing Decorated style. The unorthodox tower occurs in several other churches

24 Abergwili, 1843

25 Abergwili, interior. The standard early details modified to fit a Welsh plan type, with unusually heavy open timber roof.

26 Chesterfield, restored 1842-3. The roofs are not old: the benches with their fleur-de-lis ends are of Scott's restoration. The plaster was removed subsequently: the rood and screen is of 1918: and there was a fire in 1961 after this photograph was taken. So what we now see is very different from how Scott left in in 1843. National Monuments Record

27 St Mary, Stafford, view in 1806 before restoration National Monuments Record

28 St Mary, Stafford, as restored 1842-5
National Monuments Record

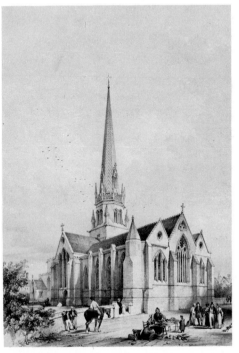

29 St Mary, Stafford. Perspective
of Scott's original proposals for
restoration. The west front and
south transept were not altered,
the spire was not built, and
there are other differences
National Monuments Record

end of Scott's life. He spent much time in Germany in 1845 and 1846. In April he set off via Belgium, stopping to study the public buildings at Ypres: from there he travelled by diligence to Minden to visit the quarries supplying the job. In September he was in Hamburg again to attend the ceremonial laying of the foundation stone. In the course of his trip to Germany in 1847, he reached Prague.

The church was consecrated in 1863, although the south aisle was incomplete. The tower was built, with some subsidence trouble, in 1876-7 and the baptistery in 1878-80.[4] The building was well exhibited: two views were in the Royal Academy in 1847, an excellent model by Salter was advantageously displayed at the Crystal Palace, and views were shown at the Paris exhibition of 1855.

The original estimate of £85,000 was far exceeded: £175,000 was spent up to 1868, £5404 7s 9d on the tower and £3602 on the baptistery, in all over £184,000, but even this is almost certainly not the complete figure.

The reaction of the Ecclesiological Society to this cathedral was strange: it was deemed a sin to use such a building for 'one of the worst sections of an heretical sect'.[5] The Society earnestly hoped that Scott's example would not be followed. Scott wrote a letter, refused publication in *The Ecclesiologist*,[6] noting that the Protestant Church embraces 'persons professing almost every variety of doctrine from the Romanist to the Socinian'. He then proceeded to argue the orthodoxy of some Lutheran opinions, the ecclesiological rectitude of Lutheran churches in general, and the correctness of the citizens of Hamburg in selecting a Gothic cathedral rather than a pagan temple. Scott hoped that his building would be instrumental in banishing the few lingering remnants of un-Christian practice in the Lutheran church.

The Ecclesiologists were nonplussed, for they were used to laying down the law. Though they dropped the matter, Scott claimed that they persecuted him for many years afterwards: there was indeed a degree of coolness for three or four years, and Scott may have found the argument useful in reinforcing his Evangelical connections.

In the wake of success, Scott and Moffatt had grown apart. Scott, increasingly poised and well-connected and with a large job to keep the office running, had less need of Moffatt's energies; he was doing a better class of work than institutions. Moffatt's rudeness gave offence to clients. The extravagant Moffatt and the always insecure Scott both needed money: Scott sought more church work, and Moffatt turned to speculation in railway shares. Mrs Scott was instrumental in their agreeing to a dissolution from the end of 1845,[7] dividing the work and their bank overdraft between themselves.

Moffatt later designed an odd and rather appealing house in Park Lane, the facade of which consists mostly of a great Perpendicular bay window rising through two storeys. In 1847 he was embroiled with the District Surveyor for St Pancras over a block of model dwellings for the Association for Improving the Dwellings of Industrious Classes. He successfully competed for, and built, Earlswood Asylum near Redhill in Surrey, and in 1855 Taunton Assize Hall was under construction. He actively propagated the idea of 'new towns', and competed for work in connection with the drainage of London in 1850. He was involved in projects, probably speculative, for housing estates in London's suburbs and in the West Country. He drank heavily, and was imprisoned in 1860 for debt. Scott, appealed to, contributed towards Moffatt's legal fees and probably continued with subventions. Moffatt continued to enter competitions, but Scott eschewed all but the largest and most prestigious.

For some years Scott was financially straitened. He had little capital, an office to run, a family to support; his absence in Germany had slowed the flow of church work. Only four new jobs are traceable to 1845, and eight to 1846. By 1846 the great expansion of church building was in full flood. About the middle of the year there were 400 new churches under construction, and even an obscure and not particularly competent provincial practitioner like E. H. Shellard of Manchester had twenty-nine on his hands at once. Scott had only fifteen, plus perhaps ten restorations.

Until he was forty-four and could cautiously regard himself as a success, with major works brought to him, his life was one of unceasing labour and continual worry. He had worked up to twenty-seven fresh jobs in 1855, and in the intervening ten years built approximately fifty new churches and restored seventy, besides eleven known schools and at least twenty miscellaneous works. By the end of 1850, just half of this work had been started, and the new churches began to take on a different character.

It is difficult to classify the churches built from 1845-50. Many are executed in a dogmatic early Decorated style, and most of the remainder in Early English. One group of churches were two-celled structures consisting of nave and chancel, with bellcotes, turrets, or towers. A second group consisted of town churches larger than those of the first, with towers (usually with spires) in various positions: some had separate pitched roofs to each element, others a clerestory and lean-to aisles, and many are distinguished by a characteristic simple form of internal Decorated moulding, which also appears in some restorations. The remainder of the early churches approximate to neither of these first two groups.

In many of these churches, one finds considerable copying or derivation of details from mediaeval sources. For instance at St Matthew, Islington the east end lancets are said to have followed those of Chetwode, and the tower that of Sutton St Mary in Lincolnshire. The tower and spire of Christ Church, Ealing (1850) were castigated as 'a very literal representation of Bloxham'.[8]

Of the small churches, Barnet in Hertfordshire, designed in early 1845, was a flint-faced chapel with a wooden south porch, a shingled western bell turret, and early Decorated tracery. In 1855 Scott enlarged it by adding a north aisle to both nave and chancel, thus producing another Farncombe-type building with many pitched roofs. The parsonage, neither classic nor recognisably Gothic revival, is probably also by Scott and Moffatt. Moulsford in Berkshire was rebuilt by Scott in 1846, on the old foundations, with an added aisle, and its original wooden spirelet was re-used. Hixon, Staffordshire (1848) has a north tower. Chantry, near Frome, Somerset (1846) was given to the new parish by Mr Fussell the local ironmaster, and has a crocketted spirelet, more sophisticated than the normal bell gable, and a leaded roof; artistically it must be counted a great improvement on many earlier examples of smaller churches.

Of the larger churches, Christ Church, Ramsgate is of Kentish rag in the Early English style, a plain church seating 950 with an aisled nave and a chancel, each element with a roof of the approved steep pitch, and a north-east tower with a shingled broach spire. It was built at the low cost of £5300, at the same time as Pugin's church of St Augustine was being erected in the same town.

Holy Trinity, Watermoor, in Cirencester, bears a casual resemblance in massing to Farncombe: this too was built in three stages. The original building, begun in 1847, had a bellcote, supplemented by a tower in 1851, a spire in 1852, and a south aisle in 1860; the vestry is by John Oldrid Scott in 1903.[9] This is a pleasant stone church with a great deal of modelling, many tiled pitched roofs, a well-buttressed south-west tower with a plain parapet and spire, and windows after both the Early English and the Decorated styles. Internally, the arrangement of roofs limits the apparent height of the nave: the heavy timbers rest on foliated corbels, and the weight of the detail is well matched to the proportions of the structure. It is a much more pleasing interior than that of St Mark, Swindon, and the progress shown in four years is remarkable.

St Matthew, Islington (1847) was in the Early English style and was sited on an open space in the middle of the City Road. The church was always well regarded, and even *The Ecclesiologist* went out of its way to describe it as 'certainly the best new church which has yet been built for our communion in London (perhaps the best absolutely)', followed by a detailed report.[10] Street had worked on the church as assistant.

Sewerby, near Bridlington in Yorkshire, also of 1847, is an example of Scott's more unusual work of this time. The client, Yarburgh Graeme, would have Norman and nothing else. Scott, after a struggle, pocketed principle, designed an original and rich essay in that style, and twenty years later spoke scathingly of the 'fads' of his employer. The church has a broad aisleless nave (which Victorian churches needed but very rarely got), chancel, north transept, and a south tower with a leaded broach.

In 1846 a great fire burned most of the town of St John's in Newfoundland. Bishop Feild crossed the Atlantic in the autumn to obtain plans for a new cathedral and, possibly through the Ecclesiological Society and brother William, the work was entrusted to Scott, although J. M. Derick had previously done some designs.

The site had an enormous cross-fall, mouldings and mullions were prohibited because of the great risk of frost damage, and work would be intermittent due to the inclement weather. This might well have produced a new style, but Scott found late first pointed infinitely adaptable, especially on account of its plate tracery. He designed a cruciform scheme with central tower and aisled chancel, nave, and transepts. Scott drew many of the drawings himself, and the design was exhibited at the Royal Academy in 1848 and at the Architectural Association in 1849. Progress was slow: the nave was started in 1848, and the choir and transepts were completed only in

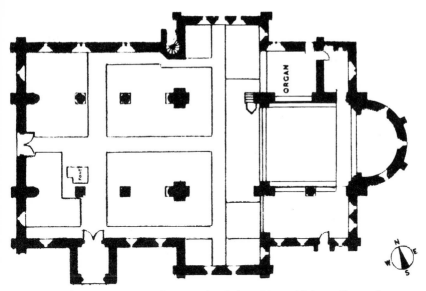

Alderney, about 1850. An early example of the wide apsidal cruciform plan.
Arc. Ass. Journal, lxvii 162

1880, under John Oldrid Scott.[11]

St Anne, Alderney (1850), given to the island by the Rev John le Mesurier, the son of the last hereditary governor, was a wide building with a short clerestoried nave, short transepts, a central tower with a pyramidal roof, but with separate roofs to the chancel and its aisles, and an apse. Scott built the church of granite with dressings and quoins of Caen stone, easier to work but less resistant to weather, and a slate roof. It was executed in a stern Early English style with unusually small windows, possiby modelled on churches in Normandy. This type of church was further developed in the mid-1850s.

Scott's thirty-six or so restorations of this period vary immensely in scope; not all were undertaken on conservative principles. Many involved considerable expenditure in rendering decent large and decayed structures, or in reconstruction and remodelling, or in making the structure safe. Churches of unfashionable periods could be radically altered. Occasionally little but refitting took place, and in some cases it is difficult to discern what exactly was done. And Scott had to deal with many forceful and eccentric clerics.

At the Perpendicular church of St Mary, Nottingham, restoration work began at the end of 1845, Scott and Moffatt having been appointed after the dismissal of Cottingham,[12] who had prepared designs. Three tenders of about £5000 had been received, together with another of £2800, the last of which builders was appointed to undertake the work. Work went on until 1848 and eventually cost about £7000. The west end of 1762[13] was rebuilt in Perpendicular, despite the finding of Norman capitals, the clerestory was renewed, and the central tower had its piers rebuilt. Scott returned in 1865, and spent over £5000 restoring roofs, recasing internal walls, reflooring, and refitting. The result is a pleasant church in which it is difficult to detect Victorian interference.

In 1847 Scott was at last asked to undertake the restoration of St Andrew's, Bradfield[14] in Berkshire, where his friend Thomas Stevens was rector. The eccentric Stevens had decided views on architectural style, and insisted on Early English, it being his habit to use the term 'square abacus' adjectivally to denote anything manly, straightforward, real or honest, whilst reserving 'ogee' for the mean, weak, and dishonest. In the end, all the old (mainly Decorated) building, except the 16th century brick and flint tower, the north nave arcade, and part of the north aisle wall, was lavishly rebuilt in Early English. Authority for the apse was found in neighbouring churches, possibly Padworth or Tidmarsh or Shinfield. The chancel was executed on a collegiate scale, with walling and apse groining in local chalk, and carvings in Mansfield Woodhouse stone;[15] the external walls were faced in Scott's beloved split flints. The church was reopened in the summer of 1848 and Scott regarded it as one of his best works.

Stevens thus had a magnificent church for choral services in his little village, so he put the village youth into surplices and trained them to sing, which they apparently did well, but there were not nearly enough of them. So Stevens founded a school, the better to fill the chancel with captive choristers, while at the same time making a little money towards the considerable cost of the restoration. At first Scott designed the buildings with help from Stevens, or vice versa. Largely Scott's is the Dining Hall of 1856, a copy of a tithe barn,[16] with great elm columns cut from the estate and in the west wall some of the earliest stained glass windows designed by the young Edward Burne-Jones. Scott, possibly to recover fees, sent his second son John Oldrid to school there from 1856-8.[17]

The finances of the school became more and more precarious, and Stevens more and more authoritarian and vague. Staff salaries were chronically in arrears, and masters enquiring when they were to be paid could be advised to read the Nicene Creed, which Stevens claimed always to have found of comfort in adversity. In 1881 Stevens became bankrupt for £160,000. The school, reorganised, survived. It is perhaps surprising that Scott thought Stevens 'a thorough man of business'.[18]

By August 1847 Scott had been appointed to restore the church of St Mary at Harrow on the Hill, no doubt at the instance of the incumbent, J. W. Cunningham, of the Clapham sect. The church, as repaired and 'beautified' in 1796, was rendered all over, with a wooden north porch, and galleries in the chancel facing west (!);[19] all the window tracery was mutilated. Scott removed galleries in the chancel and the north transept, provided a north chancel aisle and new north porch, rebuilt the nave roof on the old pattern, filled the east windows with Decorated tracery, refaced the church in flint, repaired the interior, and added battlemented parapets on nave aisles and porches. The Jacobean screen disappeared, and the old font was retrieved from the vicarage garden; the work was completed in 1849.[20]

Ellesmere in Shropshire, extensively rebuilt in 1847-9, is an example of a radical and non-conservative alteration.[21] The Norman nave, filled with galleries and insufficiently roomy for a town which had grown with the canal trade, was demolished and entirely rebuilt with aisles and a south porch, each element with a pitched and slated roof, in a correct early Decorated style, of white Cefn sandstone, contrasting with the reddish Grinshill stone of the older part. The column bases of the central tower were rebuilt and the east end repaired; the whole church was refitted. The Perpendicular north chapel roof and the chancel roof of 1822 were retained. As the work was accomplished without any significant antiquarian outcry, the Norman nave must have been in a very poor state.[22]

St Mary, Sandbach, Cheshire, was almost entirely rebuilt in 1847-9. It was not a careful restoration but the friable character of its red sandstone posed problems: Scott had much trouble with this stone, notably at Nantwich and at Chester. Although most of the building dated only from the time of Henry VII, the tower was dangerous, the interior galleried, the windows blocked, the capitals chopped off, and the roof insecure. All the old fittings and furniture were thrown out, the tower rebuilt as a copy of the original, the east end extended 40 ft. In the end, even *The Ecclesiologist* regarded it as 'so altered and skinned and transformed in a process of costly Restoration that it has almost lost all its identity...decent propriety without much heart'.[23] Nevertheless, it remained unfashionable Perpendicular even though so much work was done.[24]

Aylesbury church in Buckinghamshire, a cruciform edifice of the 13th and 14th centuries with many Perpendicular alterations, was, like many market town churches, tumbling down. As early as 1842 the Camdenians agitated for a restoration which should 'eject every pue'. Not much was done until 1848 when, following signs of the imminent dissolution of the central tower, Scott's advice was sought. Scott, no doubt with an apposite quotation of St Matthew 7.26, pronounced the church very dangerous, being founded upon sand rather than rock, and excavations for burials within the building had undermined it further. Scarcely one wall or pillar was plumb, the nave columns leant westward to a frightful extent, and the roof was dangerous. Only part of the church was used for worship, galleried and box-pewed; the remainder was partitioned off. The south transept, once a gunpowder store, now housed the fire engine and gravediggers' appurtenances. At a dinner to which Scott was invited, 'an obtuse old cleric wisely remarked "What a mercy it was that the tower did not fall during the Bishop's visitation." "Not at all", replied a witty barrister, "I'd match Sam to dodge a falling church with any man", and reverence for the episcopal bench did not prevent a general burst of laughter'.[25]

The vicar had long been annoyed by the clock striking twelve whilst he read the communion service, and the very week of Scott's visit, the sexton had devised a scheme to stop the disturbance: he drove a hook into a pew, attached a wire to the clapper of the bell, and at five to twelve tied the wire on to the hook. At midday, the bell tried to strike, and at each effort lifted up the corner of the pew and dropped it down again, with great noise and dust. The congregation, mindful both of Scott's report and the example attributed to their bishop, rushed from the church in a body, supposing it to be falling about their ears.

Scott then underpinned the tower piers, with massive shoring, and prepared plans for a complete restoration, which was started the following year with the help of a £3000 parish rate and voluntary contributions. The church was closed, and as time and money were spent in substantial quantities, there were stormy vestry meetings. The transformed church was reopened in April 1851, with many

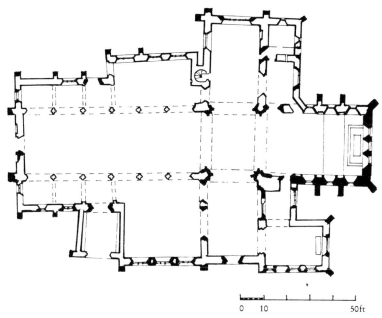

Aylesbury, restored 1850 and later. Plan: the black tint shows the areas rebuilt by Scott

fittings still incomplete. All the inside had been cleared out and fitted with open seats, the east and south walls of the chancel had been rebuilt in Early English to match the north wall, and the Perpendicular east window replaced by a triplet of lancets copied from the similar quintet at nearby Chetwode; the east end is very characteristic Scott.[26] The tower and nave were made safe, many windows were altered, the burials were re-interred outside, and the whole church repaved. In 1865, Scott reported on the state of the exterior. This project started by costing £200, soon rose to £1500, and eventually included the Lady Chapel, where, on stripping the walls, enough bits of the Decorated windows, piscina, and sedilia were found built into them to make it possible for Scott to make convincing replacements. The exterior was largely completed by 1867 and the restoration of the tower and spire followed. The choir was reconsecrated in September 1869.[27]

Scott started the earliest of his fifteen works in Cambridge in 1849. A fire had damaged the church of St Michael, and the question arose whether it belonged to Trinity College, the parish, or both. Trinity offered to repair the chancel (actually larger than the nave)

'in whatever reasonable way Mr Scott might advise',[28] provided the
parish would do the rest in harmony. The parish, hoping to avoid
any expense, demurred, prompting the incumbent, Professor
Scholefield, to reply that if Trinity were wholly responsible, Trinity
might close the church and the parishioners would have to build
themselves another. If they did not like it they might go to law, but
in any case the costs would probably fall on the ratepayers. The
parishioners agreed to the original suggestion. Though the damage
was extensive, Scott aimed to restore the fabric to its original state,
for it had all been built in one piece in the 1320s. He rebuilt the oak
roof, incorporating some old timbers, and covered it with Colly-
weston slates, removed the galleries, put in a new floor and new
arches across the aisles to support the chancel, added a north porch,
and restored and glazed the east window. The returned stalls in the
large chancel derived from collegiate requirements and *The Ecclesiologist* attempted to exonerate Scott for this, but the seating is all
unmistakably his.

Early in 1849 Scott, with the approval of the Oxford Archaeological Society, prepared plans for restoring Great Milton, Oxfordshire, a characteristic and creditable work of this period, which
completed in 1850, cost over £2000. Burnt stonework showed that
the church had been largely rebuilt after a fire in the early 14th
century. The interior was stripped of its box pews and low wooden
screen and the whole was repewed in oak, with new choir stalls
copied from those at Dorchester Abbey, though 15th century
bench ends are said to remain in the chancel. Some wall paintings
were discovered and obliterated. The chancel roof was renewed and
other roofs deplastered and boarded. The eastern half of the chancel
was rebuilt, allowing some 14th century floor tiling to remain, and
incorporating Perpendicular style sedilia reconstructed from fragments found by Scott; he did not replace them by a design in a 14th
century idiom. He reconstructed a double piscina in the south aisle
and opened out an aumbry. Pieces of a Purbeck marble altar were
found, but Low Church resistance might explain why this was not
reconstructed. Walls were underpinned. The rood screen is by
Scott.[29] The whole conduct of this work shows a considerable
regard for the mediaeval features of the building.

In contrast, Scott competed successfully for the restoration of
the chantry chapel of St Mary on the bridge at Wakefield, a building
in flowing Decorated style built about 1350, which had fallen into

decay. Work began in 1847, no doubt while he was still erecting St Andrew's. His contractor was Cox of Oxford, who, it was suggested, had received a good offer for the greatly decayed west front from the Hon George Chapple Norton of Kettlethorpe Hall who wanted it to face his boathouse. Scott was persuaded not to repair this front, but rather entirely to renew it. The new Caen stone front decayed very rapidly in the polluted West Riding air and needed further drastic attention. The old front remains, on the edge of a lake, surrounded by one of the finest rock gardens in Yorkshire. Scott later deeply regretted his action.

Coincident with the start of Scott's work at Aylesbury and at Wing in 1848, Bishop Wilberforce gave an address to the county archaeological society in the former town, advocating Low Church arrangements,[30] which was immediately followed by Scott's first public paper, on truthful church restoration. Scott's paper was a success and he gave it again at Higham Ferrers; in 1850 it was improved and published as 'A Plea for the Faithful Restoration of our Ancient Churches'. Scott sought to combat unscrupulous, unscholarly and destructive restoration: 'It is a most lamentable fact, that there has been far more done to obliterate genuine examples of pointed architecture by the tampering caprices of well-meaning restoration than...by centuries of mutilation and neglect'.[31] But here we come upon the confusion and lack of intellectual rigor pervading Scott's writing. One should preserve parts of a building of various ages to show its history, but one may remove decayed later portions to restore earlier. Even a mutilated original detail is of greater value than if restored, but the true object of restoration is to replace mutilated features and if they cannot be recovered from within the church, one ought to use contemporaneous nearby churches as a guide. He accepted the replacement in 1832-41 of the Norman west tower of Canterbury Cathedral by a new one to match its Gothic fellow because of the perfection of style of the latter (though he might not have done so twenty years later). But, given the poor state of many churches and the widespread liking for new Gothic detail, it was encouraging that conservative principles had at least been stated, even if they were not invariably adhered to.

In August 1847, Scott was appointed as architect to the restoration works at Ely, his first Cathedral. James Essex, the most scholarly of the 18th-century Gothicists, had worked there in 1757-

62,[32] and Blore later: much work had been done from about 1844 under the superintendence of Dean Peacock and Professor Willis, the antiquary, but with no professional assistance, as the professional journals pointedly remarked. The south transept had been repaired, Bishop Alcock's chapel rebuilt and Prior Crauden's repaired, the east end had been altered and the reredos removed, the tower ceiling was opened out and the choir vaulting repainted.

When the Dean came to refitting the choir and restoring the octagonal lantern, he found it advisable to appoint an architect. At an early meeting he described Amiens in such terms as to make Scott rush off to France at once, though it was November. Scott knew nothing of French work, and was astonished: 'what I had always conceived to be German architecture I now found to be French'.[33]

The Ecclesiological Society watched over the progress of the works: there are sixty-one notices in their journal between 1844 and 1868, which describe the work done and the controversies which arose. One such was over the choir arrangements. Before Essex's time there had been a reredos in the third bay of the chancel: these three bays formed a sacrarium and thirty-five stalls were positioned on each side below the crossing, the easternmost six bays of the chancel being devoted to the shrine of St Etheldreda. Essex abolished the shrine, placed the organ above the fourth bay and the altar at the far eastern end, with thirty-one stalls each side in the five easternmost bays; the rest of the choir then formed part of the nave. Peacock's proposal for retaining the altar and placing the stalls in the three westernmost chancel bays, with congregational benches to their east, incurred the ire of *The Ecclesiologist*. Scott's design, exhibited at the Royal Academy in 1848, was similar to Peacock's, but the eastern two bays formed a retrochoir behind the altar. It was built thus, but counter-suggestions were made until 1851.

In mid-1849 work was in full swing. Besides the choir work, the south transept roof had been repaired. The Bishop's throne, Dean's stall, and sub-stalls were finished in March 1851, and Walsingham's superior stalls were to be restored. All the vaults were restored, and in prospect were the new altar, reredos,[34] pavement, and organ case, together with the rearrangement of the tombs of Bishops Alcock and West, the canopy work of which had been replaced. The vault over Bishop Crauden's chapel was replaced in wood as the walls could not bear stone. This left the roof and wall painting, the

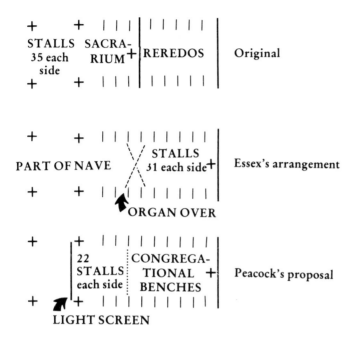

Ely Cathedral, restored 1847 on. Plans showing the choir arrangements.

opening of the arches of the west aisle and the glazing of the windows.[35]

Walsingham's remarkably early 14th century crossing lantern, of eight enormous timber posts 3ft 4in × 2ft 8in, 63 ft long, strutted together and covered in lead, had suffered from beetle and the ends of some timbers were decayed. Its restoration began in 1861[36] as a memorial to Peacock, who had died three years before. The windows and pinnacles had been altered, and nobody was sure how they should have looked, but Scott's version looks in place. Scott found mortice works which suggested the presence of a spire and revised his design to include one, though it was not built. The flying buttresses, removed by Essex, now sprung singly from the corners of the lantern, which was completed in 1865, except for the turrets and pinnacles of 1872. When in the 1950s the lantern and roofs were repaired, it was considered that Scott had done an excellent and conservative job of cutting away rotten wood and strengthening it with new.

In 1848 restoration of the old painting, traces of which had been discovered, was begun. The painting inside the lantern was completed by L'Estrange[37] in 1855, and Scott suggested St Michael's, Hildesheim as a model for the painting on the nave roof, completed after L'Estrange's death by Gambier Parry.[38]

By 1866 the transepts and west tower had been restored, St Catherine's Chapel rebuilt and the nave roof releaded. All this had cost £40,000 in cash and kind and work progressed slowly, punctuated by appeals.

Scott also designed the memorial to Dr Hill, canon and Orientalist. The original design of about 1854 was altered, exhibited at the Architectural Exhibition in 1856, and installed the same year. J.B. Philip was the sculptor.[39]

Scott has been much criticised for destructive restoration, and some of the churches he restored during this period indeed underwent drastic changes, but it is notable that little or no criticism of his actions at Ely has ever been made, and he has come in for some quiet praise.

Early in 1849 Blore unexpectedly resigned from the post of Surveyor to the Fabric of Westminster Abbey, and Scott was chosen to succeed him. 'We wish', said *The Ecclesiologist* brutally, 'that the change had taken place much sooner'.[40] Scott immediately set to work, and found Dean Buckland (whom he had encountered nine years before in connection with the Martyrs' Memorial) to be an amiable and eccentric companion, who would scamper over the Abbey roof with him. No restoration work was done until 1854 for financial reasons, but Scott in the meantime investigated the Chapter House, which was being used as a store for old Government papers, and prepared[41] a restoration of one end of the monument to Philippa of Hainault, Edward III's queen, which occupied him on and off for ten years. He found some detached fragments of the carved alabaster niches preserved in the Abbey; others were immured in the adjacent monument of Henry V — Scott made incisions into the base of the tomb and, with the help of candles and mirrors, recovered enough pieces to reconstruct the whole design.

In the course of this project, the Cottingham collection of architectural fragments came up for sale. The Cottinghams, father and son, had lived at 86 Waterloo Road, accumulating a collection of Gothic work which, as Holman Hunt unkindly but accurately put it,[42] they had 'improved' off the face of churches up and down the country. Scott knew of this, and wondered if some of the missing Abbey bits might be in the collection. Cundy, the Abbey mason, went to look, and found a number of them on the chimney-piece of Cottingham's office, he having bought them thirty-five years previously from the then Abbey mason.

It is remarkable that the Royal Commission on Historical Monuments makes only one reference to his work on this building; and that derogatory. He was by no means inactive during nearly thirty years as Surveyor. He showed several items, including the restoration of Queen Philippa's monument, at the Great Exhibition of 1851, and did much antiquarian work. In 1861 he published *Gleanings from Westminster Abbey*, a second enlarged edition, with a good deal of material by William Burges, appearing in 1863. Scott seems not personally to have undertaken antiquarian research, but he was indeed prepared to use the work of others.[43]

Besides the restoration of the Chapter House, described later, there were a number of other works. In 1849-50 the rose window in the south transept was remodelled; most likely a Blore initiative, perhaps altered by Scott in the execution.[44] Proposals for restoring the Royal Tombs in the Confessor's Chapel led to controversy: there was limited work at Queen Philippa's tomb, replacement of grilles was required in front of the tombs of Queen Eleanor and King Henry VII and induration of some of the stone with a shellac solution was thought necessary. However, most of the tombs, battered as a result of years of lack of security at the Abbey, were left alone. Also in 1849-50, the transept parclose screens were installed, as was a new choir pulpit.[45] The brass commemorating the engineer Robert Stephenson is Scott's. In 1864 the sanctuary pavement was repaired and the high altar and reredos designed. The latter was erected in 1867, a strange but successful composition with the elements enclosed in rectangles, where Scott's favourite craftsmen[46] were given rein.

In the cloisters, Scott renewed much decayed window tracery in the North Walk and refaced the South Walk, practically rebuilt by Blore in 1835. He renewed the font in Henry VII's Chapel; his new altar there, of cedar and black marble, was installed in 1870.[47] The north transept, altered extensively in the 18th century, was taken in hand in 1872[48] but Scott completed little there.

During Dean Buckland's mental incapacity, Scott dealt with the Sub-Dean, Lord John Thynne, son of the Marquess of Bath.

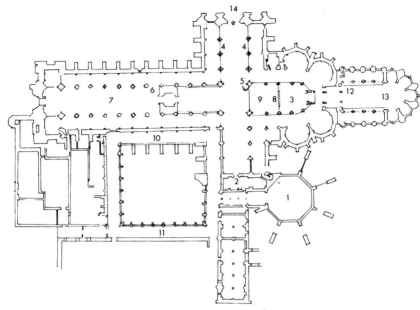

1. *Restoration of Chapter House*
2. *S. Transept Window*
3. *Repair of Royal Tombs*
4. *Parclose Screens*
5. *Choir Pulpit*
6. *Nave Pulpit*
7. *Brass to Robert Stephenson*
8. *High Altar and Reredos*
9. *Repair of Sanctuary pavement*
10. *Repair of North Walk*
11. *Refacing South Walk*
12. *Font*
13. *Chapel altar*
14. *North transept extr.*

Westminster Abbey. The plan shows the position of Scott's various works, 1849 onwards

Thynne was instrumental in introducing him to a group of noble and influential clients: the Duke of Buccleuch (himself a Scott), Earl Cawdor, and Lord Harewood. Buckland's successors, Richard Chenevix Trench and Arthur Stanley, another antiquarian researcher, were both on good terms with Scott.

Scott, though typed as a church architect, sought to gain recognition for revived Gothic as a suitable style for larger secular buildings, and wished for a more broadly based practice. He entered in 1847 the competition for the Army and Navy Club premises in Pall Mall with a design, surprisingly, in flamboyant French Gothic, possibly inspired by the Hôtel de Ville at Calais. Of the sixty-nine designs exhibited in April 1849 the only other in Gothic was by

George Truefitt. Scott lost this competition to George Tattersall: the work was eventually done by Parnell and Smith.

Scott won the competition for Brighton College in 1848; this was thus his first scholastic work. The first stage, an open quadrangle with cloisters, in 'Collegiate Gothic of the fourteenth century'[49], was built between June 1848 and January 1849. The principal's house was completed in 1854, the chapel in 1859, the dining hall in 1863.[50] Scott's original block is in flint with stone dressings, successful in its massing, and in contrast to the exclusively late Georgian and early Victorian stucco of Kemp Town.

In 1849 Scott, with more than the required seven years' practice behind him, was elected a Fellow of the Institute of British Architects, the prestigious if still adolescent professional body.

4

Success,
1851-56

In the late summer of 1851 the forty years old Scott embarked on his
'grand tour' through Italy. He set off alone through Ghent, Aix-la-
Chapelle, and Cologne, sketching at each. In Berlin, where he
had been mistaken for Sir Walter Scott by the hôtelier, he met his
friend and fellow architect Benjamin Ferrey[1] and they proceeded by
road to Dresden, Prague, and Vienna (where they sketched St
Stephen's Cathedral), thence by rail to Trieste, where they took
ship for Venice.

'At Venice, all was enchantment!' They sketched the Ducal
Palace, and Scott was so awed by St Mark's, 'the most impressive
interior I have ever seen', that he filled sixteen pages of his sketch
book with details. He grew to regard Venetian Gothic in a much
more favourable light, but Ferrey was continually heard to mutter
'Batty Langley!'. They called upon John Ruskin, still at work on
The Stones of Venice, and Scott renewed the slight acquaintance of
eight years before, meeting *en passant* the twenty-two years old
Lord Dufferin, the future Viceroy of India, and twenty-seven years
old Sir Francis Scott. The young Anthony Salvin Jr., the architect
son of an architect, joined the party for a while as an interpreter.

After three days in Venice, the party progressed to Padua. Scott,
rising at dawn so as not to lose sketching time, saw out of his hotel
window a splendid Gothic domestic ruin. Closer examination
proved it to be a *trompe-l'oeil*, a sham painted on the yard wall, as
Scott discovered with some mirth. Vicenza, Verona, Mantua,
Modena, Bologna, and three days in Florence followed, with Siena
and Pisa thereafter. At Genoa, Scott was pleased to find that the
western part of the Cathedral exhibited many French characteristics. With November snow covering the Carrara mountains they
turned north, stopping at Milan before proceeding home.[2]

Scott had nowhere paused to look closely at Classic or Renaissance architecture. Italian architecture was Romanesque or Gothic, and its study was essential to the British revival. He would not countenance plagiarism, and would not have built a building in pure Venetian Gothic such as Somers Clarke's offices at the corner of Lothbury in the City. Rather, he found a mine of details, of ways of using materials, which would be of service in clothing the fabric of a building.

Refreshed and invigorated, he thought again of the Cottingham collection, which had not yet found a buyer. He had written to *The Builder*[3] proposing that the Government purchase the collection as a necessary adjunct to the education of carvers, architects, and others, but this expensive suggestion met with silence. Then 'A strange person, Mr Bruce Allen' came to see Scott, and meetings between several architects produced a scheme for an architectural museum, with Allen to be curator and to carry on his own School of Art within it. Scott energetically wrote circulars to everyone, begging donations and subscriptions. Blore did not respond. Street discouraged the idea as tending to copyism, and Butterfield gave very cold support. Scott collected £500, a list of subscribers, and many specimens; he lent his own collection and employed agents to make casts of details. In March 1852 (before the formation of the Victoria Embankment) the Museum was established in the loft of a wharf at Cannon Row. Lectures by Ruskin and others were held amidst the specimens, and the annual *conversazione* chaired by Earl de Grey, President of the Institute of British Architects, could involve 600 people.

Scott was enthusiastic. He wrote a lecture urging architects not to use conventional Early English foliage, but rather to make their own ornaments from natural forms; for instance, he himself used zinnias and other florists' flowers at Shalstone and Ranmore. He studied botany: 'I remember longing most earnestly to discover a leaf, from which one might suppose our Early English foliage to have been derived. The nearest I could find was an almost microscopic wall fern, and certain varieties of the common parsley. One night I dreamed that I had found the veritable plant. I can see it even now, a sear and yellow leaf, but with all the beauty of form which graces the capitals at Lincoln and Lichfield. I was maddened with excitement and pleasure; but... I awoke.'[4]

Carvers and students came to the Museum to be taught art from ancient models and 'acquired a degree of skill and taste in the drawing of architectural ornament which had never before been reached nor has (since the removal of the museum) been retained'.[5] Enthusiasm and finance did not match, however, and two years later the concern was in debt. Earl de Grey, Scott, and Clutton waited on the Prince Consort, who lectured them on the poor state of architectural education in the country, and referred them to Mr Cole of the Department of Science and Art, which subscribed £100. In 1856, with the establishment of the museums at South Kensington, no further subsidy was forthcoming, though the Architectural Museum was assigned space for three years in one of the temporary buildings known as the 'Brompton Boilers'. The Department was prepared to pay the curator's salary if the collection were made over to it, but the Museum rejected this. In 1860, because of structural difficulties and because many of the casts were duplicates of those purchased by the Government as examples for the Houses of Parliament, the Architectural Museum was asked to leave. After considerable negotiation, the collection was loaned to the Department, and rearranged and the Museum was allowed to continue holding lectures there.

Scott was disgusted, and took this as a personal slight. He remained as treasurer to the body to the end of his life, by which point it had had something of a renaissance and had attained the dignity of the Royal Architectural Museum and School of Art, with premises in Westminster, but he took care never to get involved with such a voluntary or philanthropic body again. Rather, he perfected techniques to make it easy for others to take up and work on causes dear to his heart.

Among Scott's twenty-five new churches of this period, Resurrection, Longton, in the Potteries is innovatory for 1853.[6] The original small building of red and blue brick, with red and white brick in the interior, and a cross-gabled polygonal apse, represents a very early use of Frenchified forms and polychrome brick.[7] Although Scott had used the traditional feature of black or blue diaper of clamp burnt bricks in his workhouses, the mid fifties was an early date for the use of machine-made coloured brickwork and production of hard, regular red, blue, yellow or off-white bricks, in Staffordshire or in Suffolk, was only in its infancy. Even William Butterfield, the most prominent advocate of polychrome, had done little in this line at that date; the same is broadly true of S. S. Teulon and of William White, a younger man once in Scott's office. Scott himself later used much polychrome brickwork, at, for instance, Yiewsley (1858) and Ottershaw (1869): the Ecclesiological Society approved of colour.

Four further small churches make an interesting contrast. Shippon, near Abingdon (1855) is a small two-celled chapel with rock-faced walling, hard mechanical Decorated detail, a four-bay nave and a two-bay chancel plus vestry and a crocketed flèche over the chancel arch. The inside is white and plastered, with the trussed rafter roof which had become a standard pattern for small spans and cheaper churches. It is not an attractive building and perhaps was designed by someone in Scott's office. Bylchau, Denbighshire (1857) is another simple church, single-celled and rock-faced in dark green, with three pair of lancets each side and a western bell gable, a throwback to fifteen years before

In contrast to the simplicity of Bylchau, Trefnant (1855),[8] seven miles away, though small, is very rich. The component parts each have a pitched and gabled roof of green slate, ending in parapets crowned with ornate crosses, and there is a central bell gable. The exterior is limestone laid in random courses, and the Decorated windows are sometimes fancifully detailed. The interior displays polished marble pillars, plastered walls, and much carving of foliage and of heads. The whole is well balanced and in scale; even the trussed rafters have turned uprights.[9]

Scott's work at Trefnant led perhaps to his restoration of the nearby church at Henllan, though it is not known precisely what work was done. In 1862 he designed St Barnabas, Bromborough, towards which Charles Kynaston Mainwaring, the husband of one of his patrons at Trefnant, gave £2000. An apsidal variant of Trefnant was built, again with Mainwaring family funds, at Welshampton in Shropshire in 1863.[10] Gibson's large and rich church at Bodelwyddan, also a private benefaction, may have been erected to rival Trefnant.

Woolland in Dorset is not dissimilar from Trefnant. Scott's second design was accepted, the old building was demolished in April 1855, and the new foundations set out in May. J. T. Irvine, a young native of the Shetlands who had studied at the Academy schools, was appointed clerk of works at £2 12s 6d per week, a good wage. A. H. Green of Blandford had finished the building work by the end of 1856 at a cost of about £1800, against an estimate of £1658. The architect's fees and expenses came to £104 15s 0d. The church is of a familiar form: second pointed, with a nave and rib-vaulted chancel with a north chapel and a polygonal apse, as well as a western polygonal bell turret. The rich interior has twenty-six columns of Purbeck marble and three of Derbyshire fossil, foliated capitals, and stained glass.[11]

St Andrew, Ashley Place, Westminster, started in 1855, is unusual. It was modelled on a German 'hall' church, with gabled nave aisle windows, a three-sided apse and Geometric Decorated tracery. There was no tower, nor nave clerestory, nor transepts, but only a flèche over the crossing and a west gallery. It was probably more imposing inside than out.[12]

The period ends with an important group of ten large churches, middle pointed, cruciform, with towers and spires, usually with apsidal chapels, all ultimately deriving from Alderney, and, at several removes from St Giles, Camberwell. Some are very dull; others among Scott's *chefs-d'œuvre*. St Mary, West Derby, Liverpool was exhibited at the Royal Academy in 1851, but built only in 1853-6. This large (143 ft long) church with a central tower provides little cause for enthusiasm: one cannot help thinking of the more successful churches which Edward Buckton Lamb was designing, loathed by the Camdenians but well-suited to the usages of the time. Weeton near Harrogate[13] and Holy Trinity, Rugby, both begun in 1852, were to this cruciform plan but neither had apses. Similar also were St Paul's Episcopal Church, Dundee of 1853-5 and St Mary, Stoke Newington, North London of 1855-8. These churches had three-sided apsidal chapels and west towers, and each bay of the nave aisles was separately gabled on the exterior, a feature unusual in England and borrowed, like other details in this group, from North Germany. The chapter house at York, itself heavily restored ten years previously by Sydney Smirke, furnished much of the detail for St Paul's, except for the tower, which was modelled on that of the still-extant Old Town Church, but crowned with a spire. The interior was seated with chairs, an innovation perhaps confined to Scotland at the time: in England, considerable sums were being spent in repewing with benches, and when an attempt was made to use chairs at Sudbury, Suffolk in 1858 it was legislatively thwarted.[14]

Stoke Newington is disappointing and ordinary, partly because of the use of squared rubble walling — Kentish rag, with cut stone dressings. The contrast between the stones makes nonsense of the detail. The whole exterior is papery and lacks modelling, especially around the windows. The tower and spire, added in 1908 to a design by John Oldrid Scott, are the best parts of the building.

St John, Leicester (1853-4) was of this type, with a north-east tower. The spire, of bands of coloured brick, was criticised and later removed. Christ Church, Swindon (1851) has a western tower with broach spire but a square-ended chancel.

In 1854 the headmaster of Harrow School sent for Scott, as the school had outgrown its red brick, Elizabethan-style chapel, designed by C. R. Cockerell in 1838. Scott prepared two schemes, of which the more costly, middle pointed in Bath stone and flint, was chosen. The apsidal chancel, 'a miniature of the choir of Cologne', and aisles were built around the old building, which was later pulled down and replaced by a new nave. The flèche over the chancel was added in 1865, the transepts by Aston Webb in 1903 copying Scott's work exactly.

This series of churches led up to All Souls, Haley Hill, Halifax. Paid for by Col Edward Akroyd, MP, it was designed in 1855, started in April 1856, and completed in November 1859.[15] It is cruciform, with a square-ended chancel and an engaged and buttressed north-west tower with crenellated pinnacles on which is set a spire with lucarnes. The nave is high and clerestoried. The clustered nave columns have stiff-leaved capitals; the triforium has marble columns; in between, saints peer out of roundels. There was painting over the chancel arch and the reredos is uncommonly well integrated. The roofs, a panelled timber vault in the chancel and trussed rafters elsewhere, cover a Decorated richness. The pulpit is a fine work of Italian Gothic type in green and white marble. In size it is comparable with a large Lincolnshire parish church such as Heckington. One may judge Scott by this major work, for he himself regarded it as 'on the whole, my best church'.[16]

At this time Scott's activity as a restorer of major town churches is most marked. During these five years some two dozen church restorations were started. A characteristic of this time is the provision of apsidal chancels, often of a French character, and not infrequently polygonal, rare in English mediaeval work, in restorations as well as in new churches. After such early examples as

Bradfield, Kiddington, Hamburg, and Alderney, such apses became more common: Scott used about forty between 1852 and 1867, starting with that, pentagonal and French, at the now demolished Cambridge Cemetery Chapel.

In 1855 at Hampton Lucy, Warwickshire a richly detailed and externally gabled apse was added to Rickman's 1822 church and the fine stained glass east window was enlarged and reset in three sections. At Mold in North Wales the chancel was extended with an apse, in addition to considerable general restoration. Scott added a polygonal apse to William Hurst's 1827 Christ Church, Doncaster.

The Camden Chapel at Camberwell in South London, a brick box of 1797 enlarged in 1814, received a chancel in 1854. Scott apparently discussed the matter with John Ruskin and furnished an apsidal High Romanesque design in polychrome stonework, suggested by S. Fermo at Verona.[17] This was the pattern for several works in the 1860s, such as the similar remodelling of the chapel of King's College, London, or the chapel of Partis College, Bath which was given a basilican character and apse in 1862. Scott's work also may be the 1860 conversion of the library of the classical mansion of Hawkstone, Shropshire into a chapel with an apse 'decorated with much alabaster'. But he never seems as happy with this sort of work as, for example, the eccentric S. S. Teulon.

At Newark, one of England's great parish churches, Scott effected a major restoration from 1852-5. He reseated the Perpendicular building, removed plaster ceilings, and moved the organ, but the considerable amount of other work which was done, at a cost possibly exceeding £6000, was undertaken so tactfully that it now passes unnoticed.

At Melton Mowbray, one of the four parish churches in England with aisled transepts, Scott, together with his son John Oldrid, worked at intervals up to 1890, at the immense total cost of £24,000. Scott was commissioning glass in 1850 and as late as 1865 the building was said to be vast and dilapidated. By 1872 the whole church except for the south transept and the upper part of the tower[18] had been repaired.

Scott was appointed to repair the chancel of St Peter, Northampton and in 1850 he was pulling down its 'most ruinous' 17th-century east wall, having designed a new chancel in the Decorated style. It turned out that a great deal of old stone had been used by the 17th-century builders, and enough Norman material was recovered to make it possible to rebuild a convincing work in this style, a longer chancel on the old foundations. Refitting was then done, and the church was reopened in 1852.[19]

In 1854 the central tower of Great Malvern Priory, a Perpendicular structure designed on similar lines to those of Gloucester Cathedral, was found to be unsafe, and Haddon the local architect in charge could find no builder to repair it. Scott made some proposals, found a builder, McCann from Amesbury, and after a year's delay the work was undertaken. There followed nine or ten years later a general conservative repair of the stonework, removal of the pews, and repair of the 15th century encaustic tiling on the wall behind the altar. In 1868 dry rot was located in the north transept roof and the clerk, looking for a gas escape in the vestry with a lighted candle, found it. The resultant explosion damaged structure, vicar, clerk, and verger. Haddon did the repairs to the first of these, with Scott as consultant.

Scott restored another red sandstone church at Nantwich, Cheshire during 1854-61. Decay forced extensive renewal and wholesale forgery of details: none of the carving is other than modern. He also, it is said, 'restored' the western doorway and

Eastnor. Rectory, 1849. The pair of unequal gables is characteristic. Many other details derive from the workhouses
Redrawn from a drawing in the Hereford and Worcester County Record Office

window back to 13th-century forms, earlier in style than the rest of the church, and wished to destroy the clerestory. Less reprehensible, though changing the appearance of the church much more, was the usual wholesale slaughter of galleries and pews.[20]

Scott, having already built a new rectory at Eastnor, Herefordshire, rebuilt the church there in 1852, in Scott Decorated style, with an east window like that of nearby Ledbury, screens, good quality materials, and some interesting furnishings. The interior is extremely dark. Penshurst in Kent represented a not dissimilar, less drastic operation, and French detail is discernible there.

He was less severe at the Norman church of Forest Hill in Oxfordshire. He left Parker's east window of 1817 alone and added a north aisle and vestry, rebuilt the south chancel wall, threw out the nave ceiling and the gallery, and refitted the church, moving all the monuments. Farnham in Yorkshire is another sympathetic restoration of a small country church. Scott reroofed it to a higher pitch, and supplied a tactful new chancel arch, stained glass, and Minton tiles to the chancel floor.[21]

At Shinfield, Berkshire, the 'Our Village' of the 19th-century writer Miss Mitford, Scott in 1855 removed much 15th-century work from the church, sparing the brick tower. He replaced the brick arcade of the south aisle by one of his standard simple Decorated arcades with rather squashed columns. He turned the apse into a proper chancel — a strange reversal of his action at nearby Bradfield — faced in flints like the nave. Most windows, including some very late Perpendicular examples, remained, but the coldly Decorated west aisle window is obviously added. Scott resisted the temptation to rebuild the whole in a correct Decorated style, and the image of an attractive church with items of all periods is pleasantly maintained.

Scott did a great deal of work for Jesse Watts Russell at Ilam, Staffordshire, in the 1850s. In 1854 he provided the village school, Gothic with a flèche, a steep tiled roof, and a front gable encompassing a pair of doors, to prevent the mixing of the sexes. In 1855-6 he worked on the church, adding a north aisle, reseating the nave, raising all the roofs except that of the 1831 mortuary chapel, rebuilding the east wall with characteristic Early English lancets flanked by detached shafts. He furnished a new chancel arch and a new reredos, and gave the tower, unusually, a saddleback roof, as he had recently done at Queenhill, Worcestershire.[22] The only remaining altar frontal by Scott is here. Scott may well have designed many of the picturesque cottages in the village, with stone ground floors and tile-hung upper floors — what other architect used tile hanging at this time?[23]

Scott's most famous rebuilding of the 'fifties, at St Georges, Doncaster, followed a disastrous fire in February 1853, caused by an overheated stove pipe. The church was uninsured. £14,000 was raised quickly, in this prosperous railway town. But difficulties arose, in the person of Edmund Becket Denison, later Lord Grimthorpe. Denison hated architects, and made Scott's life a burden by having his say about the style of the church: he insisted that the window tracery should be coarser than Scott intended and suggested the mechanical design of the east window. He designed the clock, but he was good at clocks. Scott could not cope with Denison, pathetically referring to him as 'my friend, but also my tormentor'.[24]

Scott's photograph of about this time in the vestry at Doncaster shows a plump and balding man, dressed with modest eccentricity, bearing a worried look, a presence which might not quell a general foreman but which, on infrequent visits to the site or the committee rooom, would impress with its air of candour and learning.

Scott decided against an exact restoration in Perpendicular, and also against a reversion to the original 12th century design (which would, moreover, have had no tower). He compromised, choosing 'the early part of late middle pointed'. The tower is rather later than the body of the church: Scott had a great regard for the original tower and wished to reproduce it. The new church was not to have galleries like the old, and therefore had to be larger, and for stylistic reasons, less wide. The Steetley limestone, selected for its fire-resistance, has not stood up well to the pollution of a northern industrial town.

The Ecclesiological Society found the church 'like nothing we have ever seen before'[25] and one is inclined to agree. The interior is even less satisfactory than that of Swindon (1843). The form of the new building is less gainly than that of its predecessor; however familiar Scott was with French detail, he could not yet handle a lofty interior of French proportions. The wide, open spaces of the typical Victorian church combine with coarse detail and carving, especially of the foliated capitals, to make the whole seem out of scale, and the large proportions, inside and out, are ruined and made petty: it is hard to believe that the 170 ft central tower is among the country's highest, until one views it from five miles away. Some of this coarseness may be due to Denison, but the building is nevertheless a large and valuable monument of Victorian achievement.[26]

Work began in October 1853; consecration took place in October 1858. Scott had read a paper to the Oxford Architectural Society giving 'An Outline of the recent investigations of the ruins of Doncaster Church', showing that there were lots of Early English bits in a structure largely Perpendicular. Denison, in 1854, gave 'Lectures on Gothic Architecture, chiefly in relation to St George's Church, Doncaster...' at the Town Hall, later publishing them as a pamphlet of 111 pages. It was rather as if Scott had read a paper on the legal position of the Great Northern Railway's shareholders, with special reference to Mr Redpath.[27]

Other work in Doncaster followed,[28] but Scott refused the new Doncaster cemetery, believing it impossible to design worthy buildings for only £1500.[29] The church of St James, Doncaster, however, involved both Scott and Denison. This, like that at Swindon, was erected for the benefit of the workers at the railway locomotive factory, and there were again loud wails from the shareholders that their money should thus be thrown away. Eventually, Denison and his father paid for the church, Denison and Scott designed it in 1857, and it was consecrated on the same day as St George's in 1858. The oddity of this church is best seen in the detail: the turret sits uncomfortably on half the aisle roof, the aisle west window, totally out of character with the rest of the church, suddenly becomes five lancets, the relieving arch under the turret completely loses its pier in the north wall. Scott must have been greatly embarrassed.[30]

If 1844 had been Scott's *annus mirabilis*, 1855 rivalled it. It opened by his being asked in quick succession to superintend restorations at Hereford, Lichfield, and Peterborough cathedrals, beginning a period of intense cathedral-repairing activity which lasted until the end of his life: he more than inherited Cottingham's mantle. He was totally unconcerned in only three of those of the Old and Monastic foundations; St Paul's, Carlisle, and Llandaff. Perhaps he consciously collected cathedrals. Certainly, to understand the history of these, and many other, mediaeval buildings it is necessary to know what Scott did, and why.

At Bristol in 1859 his advice was asked and disregarded and he took umbrage. He reported on Norwich, was associated in name with Ferrey at Wells, and designed furniture at Lincoln and York. Work at the remaining eighteen varied from choir fitting to the most extensive alterations.*

Hereford Cathedral was a Norman edifice with many additions and alterations up to James Wyatt's west front and triforium of 1786, which had upset Pugin years before. During 1841-51, the Cottinghams had saved the central tower from collapse and repaired the nave, sanctuary and most of the Lady Chapel. The younger Cottingham had designed the reredos. Scott picked up where they had left off, restoring both sets of transepts, the choir aisles and the north porch. He rearranged the choir and replaced the monuments which Cottingham had removed.

The north transept was altered; the west and north windows, and the decayed buttress caps and string-courses were renewed; the embattled coping was replaced by a plain one, and a new cornice was placed on the staircase. The Norman work had been overlaid by later and 'some lost features' were recovered. The circular windows to the eastern triforium were converted back from Perpendicular, the pieces having been found in the wall round about.

The choir roof was reformed and the parapets, raised by Wyatt, were lowered again. The remainder of the Lady Chapel was rebuilt; Scott found some of the pinnacles stored in the crypt. Much structural work was performed to the south-east transept, the choir south aisle roof was repaired, and the destroyed roofs of the Vicar's Cloister were replaced (presumably a conjectural restoration), while those of the Bishop's Cloister were renewed, the destroyed battlements being rebuilt on the evidence of a surviving fragment. Such of the old monuments as could be were replaced in their old positions.

Cottingham had removed the choir stalls and stowed them in the crypt, whence Scott had to disinter them and fit the pieces together like a three-dimensional jigsaw. As at Ely, they had originally occupied the crossing and projected into the nave, but, under pressure from vista-mongers and those who wished the choir not to

* So Ely in 1847 and Hereford, Lichfield, and Peterborough in 1855 were followed by Durham, Chester, and Salisbury in 1859; Chichester, 1861; Worcester, 1863; Gloucester and St David's, 1864; Bangor, 1866; St Asaph, 1869; Exeter and Oxford, 1870; Rochester, 1871; Winchester, 1875; and Canterbury, 1877. To this list, like a roll of battle honours, must be added new cathedrals and churches raised to that status.

be used for congregational purposes, they were replaced eastwards of the centre of the crossing, and Skidmore's iron screen[31] was placed to their west. Scott, writing ten years later, expressed doubts about his re-arrangement of the choir: 'For ordinary purposes, this was a gain; for great diocesan use it was a loss. From an antiquarian point of view it was an error. I leave it to others to judge of it. I confess I do not think I should now do the same.'[32] The official reopening of the choir took place at the end of June 1863, even though much work was still under way.[33]

Lichfield Cathedral had been much altered by Wyatt during 1788-95; he converted the Early English choir 'by the help of cement, spikes and tar-cord'[34] to a replica of the nave, removed the old altar screen, extended the choir through the Lady Chapel, and fenced it about with partitions. Sydney Smirke subsequently removed part of Wyatt's patchwork in the choir and was stumped. The Chapter appointed a committee to consider the matter, and Scott found himself appointed to do the work. He prepared designs in 1857-8, and from slight indications on the stonework was convinced that he had been able to recover the earliest design. All Wyatt's woodwork was removed. Scott erected a new altar screen and one of Skidmore's metal screens, and, rather against his inclination, demolished Wyatt's macaronic reredos in the Lady Chapel, which he ultimately replaced with one of his own design.[35] Excavations for the flooring revealed the foundations of a former apse in the middle of the choir, but no one seems to have suggested that the east end should therefore be truncated. Drawings of the choir were exhibited at the Royal Academy in 1862, and some of the choir pavement was at the 1862 International Exhibition.

Professor Willis, on visiting the Cathedral, discovered on the transept triforium string-course the setting-out marks of the Early English vault which had been altered in the 15th century, took notes, and neglected to inform Scott. Later, the mason, looking for work for his men, renewed the stones. Willis complained to Scott, who complained to the mason, who said that, as Willis had taken notes, he saw no need to preserve the stones. Willis's notes had been lost, and the evidence had thus vanished. Scott was much vexed.

In 1866 Scott advised against raising the north side of the nave, instead securing a careful recording, by drawing and photograph, of the nave interior before it was repaired. The great west window, from the time of Charles II, was replaced by one, said Scott, more in character, though possibly a little too late in detail. The Lady Chapel was restored and Wyatt's plaster Gothic was cleared away. Monuments were later constructed to the north of the altar, incorporating old canopies formerly belonging to the choir screen. Matters rested until 1877, when Scott began work on the west front.[36]

At Peterborough, Blore had rearranged the choir about 1827, after which nothing seems to have been done until Scott's appointment. Money was short and Scott's work was conservative and modest.[37] He painted part of the choir roof and repaired underpinned aisles in nave and eastern transept, and secured the north nave wall.[38]

In 1855 the newly-formed London and Middlesex Archaeological Society placed Scott on its first Council, and in December of that year he was elected to Associateship of the Royal Academy, a body to which only three architects were elected between 1847 and 1870. By the end of the year, Scott's letters reflect the years of unremitting toil and show distinct signs of strain; he became seriously ill and was for a time confined to bed. But the situation is different from that of years ago. New commissions arrive at a rate of one a fortnight; clients write in asking Scott to act; Wyatt and Burlison dash around the country keeping everything under control. Wyatt reports to the office from Woolland that Burlison has met him at Cirencester and is going to Cheltenham on Thursday. 'Mr Wyatt knows the particulars more correctly than I do', writes Scott, and despairingly, in October, 'Mr Burlison is abroad'.[39]

Perhaps the assumption of greater responsibility by younger men accounts in part for the greater emphasis on foreign forms and details during the period from 1855-72. Some German examples have been noted, but French influence, never entirely absent since 1847, became more pronounced, even if Scott's office was relatively timid by comparison with, for instance, Pearson's bold use of French prototypes. Scott suggests that his first use of French detail was in 1849 when some capitals at Hamburg were based on those of the Sainte-Chapelle.

It is instructive to compare Scott with his counterpart and contemporary in France, Eugene Viollet-le-Duc (1814-79). Viollet-le-Duc, the son of a wealthy government functionary, after much travelling, drawing, and teaching, joined the Conseil des Bâtiments Civiles, a branch of the government department responsible for the care of historic monuments. In 1840 he reported on the Abbey of Vezelay and was appointed Inspector for the Saint-Chapelle; in 1844 he and Lassus were appointed to restore Nôtre-Dame in Paris He became an active Gothic propagandist in the French battle of the styles, with an especial affection for the Gothic of the 13th century, which he thought peculiarly perfect. He was of an academic bent and lacked practical education; his restorations are more destructive than Scott's. He believed that restoration was not just to preserve, repair, or remodel an old building, but actually to 'reinstate it in the complete state'. He worked at Amiens, Chartres, Rheims, Clermont-Ferrand and elsewhere, and his *Dictionnaire Raisonné de l'Architecture* was published in ten volumes between 1854 and 1868. His *Entretiens sur l'Architecture* can in part be compared with Scott's own *Remarks on Secular and Domestic Architecture*. He had also a great influence in England: he was awarded the Gold Medal of the Institute of British Architects in 1864. 'We all crib from Viollet-le-Duc', said Burges.[49]

30 Wasperton, 1843. Addition
of a north aisle in Scott's
mature early Decorated, together with other alterations,
to a village church

31 St Nicholas, Hamburg. View
Illustrated London News,
9 August 1845

32 Barnet, Christ Church parsonage, about 1845. The curiously eclectic character of the details is notable

33 Newfoundland Cathedral, 1847 on. An early view of the design *Illustrated London News*, 23 June 1849

34 Alderney. A contemporary view
Illustrated London News, 5 October 1850

35 Bradfield, restored 1847-8. There are many characteristic Scott features —
apse, early Decorated windows, south porch, flintwork, many roofs

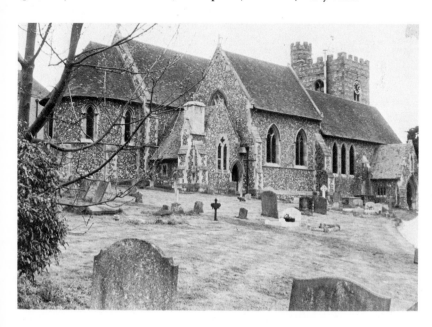

36 Bradfield. Apse roof, interior

37 Harrow. Church, restoration 1846-9, at top. School chapel 1855-6, transepts by Sir Aston Webb later. To left Vaughan Library, 1861-3

38 Aylesbury, interior after restoration. It seems that everything visible has been repaired or restored by Scott
National Monuments Record

39 Ely Cathedral. A view from the South East prior to Scott's restoration, showing James Essex's cladding of the lantern
National Monuments Record

40 Ely Cathedral. Drawing by J. Drayton Wyatt of the Octagon proposed to be restored by Scott

Victoria and Albert Museum

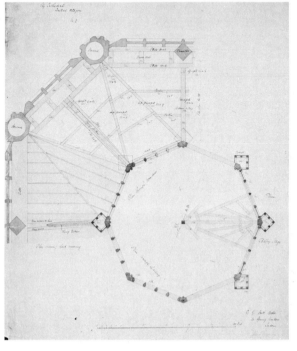

41 Ely Cathedral.
Contract drawing of
lantern restoration,
1862
Victoria and
Albert Museum

42 Ely Cathedral.
Drawing of lantern
construction
Victoria and
Albert Museum

43 Westminster Abbey, reredos, 1867. Figures carved by H. H. Armstead,
mosaic designed by J. R. Clayton, executed by Salviati
National Monuments Record

44 Westminster Abbey. Drawing, probably by C. R. Baker King, of the eastern
door to the north transept. Scott restored the doors, Pearson the remainder of
the transept elevation.
Victoria and Albert Museum

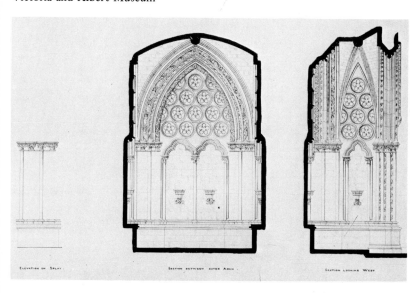

45 Westminster
Abbey. North tran-
sept, with one of
Scott's doorways in
position but the upper
part before alteration
by Pearson
Guildhall Library,
City of London

46 Resurrection,
Longton. A good but
altered example of
Scott's polychrome
and apsidal small
cheap church
Eric Tansley

47 Trefnant, 1855. Detail at junction of chancel and nave, including the characteristic bell gable over the chancel arch

48 Trefnant, interior looking east. A rich, expensive, middle period Scott interior, with polished marble and granite, stylised foliage capitals, encaustic tile floors, standard arcade sections, corbelled columns under the chancel arch, decorated tracery, and much else

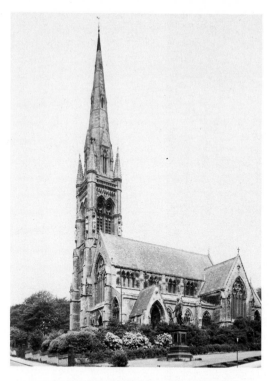

49 All Souls, Halifax, 1856-9. 'On the whole my best church'
G. Barnes

50 All Souls, Halifax. Interior. Drawing by J. Drayton Wyatt
The Ecclesiologist, xxi, 84

51 Camden Chapel, Camberwell, altered 1854. A polychrome apse added to a
ritually imperfect building
The Builder xii. 363

52 Eastnor, restored 1852. View from the North West: all visible except the tower substantially rebuilt by Scott

53 Newark, restored 1852-5 and later. A large Midlands church after repair, stabilisation, and refitting by Scott. The seating is clearly Victorian, yet possibly because nearly all the visible detail is Perpendicular, the interior does not seem to bear Scott's impress
National Monuments Record

54 Hampton Lucy, addition of apse, about 1857. A work showing decided French influence, yet containing much English detail

55 Shinfield, restored 1855-6. Scott has given the south aisle a pitched roof, built up the gable and inserted a Decorated window. He has not altered the debased tower

56 Shinfield, interior. The arcading, benches and tile floor are of the usual kind. The east window remains Perpendicular

57 St George, Doncaster. The old church burned in 1853
The Vicar and Churchwardens, St George, Doncaster

58 St George, Doncaster, 1853-8. Perspective drawing. The church is glamourised, a criticism often made of Scott's drawings
The Vicar and Churchwardens, St George, Doncaster

59 Hereford Cathedral, screen, 1862. Made by Skidmore. Brass and iron, now removed
National Monuments Record

60 Lichfield Cathedral, interior, restored 1855 onwards. The screen, reredos, and other furnishings are Scott's, a nineteenth century complement to the structure, which, thanks to skilful repair, seems totally mediaeval
National Monuments Record

5

Man of Business,
1856-59

In 1856, the Scott family moved again; with five sons more space was needed. Scott was then writing a book on secular Gothic architecture, largely while travelling. He did not, as had Pugin at Ramsgate ten years before, build an exemplar of the views expressed in his works, but rather moved into a plain and irregular late 18th-century stuccoed house at the top of Hampstead, Grove House, or the Admiral's House, upon the railed roof of which the colourful Admiral Barton had been wont to pace as upon a quarter-deck sixty years before.

Scott's book, *Remarks on Secular and Domestic Architecture, present and future*,[1] was published by John Murray late in 1857, dedicated to Beresford Hope,[2] the Ecclesiologists' man of affairs and MP. A new, revised, edition was made in 1858, but by October it had been remaindered. Scott argued that vernacular domestic architecture was wholly unworthy of the state of contemporary civilisation and required thorough reformation, to be effected by ending the unnatural division between church and secular architecture and by recognising the Gothic style as 'free, comprehensive, and practical, ready to adapt itself to every change in the habits of society, to embrace every new material or system of construction, and to adopt implicitly and naturally, and with hearty good will, every invention and improvement'.[3] This was in a sense a rationalisation of his own wish to design great public buildings and country houses, thereby to achieve a broadly-based practice.

Scott asserted that even the humblest dwellings were worthy of careful design, and lamented the fall in standards: 'The great war . . . has been the deluge'[4] — the years of conflict from 1793-1815 had swept away the feeling for domestic architecture. In addition, Scott castigated 'the wretched creations of speculating builders in the neighbourhood of London'.[5] All had been well until Classical forms were introduced into England, when fantastic ornamental forms developed. The 'Gothic Revival' had been unsuccessful: residences masqueraded as castles; there was no unity of purpose or style; boldness was wanting; and architects were divided into Ecclesiastical and Secular. Then follows the contradiction: architecture was most perfect in the late 13th and early 14th century, so all buildings should be designed to be of that period, with plans altered to suit present needs. A square-headed, double-hung sash window without mullions may yet be Gothic, and one is to have the freedom to create new details if mediaeval patterns do not suffice. For Scott, Gothic 'is especially the style of all others whose great principle is to decorate construction'; [6] he notes that he designs elevations by drawing out the windows first, adding decorative features when these are correct.

In a discursive chapter on materials, Scott admits to having built a large parsonage of cob thatched with reeds.[7] Iron and glass, much in the public eye after the Great Exhibition, are considered of great importance to the Revival.[8]

Chapters on buildings in the country and in towns display a reaction against classical taste as enshrined in the Building Act of 1777. Scott finds London's Gower Street insipid, and prefers each house to have its own distinct elevation, differing in height and outline and terminating in a varied skyline. By pulling down portions of streets and rebuilding them in uniform masses, one deprives the streets of the only good quality they possess: the Rue de Rivoli is dull indeed!

The study of Italian Gothic is advocated for public buildings in towns; an ideal public building would have the form of an Italian renaissance palace, but with Gothic decorative details. Commercial buildings, on the other hand, might be modelled on the warehouses of North Germany. Scott vents his spleen over Alnwick Castle, then being redecorated internally by Italians, rather than in the national style, and disapproves of stuccoing or veneering.

Scott had a number of opportunities to practice these theories in the immediately following years.

About 1855 he worked at Pippbrook, the home of W. H. Forman, at Dorking, Surrey, adding a billiard room, library, and porch to the existing Georgian-style house. He removed almost all the windows and their surrounds, together with the fireplaces, substituting new ones in a coarse 14th-century type Gothic.[9] The additions are in a similar stone, and are of a similar scale, to the original house. Scott later added a museum[10] to the north, a much more effective building, with Decorated details and a painted roof; a fine perspective by Drayton Wyatt was exhibited at the Royal Academy in 1858. This is typical of a number of similar works, many of them little known.[11]

In 1855 Scott won the great competition for the new Hamburg Rathaus (town hall). This German or Flemish looking design, resembling the Cloth Hall at Ypres in composition, was his second essay in secular Gothic for a large public building. It was designed in white stone and red granite, with three courts, and thirteen bays of plate-traceried windows above arcading on each side of a 300 ft central tower with a spire. Like many other of Scott's similar projects, the scheme came to nothing; the money was used instead to improve the city's canals.[12]

Scott's designs of 1856 for the town halls of Bradford and Halifax were also unexecuted, but his design for a training school for Anglican clerics at Peterborough was built, showing how Gothic work could be adapted to meet limited funds.

Scott's *début* as a town planner came in 1855, when Col Akroyd, the Halifax manufacturer, commissioned him to build Akroydon. Scott's preoccupation was with the style of the buildings, and he was unskilled at relating them to each other. He laid out a double row of cottages separated by a rear access path, surrounding a large grass square. This was an improvement on much contemporary work, but showed insufficient thought over the problem. Scott's former pupil, Crossland, carried out the work but Scott also designed All Souls' vicarage nearby.

Scott began the Vaughan Library at Harrow School in 1861. Polychrome runs riot, with patterned roof slates, red brick walls laced with vitrified blue and yellow, stone window tracery and dressings, and an entrance flanked by polished grey and pink marble columns. This is a microcosm of Scott's developed secular style: heavy detail and plate tracery, unmistakably of the 19th century. The library is a pleasant and accomplished little building, though the combination of gabled porch surmounted by gabled rose window is extraordinarily clumsy.

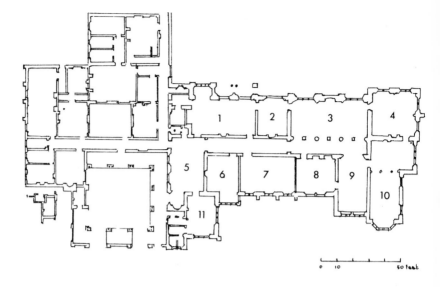

1. Dining Room
2. Cedar Room
3. Music Hall
4. Drawing Room
5. North Staircase
6. Morning Room
7. Chapel
8. Billiard Room
9. South Staircase
10. Library
11. Business Room

Kelham Hall, 1858-62. Plan. The left-hand stable block remains from the earlier house

New country houses were not a major part of Scott's practice. In 1858 he began Kelham Hall near Newark, producing a picturesque outline with a tower and a square block, a multiplicity of windows, many with plate tracery, a steep pitched roof, and Tudor chimneys. The external ornament is eclectic 13th or 14th century; the interior rather earlier. The main rooms are rib-vaulted, and the whole is of harsh brick, slate, and stone. The fireproof construction is of great interest. Even if the result lacks the discipline of Salvin's Thoresby, or the richness of Teulon's Bestwood, it is an improvement on the castles built by Hopper and Blore.

Walton Hall in Warwickshire, built for Sir Charles Mordaunt at the same time, has many similarities to Kelham: a rectangular three-storey block has a two-storey service courtyard attached to one corner. Two towers are contrasted in shape and size. The building, which cost £30,000, is of stone roofed with slate, with eclectic Gothic detail.

The planning of this sort of large country house had already been

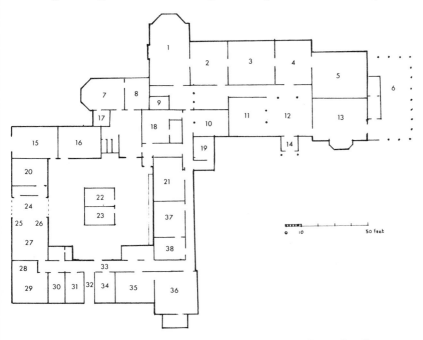

1. Dining Room	14. Porch	27. Brushing Room
2. Ante Room	15. Coals	28. Dairy
3. Drawing Room	16. Brew House	29. Dairy
4. Ante Room	17. Strong Room	30. Bacon
5. Library	18. Butler's Pantry	31. Stores
6. Conservatory	19. Store Room	32. Entrance
7. Sir Charles Room	20. Bake House	33. Passage
8. Staircase	21. Servants' Hall	34. Cold Meat
9. Area for Light	22. Meat Larder	35. Scullery
10. Servants' Staircase	23. Game Larder	36. Kitchen
11. Principal Staircase	24. Gateway	37. Housekeeper's Room
12. Entrance Hall	25. Oven Sticks	38. Still Room
13. Billiard Room	26. Charcoal	

Walton Hall, 1858-62. Plan. There are similarities with Kelham, and the arrangement of the rooms follows precedent. But the elevations are treated less in the 14th century Gothic and more in the spirit of Gothic Architecture, Secular and Domestic well systematised, with architects such as William Burn, Blore, Robert Kerr, Anthony Salvin, or S.S.Teulon producing these buildings prolifically. Scott was content to base his plans on well-tried precedents. The general arrangement of Walton or of Capesthorne (an unexecuted project of 1861) has similarities to that of a Burn house such as Whitehill, built twenty-five years previously.

In 1856 the House of Commons suggested that all the government offices be associated in one large block, and instigated a public competition for buildings for the War and Foreign Offices. No fewer than 220 designs were submitted, 210 of which were Classical in style and ten of which were Gothic. The Commission[13] appointed to consider them voted thus:

Foreign Office	War Office
1 Coe and Hofland	Garling
2 Banks and Barry	Boitrel d'Hazeville
3 Scott (Gothic)	Rochead
4 Deane and Woodward (Gothic)	Pritchard and Seddon (Gothic)
5 Bellamy	Brodrick
6 Buxton and Habershon	Habershon
7 Street (Gothic)	Dwyer

Scott's entry bore a motto from Horace: *Nec minimum meruere decus vestigia Graeca ausi desirere et celebrare domestica facta*, and was to be the vindication of the views expressed in his latest book. He approached the problem by designing details of Gothic windows doors, and other features, practical for use in a public building but leaning towards the fashionable French Gothic. He assembled these into a building containing gables, dormers, and high pitched roofs with a certain regularity of massing, at which point an opportunity for a trial run appeared, as Akroyd had asked him to design a town hall for Halifax. The drawings for this went to the Royal Academy exhibition in 1857, but Akroyd's influence did not prevail, and Sir Charles Barry got the job, his last work.[14]

At the same time, there were difficulties over the government offices. The cost of purchase and clearance of the competition site would exceed a million pounds, a vast sum, and it transpired also that the India Office would have to be accommodated on the site. The War Office scheme was dropped. The result was that the

Parliamentary bill to secure purchase of the site met resistance from the Opposition and was withdrawn.

The First Commissioner of Public Works stated openly that the Government could not be bound to employ the first prizewinner, and it came out that the architects on the Commission had drawn up a list, overruled by the lay majority, on which Banks and Barry were placed first for the Foreign Office, Scott second, and Coe and Hofland only sixth. Scott was also second for the War Office, and the architects considered second for both as a higher position than first for only one. Scott was resigned to accept his near-miss until Lord Palmerston decided that the elderly Pennethorne, architect to the Office of Works, should do the job. Scott then went to see Beresford Hope, who got the professional members of the Commission to send a deputation to the First Commissioner. Due to a providential change of government, this was now Lord John Manners, by some accounts incompetent, but known to and well disposed toward Scott.

In such a combination of chaotic circumstance it was necessary to appoint a Select Committee. Of its members Hope, Akroyd, Lord Elcho, and Stirling (the only member of the original Commission on the Committee) supported Gothic and Scott; William Tite, MP for Bath and architect of the Royal Exchange, led the Classic party. The Committee reported inconclusively in July 1858: the matter had been discussed at great length as one of Gothic versus Classic, but it left the Government to do the choosing. This helped no one but Scott because, the Bill for purchase of the site having been reintroduced by the very party which, in opposition, killed it, the appointment was made by the First Commissioner.

It was now November 1858, and Scott was instructed to revise his design, as the India Office had replaced the War Office in the western part of the site. The Secretary of State for India, Lord Stanley, was in favour of Scott's appointment for this building also, and Scott agreed to associate himself with Digby Wyatt, the official architect to the India Office. Designs for both buildings were approved, and working drawings were being prepared, when Tite in the Commons, branded the Gothic style as inconvenient and expensive, largely because it did not utilise double-hung sash windows, and aggressively championed the Classic cause once again.

The Commissioner made it clear in his reply that the architect was pressing on with the drawings, and avoided the matter of style. Beresford Hope came out strongly for Scott and Gothic: the provision of convenient windows had been Mr Scott's especial care. Mr Coningham thought Gothic a barbarous style for the enlightened times of the mid-19th century. General Thompson considered that the country might soon be involved in a European war, and it would be better to postpone the entire scheme. The seventy-four year old Palmerston, the Opposition leader, rose to speak:

Viscount PALMERSTON: I have never heard a less satisfactory explanation, both as regards the selection of the architect and the choice of the style in which the Foreign Office is proposed to be built, than that given by the noble Lord the First Commissioner of Public Works. The reason last assigned, that of the Hon Member for Maidstone (Mr Beresford Hope), for the choice of Mr Scott was, that he was always second in all the trials which had taken place, that he was second competitor for the Foreign Office, and second also for the War Office, and that therefore he ought to be put first; on the principle, I suppose that the two negatives make an affirmative. It certainly is a new doctrine. What would be said if it were applied to horse-racing, and the horse which ran second in two heats were held to be entitled to the cup? Then, again, Mr Scott was chosen because he was second competitor for the Foreign Office and for the War Office; but it now appears that there is to be no War Office, and the Foreign Office alone is to be built; and therefore Mr Scott is reduced in point of claim, and we are told that he has been chosen to build a Foreign Office because his plan for that building was second best. With regard to the Gothic style, we are told that it has been adopted because it is the national style, suited to Teutonic nationalities, and all that sort of thing. If that theory of nationalities is to be carried out in our public buildings, the noble Lord the Secretary for India, in building his new office, should be lodged in a pagoda or a taj-mahal. That would be adapting the national style to the department over which he presided; and as Mr Scott cannot be expected to be well acquainted with that style, the noble Lord should invite, as most competent for the purpose, the aid of some architect from India to decide as to what will be best for an Indian office. In my opinion no satisfactory reason has been given why the architects, whose plans were better than those of Mr Scott, should have been set aside, and Mr Scott selected.... I quite agree with the Hon Member for Brighton (Mr Coningham) in his protest against the selection of the Gothic style. In my opinion it is going back to the barbarism of the dark ages for a building which ought to belong to the times in which we live. And what, let me ask, is the reason alleged? It is said it is the intention to fill up the entire space between Downing Street and Westminster Abbey with buildings, all of which are to be Gothic, and that therefore it is desirable to begin with a Gothic Foreign Office.... But if the principle of congruity is to be applied to the future why not apply it to the present? The neighbourhood of Downing Street is full of buildings of totally different styles of architecture . . . . in order to complete the "congruity", we should have to Gothicise the Horse Guards and apply Gothic exteriors to all the buildings in the neighbour-hood. At present all the buildings in connection with the public departments and Downing Street are in different styles — in fact all the principal buildings in London are various in their architectural types. There are the Treasury buildings, the Horse Guards, the Admiralty, the Banqueting House — one of the finest specimens of architecture to be found anywhere — these are to be contrasted with a building which after all does not answer the description of the noble Lord who talks of a "national style", for it appears not to be English Gothic, but, as stated by the Hon Member for Maidstone, Italian or Lombard Gothic. I have not had the advantage of visiting these climes lately, and therefore I do not exactly know what the peculiarities of Lombard Gothic are, but it combines, I suppose, all the modifications of barbarism. Look, too, at the street of palaces, Pall Mall, where the clubs vie in splendour with each other; take St Paul's and Somerset House, and I venture to say that they are handsomer, in their respective styles than either Westminster Abbey or the new Houses of Parliament. The Houses of Parliament are no doubt very beautiful, but I think it was a great mistake, both in point of expense and accommodation, to make them Gothic . . . I hope, however, that the decision of the noble Lord is not irrevocable, and that he may be induced to modify his views. I find, upon re-reading the Report of the Committee, that Mr Scott has studied the Greek and Italian style of architecture as well as the Gothic: and if it is finally determined that he is to be the architect, as he is a person of great talent, I have no doubt he may be able to make as handsome a design in the Latin or Grecian order, as this Gothic one which the noble Lord favours. If Mr Scott be the architect, I hope he will be told to put a more lively and enlightened front to his buildings, than that which he contemplates, and that we may see them in harmony with the other public buildings of the metropolis, either of Greek or Italian architecture, and that the noble Lord opposite will not insist upon erecting a Gothic Foreign Office in Downing Street.[15]

After this the House went on to consider the Native Princes of India, and Scott wrote a long letter to *The Times* in his defence. On 18 February it was debated again: Manners blamed all the difficulties on the previous Government (it had become a party matter, with the protagonists on the wrong sides) and inferred that Scott's scheme was the only possible. Palmerston pleaded for a light and airy building, castigating Scott's houses in Dean's Yard as 'hideous'. Scott was nettled, and dismissed it as 'a quantity of poor buffoonery which only Lord Palmerston's age permitted'.[16]

Manners decided that Scott's completed drawings should be exhibited, no doubt relying on being able to state categorically that it was too late for alterations. Pamphlets flew: Scott versus Barry. Coe's scheme ('a flash affair', said Scott) had no friends and everyone dismissed him and Hofland as incompetent for so great an undertaking.

European affairs now took a hand. Lord Derby's Government fell, France invaded Italy, and in June 1859 Palmerston's Whigs took over. The exhibition of Scott's drawings and model took place in July, whereupon Palmerston sent for Scott, to inform him that while he had no wish to disturb the architect's appointment, he would insist that Scott create a design in the Italian style. A deputation of MPs waited on Palmerston to advocate Gothic, and more pamphlets flew.

The Supply Votes for the Civil Service Estimates in August were made the excuse for again considering the matter of style, filling twenty-three columns of Hansard,[17] even though the vote was for the site and foundations of the Foreign Office, not the superstructure. The estimate for the building was now £310,000 including lighting, contingencies, and fees. Lord Elcho warned Palmerston against jettisoning Scott and Gothic: the Foreign Secretary sat in imminent danger of immolation beneath his own decrepit roof, and the Government had only a precarious majority of six: should this vanish after an Italian design had been produced, delay and waste of public money might ensure. Most speakers in the debate were for Gothic, but Palmerston, carefully coached by Professor Donaldson of University College, asserted that since there were so many public buildings in Classic and so few in Gothic, the latter might be suitable for a Jesuit College but not much else. But, if Mr Scott were a clever architect he could make Classic elevations to fit his Gothic plans; the present difficulties were none of his own fault but were entirely due to Manners. The First Commissioner made a temperate reply, recalling that when Dr Newman had been called upon to decide on the design of a new building for the Jesuits in Dublin, he had said that the Gothic style was not so much in accord with the real Ultramontane spirit as the Italian style. No one has recorded what the Irish members thought about it all.

It appeared that the balance of opinion was in Scott's favour, with only Palmerston and Tite opposing Gothic. The Royal Institute of

British Architects, however, was rent in two, and a further deputation, led by Smirke, F.P.Cockerell, and Donaldson, waited on Palmerston, this time in the Classic interest. Palmerston sent again for Scott, informing him that he was thinking of appointing Garling as coadjutor, to design the building in Classic style. Scott wrote a letter dwelling on his position as winner of two European Competitions, an ARA, a Gold Medal of the Institute, a lectureship at the Royal Academy, and declined any such arrangement. He then retired with his family to Scarborough during the Parliamentary recess: this was his first long holiday since entering practice in 1835.

Scott discounted the chance of a change of government, and accepted that Palmerston would not change his ideas. He prepared a semi-classic design, 'Byzantine, in fact toned into a more modern and usable form, by reference to those examples of the Renaissance which had been influenced by the presence of Byzantine works'. 'To resign would be to give up a sort of property which Providence has placed in the hands of my family', which would simply reward Barry for his unprecedented attempt 'to wrest a work from the hands of a brother architect'.[18]

Scott showed the scheme to Palmerston, who was civil but said little, for he had quietly instructed Garling to prepare a Classic scheme, which was sent to the Office of Works. Scott complained, and wrote to all the MPs who supported him. Scott's semi-Byzantine design, modified to be less Byzantine, was referred to the joint opinion of C.R.Cockerell, Professor of Architecture at the Royal Academy, Fergusson, the architectural historian and Burn, Cockerell 'lectured me for hours on the beauties of the true Classic, going over book after book with me, and pouring forth ecstatic eulogies for his beloved style of art. I did not argue against his views, which I respected, but rather took the line of advocating variety and individuality, of each man being allowed to follow out his individual idiosyncracies'.[19] Fergusson favoured Scott; Burn considered him ill-used. The report commended the new design, which went before Parliament in the summer of 1860.

The Commons, like Scott, disliked it but approved it after yet another debate on style. The matter had become tedious: the India Office was looking for a new site, and was placated only when offered half the front to St James's Park. On 8 September Palmerston told Scott that the scheme must be entirely altered, and that his appointment would be cancelled if he refused to prepare the new scheme in 'the ordinary Italian': the design lately approved was 'neither one thing nor t'other—a regular mongrel affair', and he would have nothing to do with it.[20]

In the face of this peremptory and unconstitutional action a man more sure of himself might have faced it out, but Scott's instincts were always for compromise. He took the advice of Hunt of the Office of Works and Wyatt of the India Office. Both considered that the employer had the right to dictate the style of a building. Scott bought some costly books on Italian architecture to refresh his memory, paid a visit to Paris to study the Louvre and other important buildings, and spent the autumn and winter preparing a true Italian design. He took care to prepare alternative Gothic elevations, which he sent to the Academy the next year.

In July 1861, five years after the competition was first announced, Scott's designs were once again hung in the Palace of Westminster. He had tried unsuccessfully to have his Gothic alternative hung as well. Lord Elcho, outlining the history of the case, moved that the Italian design was not desirable. Buxton, the Secretary of State for India, seconding, said that it was not ugly but dull: he would prefer a good Scott Gothic to a bad Scott Classic. But why had Lord Palmerston only last Thursday ridden in a flood of rain for twenty-two miles to lay the foundation stone of a Gothic building, the Vaughan Library at Harrow, architect Mr Scott?

'Sir', said Palmerston, 'the battle of the books, the battle of the Big and Little Endeans, and the battle of the Green Ribbands and the Blue Ribbands at Constantinople were all as nothing compared with this battle of the Gothic and Palladian styles. If I were called upon to give an impartial opinion as to the issue of the conflict, I should say that the Gothic has been entirely defeated.'[21] Everyone had been quoting this or that building in support of their choice, and Palmerston concluded that if he had sunk his principles so far as to lay the foundation stone for a Gothic library, his opponents should do the same for a Classic Foreign Office. 283 members voted in the Division, and Lord Elcho's motion was lost by ninety-three. A further thirty-three columns of Hansard had been filled.

The House thereupon went into Committee of Supply, and the first estimate was for £30,000 out of the £200,000 the Foreign Office was now expected to cost. Palmerston, professing himself keen to build without further delay, jettisoned Pennethorne and Garling. Work started in 1862, but, with various difficulties, it proceeded slowly, being completed only in 1875, nearly twenty years after the competition.

The Foreign Office has seldom been regarded as great architecture, and it was not regarded as convenient by its original inhabitants. T. G. Jackson of Scott's office, on the other hand, said 'though he nearly broke his heart about it, I think that building is the finest thing he ever did'.[22] Sir Reginald Blomfield regarded it as 'one of the most boring buildings in London, of vast size, but petty in conception'.[23] He compared it adversely with Norman Shaw's New Scotland Yard of 1887, a building based upon a not dissimilar problem. Street thought that the tower of the Foreign Office ruined the view of the Houses of Parliament from Regent Street and Waterloo Place.

The Whitehall facade and the St James's Park facade (based on a design by Digby Wyatt) do seem to belong to different buildings. On Whitehall, a three-storeyed elevation has a three bay central feature crowned by a group of statuary, separated by six bays each side from heavier corner pavilions. Five floors are contained in three storeys. The slightly rusticated lower storey, with round-headed window openings, is notable for the rosette ornaments on the window surrounds, perversely reminiscent of the ball-flower ornament at Ledbury, and for the sculptured spandrel groups.[24] Scott's facade has no relationship with Barry's Treasury elevation on the north of Downing Street, which is lower, with Corinthian pilasters through its full height.

Scott's elevation to Downing Street is in two pieces with a curved feature at the junction, but it cannot be appreciated from the narrow street, with buildings of a totally different scale opposite. The Park elevation is higher, because the ground falls towards the Park, and there is the rather forced irregularity which one associates with Scott's Kelham and Salvin's Thoresby: blocks, one possibly of a Venetian character, break forward; there is a curved feature and a tower. The regular Whitehall facade design creeps around the corner, but is replaced by a variety of window treatments, with and without columns. The intention was to make a picturesque composition to be viewed from the Park, which, in winter, is successful. The long elevation in King Charles Street is seen only in perspective and is relieved by slightly projecting corner pavilions and three bays, the central crowned by too small a pediment. This feature, derived from Le Vau's 1650 work at the Louvre, is echoed in the Downing

Street entrance and within the central courtyard. The decision not to use a pediment on the Whitehall elevation was correct.

Scott's regular facade has been complemented by that of Brydon's less dry Ministry of Health of 1898 on the other side of King Charles Street, creating the effect of a monumental street, unusual in England. Now that Scott's building has been cleaned one can better appreciate the massing and the detail, whilst the oppressiveness of the design is gone: after a hundred years it can be judged for its virtues or shortcomings as architecture.

From 1856-9, new churches were started at much the same rate as before, but the rate of restorations doubled. Of the new works, Leafield, Ranmore and Richmond are among Scott's best designs.

Leafield, in North Oxfordshire, of 1858-60 may be contrasted with Trefnant of three years before. Leafield is a high pitched church with clerestory, lean-to aisles with (German?) cross-gables, and a central tower with an octagonal upper stage and spire, an improvement on that of Anstey, Warwickshire, of 1856. The detail is, for Scott, delicate; the style Early English. The stone and slate are local and pleasant in colour; the interior chaste and free of polychrome.

Ranmore, built for George Cubitt, MP, in 1859, is a rather grand church in a country setting on the North Downs, with 13th-century detail and facing of round flints. It looks better here than it would in the middle of a Victorian city. The tower with its octagonal steeple supports a spire which shows up finely from six miles away. The capitals, of various flowers and plants, with ivy and zinnia naturalistically depicted, are noteworthy, but those at the crossing are strangely large, as though they had been designed for a different building. Scott probably designed the vicarage here, and certainly the schools, to which he added in 1874.

Richmond, designed in 1857-8, is a well-developed late first pointed church, high pitched, very richly detailed in a French fashion, with a north-west tower and a broach spire. At the west end of the nave stands a wheel window over a porch all enclosed in a colossal pointed relieving arch.[25]

Set against these is Yiewsley, Middlesex. Scott's beastly little two-celled church of 1858, with an apse and polychrome brickwork, now forms the north aisle of a building the remainder of which, refined and polished, was designed by Sir Charles Nicholson in 1898, deliberately, it seems, to show up Scott's faults.

The chapel at Woolwich Dockyard,[26] completed in 1859, was notable for its iron interior with galleries. Scott had used iron columns in his early church at Turnham Green and iron was common in Non-conformist chapels, but this was a daring usage for the Established church.

The most famous new church of this period was the chapel of Exeter College, Oxford. The college had employed Scott in 1855-6 to build a new library and Rector's house, after which it was discovered that the chapel was ruinous. It was, it is alleged, blown up with gunpowder,[27] since pick and shovel made no impression. The first design for the new building followed closely the appearance of the old, but the chapel as built in 1858-9 is a magnificent structure, based upon the Sainte-Chapelle in Paris, and sumptuously fitted. Scott has never been forgiven in some circles, but perhaps his work was necessary to combat that 'coarseness of manners and morals' which William Morris, an undergraduate in the college in 1855, had so deplored.

Large town churches figured prominently among the forty restorations begun during these years. Scott restored Oakham in Rutland in 1857-8, performing much work on the interior and the roofs. The 'debased' east window was rebuilt, but the rest of the Perpendicular exterior was not molested. At Holy Trinity, Coventry, Scott stripped the interior in 1856, removing the 'modern' fittings, sparing only the early 17th-century pulpit and the lectern. Open seats, stallwise benches in the chancel, painted roofs, new glass, and a Skidmore font canopy were all introduced; the organ was moved from the west end (traditional) to the south chancel aisle (correct). Scott tried without success to save the north choir gallery, but this was destroyed for the sake of more room. As the tower was unable to bear the weight of the bells, Scott designed a Scandinavian-type detached timber belfry. He worked also at St Michael, Coventry, but the church was so heavily bombed during World War II, that it is difficult to know what precisely he did here.

Scott and Ferrey spent three years from 1859 performing a drastic and successful rebuilding of the tower of St Mary, Taunton, perhaps the grandest parish church tower in England.

The west front at Crowland Abbey leaned outward to a frightful degree and suggestions for its repair had always foundered on likely cost. Late in 1856 Scott, perhaps having come across an account of Thornton's righting of one of the transept ends at Beverley Minster in 1717, offered to correct in inexpensively. He formed a timber cradle around the wall, cleared a space where it joined the rest of the building, raised the wall perpendicular with jacks, underpinned it, and joined it up to the body of the church, and all with success.

So much for the structural tours-de-force. Next, the cosmetic. At St Michael's, Cornhill in the City Scott designed a Gothic doorway in a Franco-Italian style, handsome of itself, but unsuitable for the base of a Wren tower. During 1856-60 and again in 1867 he and his collaborators coloured the roof, inserted shafts into the round clerestory windows, altered the vaults, and reopened the full length of the south aisle windows, which had been filled in at the base in 1790 to make them circular, but then placed Italian Gothic tracery in them. The marble altar and reredos are his. The interior was stuffed with polychrome, and the pulpit, pews and stalls removed. *The Ecclesiologist* was enthusiastic, and spoke about 'noble manipulation'.[28] Scott himself talked of attempts to give tone to the Classic architecture.[29]

St Alban, Wood Street had not been entirely destroyed by the fire of 1666, and was considered a good example of Wren's Perpendicular Gothic: *The Ecclesiologist* surmised that old tracery and mouldings must have been retained. Scott in 1856 added a fullblooded Decorated pentagonal apse, contrasting with the delicate old work, and both gained from the juxtaposition in a way doubtless he never intended.[30]

Scott in 1856 repaired the steeple of St Mary the Virgin, Oxford, which had been insufficiently repaired four years earlier by J. C. Buckler, and in 1861-2 refaced most of the exterior in Taynton stone instead of Headington (19th-century architects had much trouble with Oxford stone), restoring the pinnacles, battlements, and parapets.[31] The removal of the south porch, one of the few bits of English exterior ecclesiastical baroque, was contemplated, but Scott pleaded earnestly for its retention, and was allowed to patch the worst places and to saturate the stone with a hardener. This action is greatly to his credit, but curious after his work at Exeter College or his action at St Mary the Great in Cambridge, where in 1851 he replaced the Classic tower door by Gothic.

Scott in 1857 largely rebuilt the church at Cattistock, Dorset, retaining some Perpendicular windows, and adding a south aisle and an apse to the chancel, not at all French but in key with the rest of the building: indeed he found traces of a mediaeval apse. Instances of George Gilbert and John Oldrid at work on the same church at different times are commonplace, but it is less usual to find father and George Gilbert Junior at work in the same church; the latter built here in 1874 a fine north-west tower, said to be modelled on that of Charminster, in a personal Perpendicular.

We have a comprehensive view of Scott and his office from T. G. Jackson, a pupil from 1858-61:

Mr Gilbert Scott, then at the head of his profession, had come to be our neighbour and we had made his acquaintance before we left Hampstead; my father went to see him and showed him one of my sketch-books and arranged that I should go and talk the matter over with him. I went to breakfast with him and he offered to take me to the "Brompton Boilers" where the architectural casts with which he was concerned were temporarily housed. We walked across the Conduit Fields ... till we took an omnibus, from the top of which I remember he disparaged Decimus Burton's arch opposite Apsley House as "a thing one could design in ten minutes". In his disregard of personal appearances I think he outmatched my father. His negligent dress and ill-brushed hat were counterbalanced by a certain unconscious dignity in his manner and were part of the modesty and simplicity of the man. He would stand still in the middle of the road and take out a case of pencils and a notebook and illustrate by a sketch what he was saying. I was much touched by the freedom and absence of pretension with which he discussed architecture with me, a mere tyro and a youngster with the merest smattering of knowledge on the subject. He told me how he began by travelling for a year after his articles and then put himself with some large builders to see practical work for some months before starting for himself. He said he managed to keep himself after four years and that his success began with winning competitions for union workhouses when the Poor Law was revised. In that way, after winning a great many, he gradually came into notice. "Dirty disagreeable work", he said, "but the rule should be never to pick your subjects but go in for whatever offers whether you like it or not, for if you complete only for the subjects you like you will nearly always fail".

I told him of my leaning rather towards painting, but he thought it late to begin at my age, "However", he said, "there is Mr Jones of Exeter College who has done it." The Pre-Raffaelites nevertheless seemed not much to his taste; he said they painted like a school of madmen let loose. This roused me to defend them, for I was steeped in Ruskin and mad about Hunt and Millais. "Well", said Scott, "bring your pre-Raffaelitism into architecture, for it is exactly what architecture is most in need of at the present time." After this conversation I took to drawing the statuary at the Crystal Palace, for Scott had said how all-important it was for an architect to be able to draw the figure well and not to be obliged to depend on a sculptor for the statuary of his building.[32]

Scott's office was a very large one. Counting pupils, salaried assistants, and clerks, I think we were twenty-seven in all. I was put to work in the first floor room at the back with six others; there were about a dozen more in two rooms on the second floor; the ground floor front room, which also served as a waiting-room, was the sanctum of Mr Burlison, the head man, who made the estimates and surveys. Scott's own room was the ground floor back, and farther back still were the writing clerk and the office boys. The front room first floor was let to a Mr Moriarty, a barrister, a mysterious person whom we never saw. Of Scott we saw but little. He was up to the eyes in engagements and it was hard to get him to look at our work. I have seen three or four men with drawings requiring correction or approval grouped outside his door. The door flew open and out he came. "No time today!"; the cab was at the door and he whirled away to some cathedral where he would spend a couple of hours and then fly off again to some other great work at the other end of the kingdom. Now and then the only chance of getting instructions was to go with him in the cab to the station. I see I wrote at the time, "What a fine thing it is to be so busy"; but looking back from my present standpoint I find nothing in such a career to envy, and much to wonder at. It need hardly be said that it is an impossibility really to direct so large a staff as Scott's but the work had to be done somehow. The heads of different rooms were capable men with a good knowledge of construction; Scott had a wonderful power of making rapid expressive sketches and from these his men were able to produce work which, curiously enough, did fall into something of a consistent style that passed for Gilbert Scott's and which one can always recognize wherever one meets with it as coming from that office. There are many amusing tales which show the slight acquaintance he had with what came out of his office: how he admired a new church from the railway carriage window and was told it was one of his own; how he went into a church in process of building, sent for the clerk of works, and began finding fault with this and with that till the man said, "You know, Mr Scott, this is not your church; this is Mr Street's; your church is farther down the road'.[33]

To these anecdotes should be added another told by Lethaby. Scott having left town by the six-o'clock train, the office on slackly assembling found a telegram from a Midland station asking, 'Why am I here?'[34] These tales may be apocryphal, but Scott's method of practice was something which had grown upon him rather than being the result of any philosophy; indeed, he was one of the earliest men to build up a large practice without the help of official appointments. Men like Nash were 'attached architects' to the Office of Works; men like George Smith collected surveyorships to hospitals, livery companies, and other such bodies. Scott's similar appointments, such as that at Westminster Abbey, did not provide the bulk of his work, and came when he was already well established. Earlier architects, save perhaps Jeffrey Wyatt, did not keep large drawing offices where much of the work designed itself, though the principle in art is not new: Scott's office was not unlike the Rubens workshop, where many works were executed from the master's sketches and many of the assistants were themselves artists of note.

Burlison and Wyatt of course remained: the three other chief assistants were Richard Coad, John Bignold — 'a mine of information on building construction whose soul was wrapped up in the office' — and J. T. Irvine, who went as clerk of works to major restorations like Ludlow or Peterborough. Burlison's son James was there. Junior assistants included E. R. Robson and J. J. Stevenson. Bodley, Street, Crossland and Coe among others had left to practice. There were in 1858 seven pupils including Thomas Garner and C. Hodgson Fowler. Later names of note include Somers Clarke, C. R. Baker King, and J. T. Micklethwaite. Over a hundred people passed through the office, and its effect on the architecture of the latter half of the century was considerable.

In 1859 Scott was awarded the Royal Gold Medal for the Promotion of Architecture, conferred annually since 1848 upon a distinguished architect or other person whose work had promoted architecture. Late in 1860 he was advanced to Royal Academician in the place of the deceased Sir Charles Barry. That year he became a Fellow of the Society of Antiquaries.

6
Restorer,
1859-64

From 1859-63 Scott consolidated his position as restorer of major ecclesiastical buildings. Fifteen were brought to him in these years.[1]

Salisbury Cathedral, built in one operation between 1220 and 1260, except for the upper stage of the tower, the spire, and the west front, and restored in 1668 and again, destructively, in 1787-93 by James Wyatt, might well have been the great church with which Scott felt most sympathy. By the 1850s, it was in disrepair. The Chapter House was decorated by Clutton and Burges in 1856, but the raffish and eccentric Burges, though a capable and inventive designer, could restore too fiercely. Scott was appointed about 1859. His first task was the renewal of eight flying buttresses, generally using Chilmark limestone from a bed left by the old masons to form a roof whilst they quarried beneath .

The releading of the roofs was completed by the first half of 1866, and in the meantime the tower and spire, the subject of continual tinkering since 1837, had attention. Scott found that their weight was too great for the thin walls of the earlier lower storey despite considerable buttressing. He proposed to underpin with concrete and to drain the whole church, to bond the lower storeys of the tower with diagonal iron ties, and to renew all the damaged stonework piece by piece.

The foundations were completed by the end of 1864. The Chapter, alarmed by the proposals, asked a second opinion of F. W. Shields, who substantially agreed with Scott. The strengthening ironwork was duly inserted, the stonework was scrupulously repaired, and the remainder of the tower and spire underwent minor repairs. The tower piers were bent but not broken, and were left alone.[2]

In 1869 Bishop Hamilton died and, as at least £25,000 had been spent without any internal rearrangements, a memorial fund was raised for the restoration of the choir interior. Canopies and desk fronts were apparently of Wyatt's time, and the fittings were accordingly 'brought back', as closely as possible, to what may be supposed to have been their original state.[3] The walls, covered by Wyatt with yellow wash, were revealed. Scott disliked the execution of the repainting of the Lady Chapel, the choir, and the presbytery, in 1870 and later.

Wyatt had merged the choir and the Lady Chapel, supplied a screen between choir and nave supporting the organ, and placed the high altar at the east end of the Lady Chapel, which proved too far from the congregation, and at one time a portable altar at the east end of the nave had been used. After controversy, Scott introduced a new altar two bays from the end of the choir. To obtain an uninterrupted view down this long church, he replaced Wyatt's screen by an iron one of Skidmore's, removed in 1959. It is possible that the impractical views of John Jebb[4] about the propriety of using cathedral nave and choir as one undivided area had had some influence.

Reredos (now removed), pulpit, throne, organ case, Hamilton memorial, and font[5] followed. The nave interior, completed under John Oldrid Scott at a cost of nearly £7500, was the last work.[6] Gilbert Scott had been most interested in the restoration of the screens between the small transepts and the choirs, where he was able to indulge in antiquarian detective work, as indeed he had done in the restoration of Bishop Poore's tomb.

The total cost of Scott's work at Salisbury was some £60,000, spread over eighteen years. The work had been for the most part carried out in a conservative manner; he had saved another tower from damage or collapse, and had not impressed himself unduly upon the interior. The screen and the reredos, both removed, were the only items distinctly out of place.

Chester Cathedral, built of friable red sandstone, had over the centuries worn away in an alarming manner. Scott had often encountered this problem, as at Sandbach, Hereford, and Nantwich. As early as 1819 Thomas Harrison had undertaken restoration, and from 1844-46 Hussey had restored the choir. In 1859, he and Scott restored the Lady Chapel interior, replacing the

Perpendicular window tracery with Early English;[7] Octavius Hudson provided the colour decoration, and A. W. Blomfield the mosaic at the base of the east wall.

After Hussey had resigned as architect to the Cathedral, Scott was in 1868 asked to report. The Cathedral was in a sad state, with its walls eroded and honeycombed. its mouldings absent, its buttresses tottering. Scott (and Ewan Christian acting for the Ecclesiastical Commissioners) estimated that the necessary repairs would cost £22,531, desirable repairs £7000; improvements £20,000; and fees £2500. The work was in the end to cost over £70,000.

In June a public meeting was held: the Ecclesiastical Commissioners gave £10,000 and the Dean and Chapter £2000; in a month £11,600 more was promised. Seldom can there have been so immediately successful an appeal for funds. Work at once started on the Lady Chapel exterior[8] using a hard sandstone from Runcorn. Scott was much taxed by the defaced stonework, but patiently built up each part of the design of the Lady Chapel (where he found many affinities with the eastern parts of Bangor Cathedral) from fragments more protected than the rest, so that the only conjectures were the eastern gables and pinnacles. He removed the southern of the two perpendicular Chapels flanking the Lady Chapel because 'it was horribly decayed, it spoiled that side of the beautiful Lady Chapel, it had destroyed the apse of the choir-aisle, and its walls were the burial place of the details of the finer work which it had displaced; while its design was the same as that of the north Chapel which I left'.[9] In its walls he found details showing that the south choir aisle had terminated in an apse, and this was rebuilt, partly out of old material: but it was found necessary to conjecture the spire-like roof and the buttress with its pinnacle between aisle and apse. This was widely regarded as either forgery or pedantry. The cloister south wall was rebuilt, exactly on its old lines, in order to buttress the south nave aisle, and the nave aisles had to be vaulted in stone: this, as at Bath or Brecon, was intended but never actually built. The nave itself had been prepared for stone vaulting, but Scott did not trust the walls to support stone: instead he made an oaken vault. Hussey had altered the choir roof, and the Chapter insisted on its reconstruction in oak. The choir stalls, which Hussey had brought to the west of the crossing, were restored and replaced to the east, and the ancient but ugly stone screen was, against Scott's inclination, removed, replaced by an open screen founded on the design of the old; the old bits of the former screen were set up in the side arches behind the stalls, which had previously been glazed in an ineffectual attempt to quell the draughts. The organ which the screen had supported was placed in the north transept and encased in carved oak to Scott's design in 1876. The substructure of the shrine of St Werburgh was discovered acting as the Bishop's Throne, and other bits were recovered in walling at the west end pulled down in 1872. A new Throne was made, and the recovered pieces of the shrine put together in the south choir aisle: by 1930 they had migrated to the Lady Chapel. The sedilia were completed 'according to their own evidence' with the help of an old canopy unearthed by the clerk of works, strangely, among the ruins of St John's Church. Finally, the reredos, depicting the Last Supper in relief under Gothic canopies with a rectilinear tiled surround, was erected.

The large south transept was used as the parish church of St Oswald for a long time on and off until Scott built a new church for its congregation. Similar instances were not uncommon: St Faith-the-Virgin under St Paul's, or Ely, where the Lady Chapel was so used. Scott repaired the exterior, and prepared designs for the complete replacement of the south front, rebuilt early in the 19th century, which were carried out after his death by John Oldrid Scott. Internally, some capitals were carved with modern political subjects, such as Gladstone overthrowing the Irish Church. The central tower, from which bits of stone used to fall on windy nights, was restored during the earlier years of the work. Scott maintained that a spire had been intended in the 15th century but not built, and designed a lead covered timber spire to give the tower a little importance. Though a model was on view in the Chapter House in 1876, it remained unexecuted.

When in 1876 the majority of the work was done, critics began to talk of 'the new Cathedral', a reproduction of a mediaeval building by modern workmen, and to remark upon the ostentatious fidelity with which a single piece of old stone was left in the middle of nearly a whole wall of new and elaborate work.

When the King's School was rebuilt in 1876 on the site of the Bishop's Palace, Blomfield did the main part of the work, but Scott was entrusted with the west elevation, adjoining the Cathedral on the north.

Bath Abbey in the mid-19th century was Bishop King's

unfinished early 16th century Perpendicular building, patched by later hands and fitted for worship in the choir only.

Restoration started as early as 1833 under G. P. Manners: the Corporation of Bath was patron of the living and took its obligations seriously to the extent of £10,000. The interior was remodelled, apparently introducing nave galleries, the exterior extensively repaired, the prominent flying buttresses added, and a new stone screen by Blore replaced the Jacobean screen supporting the organ.

In 1860 Charles Kemble was appointed to the Rectory, and asked Scott's advice. Scott recommended that Blore's screen be placed at the west end, the organ in the north transept, the pulpit at the north-west corner, and that the nave galleries be banished. The nave was covered by a dilapidated timber roof, resting on the walls at the height of the clerestory transomes. Four years later the internal work, estimated to cost £12,000, commenced: Bladwell's tender of £5389 for the first portion was accepted, and the perilous nave roof was to be repaired, new battlements (conjectural) erected, the stonework of the clerestory, west and transept windows renewed and the windows reglazed. In the middle of 1865, at the instigation and with the monetary help of the rector, work started in greater earnest, and the plaster ceilings to the nave and its aisles were removed and replaced by fan vaulting to match the choir, as, it is abundantly clear, Bishop King had intended — a reasonable proceeding, similar to that taken previously at Brecon. The transepts were similarly treated. This operation, delayed by lack of funds, continued until early in 1869, and cost £5500. The nave floor was levelled and concreted with the monumental slabs reset, the galleries banished, Blore's stone screen removed to the west end to form an inner porch, the pillars and walls repaired, and, it is stated, some columnar mural tablets tidied away to the side walls.[10] The interior was rearranged, for Manners had spoiled the Jacobean arrangements anyhow.

The west front, with its queer 'ladder' motifs exposed to the prevailing winds, had by 1847 become almost illegible and was beginning to sink. It was underpinned and considerably repaired with the help of the local Freemasons, most of the windows being repaired and having stained glass inserted. The Abbey was reopened in 1871; items such as the font (of 1874) were added later. Total expenditure was over £21,000.[11]

At Chichester Cathedral, William Slater had restored the large south and west windows, and was still busily engaged when Dean Hook came from Leeds in 1859.[12] It had long been desired to remove the Arundel Screen in order to inspect the tower, but the Catholic Duke of Norfolk would not allow the heretics to touch it. When the screen was finally removed in 1860, the piers of the central tower were found to be ruinous. The walls began to move in January 1861, and some shoring work was done. The cracks got worse, and by 21 February the situation was desperate. Bishop Gilbert prudently had his horses removed out of danger, Dean Hook sat in his study sobbing, and at half past one the spire inclined slightly and then collapsed telescopically into the church with a cloud of dust and little noise. Hook was very upset, and threw himself, with much personal sacrifice, into the task of raising money for the rebuilding, giving the whole of his annual stipend of £1000 and, having known Scott at Leeds, now turned to him for help. Scott was appointed to restore the tower and Slater was ignored, though the tower could not have been saved from disintegration. Scott associated Slater with him in the work and shared his payments with him.[13] The cost was estimated at £50,000.

The usual amateurs wrote the usual letters to the usual periodicals advocating this or that course, but they were as usual disregarded.

Scott examined what remained, and sent George Gilbert Junior, twenty-one years old and just out of his articles, to live on the spot with instructions to salvage and identify all the mouldings and carved stones in the heap of rubble as it was cleared away. Jackson helped him. Old prints and photographs were collected, and Joseph Butler's measured drawings of 1847-8 were invaluable. Next the raw ends were shored, and when the site was clear, the ground was excavated to a depth of 13 ft, and a layer of concrete 4 ft thick placed in the bottom of the hole, on which were laid massive blocks of Purbeck stone set in cement mortar. The tower was built up, in Purbeck and in Portland stone, with iron ties at the springing of the arches. The work connecting the tower with the remaining body of the Cathedral was inserted, and the spire carried up. The design of the tower and spire was recovered in its entirety, and much old detail was re-used: the only alterations were the omission of the partial walling up of the belfry windows, and the heightening of the tower by some 6 ft, since the roofs abutting on it had in the 14th century been raised by this amount, thus as it were burying a part of the design. Said Scott: 'I do not think that a settlement of a hair's breadth shows itself. This is as admirable a piece of masonry as ever was erected, and as faithful a restoration'.[14] George Gilbert Scott Junior superintended every detail of the work, from setting out the foundations himself to refixing the old weathercock with his own hands on the spire on 28 June 1866, when the Bishop attended a celebratory service. The young Scott then went off to spend ten years as an undergraduate and fellow at Jesus College, Cambridge, meanwhile doing work for Bodley, for his father and on his own. The elder Scott, in 1870-2, helped Slater underpin and restore the Lady Chapel and that to the east of the south transept. The remaining restoration work, notably the chancel refitting, was by Slater alone, except for Bodley's screen replacing the Arundel Screen.[15]

Robert Bickersteth had been a Canon of Salisbury when Scott started work there. In 1856 he became Bishop of Ripon and Scott was asked to report on the restoration of that Cathedral.

He said the building was cracked and dangerous, the interior dilapidated. He wished to spend £17,000 on repairs, £10,000 on alterations, and £5000 on fittings. These were formidable sums, but the eventual total exceeded £40,000. He methodically worked his way round the building in the course of the next ten years; the choir was completed early in 1869 and the nave in October 1872. He underpinned and founded the two western towers and restored the crumbling detail to give the appearance of heartless perfection intended by the mediaeval masons. He repaired the exterior, rebuilt two large pinnacles at the east end and the buttresses to the north and south walls, replaced the choir roof by a leaden one of higher pitch, removed the galleries and the plaster choir stall canopies, replacing the latter with copies of a few wooden ones which had survived. The sedilia were moved to the easternmost bay. The choir was repaved and the walls stripped of plaster. The organ was re-cased. Iron girders were introduced into the tower, and new oak ceilings were installed in the transepts and over the nave. The choir received a new roof of higher pitch, and its aisle vaults were repaired. The south windows were opened up and re-mullioned. The bare outline of the work is more instructive than any commentary.

On 2 August 1861 Scott reported to a public meeting on the Abbey of the Holy Cross, Pershore. He proposed to spend over

Ripon Cathedral, internal bays of choir. Drawings by W. S. Weatherley from Scott's lectures on the Rise and Development of Mediaeval Architecture given at the Royal Academy

£4000 to repair the rump of the fabric — the nave had long been destroyed — and to make it more convenient for worship, by rebuilding the south-east aisle, strengthening the foundations, cleaning whitewash off the interior, repairing the south transept, tower and roofs, and taking down the 1846 eastern apse and rebuilding in its original style (this did not in the end take place).

The work, with Collins of Tewkesbury as builder, was done substantially during 1863-4. Certain things were added, notably the ringing stage in the tower, replacing an old ceiling; gas lighting was installed, a vestry formed, and the organ reconstructed. Scott had to redesign the pinnacles on the tower, and based them on Salisbury, which he thought clearly the work of the same hand, but he made them plainer to accord with the general appearance of Pershore. Dr Williamson, the incumbent, who largely financed this, died in 1865; as his memorial, two years later, Scott, with Clayton and Bell, decorated the west wall with mosaic, painting and glass.

At Dorchester Abbey in Oxfordshire a change of incumbent in 1858 heralded a change of architect. Various people had worked here between 1844 and 1853 (incidentally destroying the hammer beam roof of the north aisle) — J. P. Harrison, and Cranstoun, and Butterfield. The Rev MacFarlane was anxious to complete the work his predecessors had started, and during 1860-3 Scott worked at the west end of the nave, restored the south aisle, repaired the exterior, re-tiled the sacrarium in a pattern discovered in some old work, repaved the aisle, rebuilt the Tudor porch, renovated the 14th-century wall painting above the altar, and attended to the roof.[16] Years after, in 1872, the great south chancel aisle was repaired, and two years later Scott vaulted over the two altars at its east end, although it is not clear whether this groining existed in the mediaeval building.

In 1862, Scott was asked to look at St James church at Bury St Edmunds. He condemned its modern nave roof, which was giving trouble, and wished to rebuild it of flat pitch in conformity with the East Anglian Perpendicular style of the nave, but the parish insisted that it be fashionably high-pitched, in oak with nineteen pairs of principals, and hammer beams. The nave was made secure, pews and galleries were abolished, and the interior stuccoed.[17] The pavements were lowered and relaid with Minton tiles; a new pulpit was erected. This work was all completed by 1864, at a cost of £5000,[18] when Scott turned his attention to the debased chancel of 1711. One party favoured Perpendicular; the Ecclesiological Society judged in favour of middle pointed as the style for a total rebuilding, completed by 1868.[19]

In 1860 restoration of Brecon Priory Church in South Wales was contemplated. Bishop Thirlwall was no doubt responsible for Scott's presence at the meeting on 17 November to consider the proposition and Scott spoke on how the foundations needed underpinning, the tower roof renewing, the transept roofs repairing, the walls cleaning internally and pointing externally, the floors re-laying, and the screens removing. The Marquis Camden offered £1500 whereupon the meeting resolved to proceed and subscribed a further £1256 on the spot: this was unusually encouraging. A start was made at the east end, with James and Price of Cardiff as builders. The nearby quarry from where the building stone original-ly came was located and re-opened, the transepts repaired and presumably also the tower. The chancel was an unusually fine first pointed work of a French character, with triple piscinae and sedilia, an east window of five lancets, and three bays of triple arcading each side, with vaulting springers formed. The vaulting had never been built, but there was a flat Perpendicular ceiling. Scott supplied, after an interval of 650 years, the intended vaulting over the chancel, below the existing ceiling: this is perhaps his most daring and successful foray into 'conjectural restoration'. Originally the chan-cel furnishings were below cill level: an elaborate and high carved reredos was installed much later.[20]

Scott's work, finished by May 1862 and costing about £4500, left the nave and aisles unrestored. They waited until a report from Scott and a further public meeting inviting subscriptions in 1871. In April 1872 the tender of £2940 from Collins and Cullis of Tewkes-bury was accepted, and the work, though involving removal of plaster and whitewash from the internal walls and thus discovering the stairs each side leading to the former rood loft, seems otherwise conservative and uneventful. The building now shows a strange contrast between the clean light nave and the rich and heavy chancel — a contrast not due to Scott but rather that of Early English against Decorated.

In 1862 Thirlwall again sought Scott's advice, this time about St David's Cathedral in remote West Wales. His was one of the least and poorest sees in the country. Butterfield had, in 1846 and perhaps later, repaired the Perpendicular sanctuary screen and worked in the transepts, including designing the north window, but still the whole building was very dilapidated and damp—indeed it had never been the same since earthquake damage in 1248—and fears were entertained about the stability of the central tower, rebuilt after it had fallen about 1200. Scott, who had visited and sketched on previous occasions, examined carefully, and recommended work costing £30,000 to be done in four stages, spread over eight to ten years to facilitate raising the money. First, urgent attention must be given to the tower. The western supports were useless, so that the nave arches were being pushed to the west, and there were cracks in the north and south faces. Scott proposed to tie the upper part of the tower together with iron, to shore up the north and west arches (the south being already walled in) and to rebuild the west piers bit by bit. Cottingham had done this kind of thing at Hereford twenty years before; R. C. Carpenter had executed similar works at Sherborne, Bayeux was a recent example from France, and Scott himself had experience at Ellesmere, Stafford, Nottingham, Aylesbury and Hawarden, and was now so engaged at Salisbury and Darlington. The Cathedral was to be drained and the choir, seats, stalls, and organ were to be repaired.

In 1864 Pollard's tender of nearly £14,000 was accepted: Wood and Sons of Worcester must later have come along with a figure of £11,000 for they began work at the end of the year. It took a year to secure the tower and whenever Scott woke in the night, his first thought was whether it had fallen. When Clear (the clerk of works) was satisfied with this stage of the work, he, like Sir Christopher Wren's daughter, stood below the tower when the timber shores first took the weight, saying that 'if the tower fell, he would be smashed first'.[21] Nothing fell, and in the first five months of 1866 the western piers were rebuilt.

The roofs of the chapels east of the altar were extensively renewed, and that of the presbytery repaired. The east window, in bad repair, was demolished, and the pieces of its predecessor were found in the walling. The low-pitched 15th-century nave roof, of Irish oak and almost barbaric splendour, was repaired late in 1870, as were the aisle windows and clerestory, particularly on the south side. The nave was refloored with concrete in the hope of keeping the damp down.[22]

Finance was a continual worry, and by 1873 the £21,000 subscribed had been spent. Yet the west front still irritated Scott, for it
stood as Nash had left it in 1791, with timber shoring encased in
stone buttresses. After Bishop Thirlwall died, in 1874, it was
proposed to restore this to its original appearance as a memorial.
Scott, guided by old prints, rebuilt it as it now stands, a remarkably
close copy of the original, with the exception of the porch and
turrets, which must be largely conjectural. All in all, St David's
must rank as perhaps Scott's best cathedral restoration.[23]

Worcester Cathedral now presents an exterior almost entirely
renewed in mid-Victorian times, whilst the interior, notable for its
homogeneity of Gothic design, achieves this largely on account of
the Victorian replacement of Perpendicular windows, some of them
rebuilt only sixty years previously, by Early English to match the
rest of the structure. Almost all of this is due to A. E. Perkins of
Worcester who started work in 1854. He was not one of the
Ecclesiologists' charmed circle; they deplored that he was 'the
ordinary cathedral architect', not 'any first rate architect of acknowledged reputation', and stigmatised his restoration as
'destructive'.[24] The Diocesan Architectural Society, however, always warmly supported him. But when, in 1863, Perkins having
restored the choir, the question of its rearrangement arose, Scott's
advice was sought. He proposed that the solid plaster choir screen
of 1812 be removed, the organ be placed on a *jubé*, and the bishop's
throne, stalls and canopies, and reredos be replaced. Painting,
lighting and heating were to be provided.

Scott took care to have Perkins associated with the fitting out of
the church. The alabaster reredos of 1868 is similar to that designed
for Lichfield four years earlier, and contains five elaborately
crocketed niches for statues; the bishop's throne is of the same year.
The iron chancel screen was one of Scott's four famous screens: that
behind the north-east transept, of stone, is supposed to be composed of 15th-century material. Skidmore executed the choir par-
closes and metal grilles, and the organ case and nave benches were
carved by Farmer and Brindley. The altar rail dates from 1875, as
does Hardman's glass in the new west window. The choir stalls
incorporate thirty-seven misericords of the stalls of 1379.[25]

There is an intriguing remark that in 1873 'Some talented French
refugees'[26] had been engaged for the choir works, but no details are

given. The restoration was completed in 1874, having cost an exceptionally large sum — over £100,000. Scott's work was estimated at £13,000 of this but it certainly cost more.

In the 18th century a great deal of money was spent on Gloucester Cathedral, but it was in a shabby state by 1848, when restoration started under the local architects Fulljames and Waller. The west front and a few unimportant details were taken in hand: then in 1853 a planned programme of repair was started and Scott was asked to report upon the architects' proposals. He reported favourably, having a good opinion of Waller, and took no further part in the works, and so during 1855-64 the Dean and Chapter spent some £14,500. Buildings, and accumulations of earth up to 12 ft deep, were removed from around the structure and the area drained, the crypt cleansed and its windows unblocked, and coat upon coat of yellow and white wash removed from the nave interior. The vaulting thus exposed was found in good order. Some fragments of painting were found, all but one unintelligible, and the bases of some of the nave columns, replaced in the time of George III, were renewed.

In 1863 Waller, still comparatively young, resigned his position due to ill health, and Scott was brought in to act with Fulljames. Next year, heating stoves were installed, as much to preserve the fabric as to comfort the congregation, and the year after the Dean appealed for a further £50,000, the choir, transepts and cloisters particularly needing attention. As usual, the pace of restoration ran a little ahead of funds. In 1866 Fulljames too resigned, giving money to the work, and Scott carried on alone, with Ashbee as clerk of works.

Scott made no sweeping alterations to the early Perpendicular work. Waller had, years before, made careful measured drawings which were of value in recording that which had since disappeared. The south transept, supposedly dangerous, was first taken in hand during 1867-69: 'as much as possible of the ancient work is retained'.[27] In 1869-70 the south porch was then repaired, fourteen new statues by Redfern placed in the canopied niches over the door in place of a 'modern' sundial, and Scott added a central finial. St Andrew's Chapel, in the corner between the south transept and the chancel, was adorned with thirty-three figures by Roddis of Birmingham and painted during 1867-8 by Gambier Parry, who also subscribed £300 to the funds. Scott repaired the very decayed exterior, and the other side chapels.

By early 1869 the choir was under restoration, estimated by Scott at £13,000. Again, the whitewash was carefully removed from the elaborate roof vault, and a watch kept for old painting, but only fragments were found. It was repainted by Clayton and Bell according to Scott's ideas, the ribs mostly in blue and gold and the spaces between for the most part unpainted. Parry, predictably, would have painted the panels and left the ribs. Scott's views were based not upon precedent but upon what he thought would give the best appearance.

The thin but decayed stonework of the enormous choir east windows, of 1350 but already Perpendicular in style, was renewed and the 14th-century glass preserved. Some other windows were so treated. From 1869, stalls and canopies were repaired. As the desk fronts were 'modern' they were redesigned incorporating remains found in the Lady Chapel. The carving was by Farmer and Brindley. The side galleries across the transept openings were removed. The return stalls were complete and backed on to a stone screen designed by Sir Robert Smirke in 1820, bearing a 17th-century organ. Because the Dean objected to opening the screen out, and because of the return stalls, Scott left all this *in situ*, in spite of much local opposition and contrary to his usual practice. The organ itself was reconstructed in 1888-9.

The south aisle, out of plumb, had been restored to the vertical by Waller, who had intended to restore its easternmost window to match the other Decorated six. Scott repaired it as it stood.

In 1870 the south transept window was renewed. For here, and for the clerestory, Scott designed glass made by Clayton and Bell.

Scott's last works here were the font of 1876 and the high altar and reredos, unveiled in 1873. It was at first intended to retain the existing reredos but Scott uncovered the position of its predecessor, which he could not restore on the evidence available: the Freemasons then donated a new one from his design. Overall one cannot consider Scott's reredos as successful, though here the detail, based on local prototypes, is fussy rather than coarse: the figures are Redfern's. The colouring was added by Clayton in 1889. The old altar and rails were removed to the south chapel.

During this period Waller, restored to health, resumed practice, and gave Scott some assistance: then he was reinstated as resident architect and Scott retained as consultant. Between 1873 and 1879 he partially rebuilt the north transept facade and reconstructed the central tower cornices, pinnacles and parapets, and after 1892 worked on the remaining unrepaired areas, the north and south choir aisles and the Lady Chapel.

Scott was possibly involved at Windsor Castle, advising on the chapter room, as early as 1852, and in 1859 the monument to the Duchess of Gloucester in St George's Chapel was erected from his design by William Theed; he did further work from 1862.

St George's Chapel, a large and late Gothic work of 1475-1511, had had a great east window of fifty-two lights which had been entirely replaced during the reign of George III. As a memorial to the Prince Consort, the Dean and Chapter restored the window to its original form with Scott's help, filling it with glass by Clayton and Bell. *The Ecclesiologist* thought it 'one of the best windows... which has been placed in any English church since the revival'.[28]

At the same time Scott designed the reredos, to be carved by Philip in Derbyshire alabaster. The rest of his work at St George's Chapel was probably administrative in character, but there exist his drawings for the restoration of the nave roof.

Scott was called in to co-ordinate the conversion of the disused Wolsey Chapel into the Prince Consort Memorial Chapel. He designed the marble reredos, but was not personally responsible for much else in this fantastic and perhaps vulgar interior, the decorations of which are utterly characteristic of Victorian tastes.[29]

Scott's third work at Windsor was his considerable restoration of the 'horseshoe cloister', the crescent of timber framed clergy houses built 1478-81 which forms the western approach to St George's Chapel. No doubt all that is externally visible dates from Scott's work of 1871 or later.

Clearly the emphasis in Scott's church practice had changed. During the twenty years after 1845, church work came at a fairly even rate. But the amount of church restoration work grew steadily, so that from being rather less than the volume of new churches in 1845, it was three times that in 1865, and in both 1862 and 1863 fifteen new such jobs can be identified. In the twenty years, over 100 new churches and over 200 restorations were undertaken: in the period 1860-4 against about thirty new churches and about the same number of miscellaneous works (some however of considerable size), there are seventy-seven traceable restorations, many of considerable interest.[30]

In the early 1860s, Scott's fame led to his being in demand as a consultant, to advise local men. He stood in this relation, for example, to S. Pountney Smith over the ruinous Battlefield Church near Shrewsbury in 1861; to Law at works in and around Northampton; to Pritchard at St Nicholas, Great Yarmouth about 1862; to Pope and Bindon at St James, Bristol the year after; to Goddard of Leicester at Washingborough in 1859; or to John Henderson for the main hall of Glenalmond College in Perthshire in 1861-2.[31] For the schools at Glastonbury Scott furnished a Perpendicular design, to be in character with St John's Church, realised by a Mr Merrick. The danger here was that, although Scott might give of his expert knowledge of Gothic and advise restoration according to his often reiterated principles, he had no control over the execution of the work, and he might find himself in the classic dilemma of the town planners of the present time: if the work turned out well, the local men had done a good job; if badly, it was all Scott's fault. Or Scott might prepare designs and hand them over to a local man to do the work, such as at Harewood, Yorkshire, where Scott did drawings in 1862 for a drastic restoration which involved removing the plaster ceiling, two inches of wall plaster, pews and gallery, and moving monuments. The work was carried out by Parsons, Lord Harewood's estate architect. Occasionally, he even retired from a commission, like the Hospital of the Holy Trinity at Ascot, started in 1862 but carried on by Buckeridge; or Bradfield School, continued by John Oldrid Scott. Even more occasionally, he might assess a competition, as at Kenley, Surrey, in 1871 where he recommended the design of James Fowler of Louth.

It seems that in 1863 Scott senior passed on to George Gilbert Scott junior the restoration of the church and the churchyard cross at Cheddleton in Staffordshire, his first independent work, undertaken in the next year under the eye of Saville, a clerk of works from the Spring Gardens office. It was the custom in some Victorian offices to pass on such a 'setting up' job to a young man embarking on practice.

Other church restorations of this period involved widespread and expensive work to major town churches, the cost running perhaps into five figures. These were inclined to run to type: the interior would be gutted of old furnishings, galleries, and so on, especially if they were of the despised 18th century, the structure made damp-proof and watertight, and repaired, more or less heavily depending upon the state of the fabric, and new, ecclesiological, fittings supplied.

St Lawrence, Ludlow, the largest parish church in Shropshire, is outwardly mostly 15th century work in sandstone, which gave Scott a lot of trouble in those latitudes. Kyrke Penson of Shrewsbury repaired it about 1844, but when sterner measures were required, Scott was sent for, and in 1859-60 he cleaned out the interior, removing all the pews and galleries but leaving the rood screen, removing the tracery of many windows, which at the same time had stained glass introduced by Willement and others, repairing the porch, and no doubt, although there is no certain evidence, doing some general external repairs; he also exposed and heavily repaired the old stone reredos.[32]

The church at nearby Leominster in Herefordshire is a very odd building: the remains of a priory, it has three parallel naves of different ages and a north aisle. The two later naves, the middle and the south, were in 1705 after a serious fire refitted with a south gallery, box pews, three decker pulpit and what looked like theatre boxes on the north. In 1843 it took on its final unreformed appearance with the addition of a west gallery and an organ on a gallery behind the reredos and in front of the east window, to the design of John Collins. In 1863 Scott provided plans for repairing, reflooring, removing monumental tablets and galleries, and placing the organ on the floor. All the 18th-century fittings were then stripped out and the Norman nave, in a poor state of repair, was put into some sort of order at a cost of £3012, between March 1864 and July 1866.

To quote from a report of Scott's:

The external stonework is in part very badly decayed and will require general reparation. Several of the beautiful windows of the Nave, some of the very noblest of their age, have been deprived of their tracery and must be in great measure repaired. The vast west window of the Middle Nave is in a most dangerous state and must be almost wholly rebuilt. The pillars between the Middle and South Naves date from after the fire in 1690 and are a great disfigurement... Their original form is ascertained from one of their capitals which has been made use of in repairing the tower: and I would strongly recommend that they should be replaced by new ones of the original form. This would be a great improvement and would reduce the obstruction which they at present cause from their undue size. The stonework of the tower is especially bad in its condition almost the entire surface having perished and the walls become much shattered and disjoined while the parapet and pinnacles

— which seem to have re-used from some earlier portions of the church — are in such a state of decay as to be extremely dangerous. The west end of the North aisle, the only part which retains its early vaulting, is in a most shattered and dangerous condition and the remainder of the aisle is in a very mutilated and shabby state. The parapets generally demand considerable reparation and the repairs needed by the stonework both within and without are very heavy. I need hardly say that internally the stonework must be denuded of its thick coatings of whitewash but without removing the ancient painting which in many parts exists below it, much less disturbing the surface of the ancient stone. The roofs throughout are of a miserable character, dating from after the fire. The old Nave is covered by a leanto roof which is far from strong. The Middle nave has a roof of moderate pitch and in itself substantial but concealed by a wretched ceiling parts of which threaten to fall upon the heads of those below. The third or South aisle has a lean-to roof tolerably though not substantially built but unfit to be exposed and concealed by a common plaster ceiling, and the roof of the old Norman nave is of a very rude and barn-like kind. I do not like to recommend the reconstruction of all these roofs according to what may be supposed to have been their original forms partly because of the great cost and further because the Church having been reduced to a mere fragment of its original form it is doubtful how far this might produce an agreeable effect. It is indeed clear that the older nave has not possessed a high pitched roof since the addition of the present tower. I further find that the timbers, uncouth though they are, are not much decayed, while the church having externally a sort of traditional aspect which is not unpleasing, I am rather unwilling to disturb it. I am for these reasons induced to recommend such internal modifications of the present roofs as may render them as sightly as may be without going to the extent of reconstructing them. The roof of the central nave can I think with a certain amount of modification be made to look fairly well as an open roof.

And so on.

The west window of the middle nave had in fact been rebuilt by Nicholson, later the Hereford diocesan architect, in 1846 or thereabouts. Not until June 1876 was Scott able to embark upon more serious work: he cut down the south arcade piers to their present, more Gothic, form, and opened out the wall at the east end to form a further bay of arcading. It is notable that all the internal walls are now of bare stone. The east and west windows of the south nave were then renewed. This was completed at the end of 1878.[33] Very little of Scott's seating remains, to the church's benefit, and it is now extremely difficult to discern what is old work. The character of the immense, light, open area at different levels and with many columns is unusual and totally different from that of the 18th-century church. Often the major difference between the appearance of a church before and after restoration by Scott was in the furnishings.

At Holy Trinity, Hull, in 1859 the arrangements were curious: the nave was fitted as a parish church, and the choir used as a vestibule, and in that year restorations costing eventually £33,000 and taking twenty years were embarked upon. The ritual arrangements were made orthodox, the structure properly restored, and, in 1876-7, the chancel entirely refitted.

In 1860-61 Gilbert Scott did a careful and expensive job at St Mary's, Lowgate, where his cousin John Scott was incumbent.[34] The galleries were removed, a south aisle added, the brick tower encased in stone and Gothic fripperies added on top, and various other works took place. The appearance of the church was indeed a good deal improved, but the expense was a great burden to the incumbent in his last few years of life.

St Cuthbert, Darlington, had a central tower which Scott reported as being 'in a most dangerous condition' in 1861, and that year he underpinned it and saved it, also refitting the nave, removing the galleries, and repairing the exterior. The chancel was similarly treated at the same time, but the architect for this work, undertaken by the Duke of Cleveland, was S. T. Pritchett, a local man.

Another troublesome tower in County Durham was at Jarrow, the church of the Venerable Bede, where Scott, during 1864-6, made it secure, repaired the chancel (also of Bede's time) and rebuilt and enlarged the 18th century nave in a manner in keeping with the style of the rest of the building. He was later criticised for his alteration of the nave.

He was particularly active in the major churches of the East Midlands at this time. Melton Mowbray, started in 1850, was about to commence its second period of restoration. At Market Harborough, Scott did some work in 1860: the pulpit and the east window with its Hardman glass are his, and it is notable that the galleries of 1836 are still there. At Huntingdon in 1860-2 his work seems to have been at All Saints, although C. R. Baker King says St Mary's. The south side of the church was collapsing and it was reinstated, and the building substantially reroofed to the old design, among other work. The admirable iron churchyard railings may be Scott's. The church was furnished with chairs, not pews.

South side of North nave

Leominster. South side of north nave (r) and after (l) restoration in 1864

Leominster. North side of north nave before (r) and after (l)

North side of North nave.

At Loughborough in the same years £9000 was spent, and the details of the work show that most of the exterior was renewed: indeed it looks all 19th century. There is a new 13th century style east window: the transept windows now have stone mullions in place of brick. At Ketton it is said that all the tracery is Scott's except for one window: he restored all but the chancel in 1861-2.[35]

At Oundle, Scott prepared abortive plans for reseating in 1854, but eventually restored the church in 1864. The experiment of leaving a thick layer of sawdust in the belfry to deaden the sound of bell-ringing inside the church must be accounted a failure, as in 1868 it caught fire. Afterwards, in 1874, Scott rebuilt the spire.

An admitted consequence of Scott's work at St Peter's, Northampton, was his restoration of the round church of St Sepulchre, where he had before 1857 undertaken work, probably of repair. The church then consisted of the round, a chancel, and its aisles. The restoration turned out to be extraordinarily long-winded: money was collected amid disagreement, mostly over how Lord Northampton should be commemorated, and the funds collected by the 'London Committee' could not be traced. Work did not begin until 1860, when a new chancel, apse, and aisles were added to the east, and a new second aisle to the north. By now it had the Scott characteristics of that period: polished shafts and floral capitals. After this the existing chancel (now the nave) and its aisles were restored, and refitted. By 1866 the round had been stripped of pews and galleries: in 1868 it was restored and refitted, and this seems to be the extent of Scott's involvement, though some minor works took place later.[36]

St Mary, Leicester, a curious church, a mosaic or exemplar of all sorts of styles of architecture, was over-restored by Scott in 1859-61, as part of an extensive reconstruction which had started in 1844 under other hands. He rebuilt the narrow north aisle and nave arcade only partially on the old plan, with moulded arches substituted for plain, and provided a new clerestory on the model of the old, together with a new carved embattled parapet. The north chapel is his: so probably are the south porch and the organ case. He also repaired the outer walls. The south nave arcade was part of an earlier work, in the 1850s. This church is one among many which deserves a monograph detailing the 19th-century changes.

St Mary in Castro, Dover, is more interesting for what Scott did not do than for what he did. The roofless remains of a cruciform

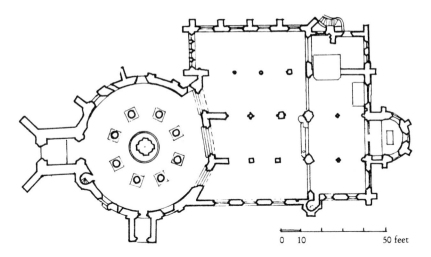

St Sepulchre, Northampton, plan. Scott after 1860 added the east end, the apse and the outer north aisle, and restored the remainder.

church of perhaps 1000, predating the adjacent Norman castle and incorporating re-used Roman tiles, were in 1859 used as the military coal store. After some agitation in interested circles the building was in 1861-2 reroofed and repaired by Scott for use as a military chapel, and the drawings showed the considerable care and archaeological research he took. What is now so prominent, and what it seems has never received favourable criticism, the elaborate polychrome mosaic decoration of the east end, is by William Butterfield in 1888-9, following his similar work at St Cross, Winchester, and based on evidence of the Norman fresco painting. It is comparable in intention, but not in execution, with such Scott interiors as St Michael, Cornhill. A dry and archaeologically correct restored Saxon church might not have been an inspiring place for worship by the soldiery, but perhaps the enrichment might have been made with furnishing rather than in compromising the building so; though mediaeval builders might have used colour in a comparable manner had they known how.

Another work of this time must be grouped with Dover for its unusual character. Christ Church, Hampstead, of 1852, architect S. W. Dawkes, vicar E. H. Bickersteth, later Bishop of Exeter, was where Scott worshipped during his stay in Hampstead. As early as 1860 the accommodation was found insufficient, the site cramped, and so Scott added a west gallery, possibly the only occasion since

1845 on which he introduced, rather than removed, such a structure.

Middleton Cheney, near Banbury, Oxfordshire, was one of a large number of village church restorations of this time. In the year from April 1864, the walls were cleaned internally and the whitewash removed (the effect of coat upon coat of whitewash covering up mouldings was disastrous and contributed to the contemporary horror of this cheap means of decoration). The mutilated nave pillars and arcades were repaired. The chancel arch, propped with timber from the screen, was rebuilt, the screen itself repaired, and a further screen erected to the south of the chancel. New oak seats were provided, the floors lowered, the chancel paved in the familiar encaustic tiles, and the nave with 18 in squares of Hornton stone. The decayed oak roofs were mostly renewed, and leaded externally; the old colouring was retained. The walls were repaired and repainted: the east wall of the south aisle, being too far gone, was rebuilt, as were the much weathered tower pinnacles and parapets. Much missing window tracery was replaced. The incumbent, W. C. Buckley, was a personal friend of Edward Burne-Jones, so the east and south chancel windows were fitted with Morris glass, and other glass by pre-Raphaelites and by Philip Webb was added later. The cost was about £3000: no doubt an entirely new church could have been had for about this sum.

In 1860 the rector of Stoke Talmage, also in Oxfordshire, had plans prepared by E. B. Lamb for a new building to replace the neglected little church where, under the previous incumbent, fowls had roosted in the pulpit during the week. The Diocesan Building Society was asked for financial help: Street as Diocesan architect, predictably, reported adversely on Lamb's drawings. '... very objectionable .... full of eccentricity, unlike any ancient building'[37] and likely to be expensive, although Lamb estimated the cost at £1000. Scott was consulted, and submitted plans for which the lowest obtainable price was £1400: for want of £400 the plan to build a new church was abandoned and Scott undertook to restore the existing structure, clearing out features which dated from the 1750s, reseating, tiling the floor, removing the ceiling (no doubt these maligned ceilings formed a useful insulating function in these cold country parishes), and adding north aisle, vestry, porch and buttresses. One rather regrets the loss of one of Lamb's remarkable churches, but Scott's additions are most tactful, and the windows on the north faithfully copy those on the south. The Perpendicular-type east window appears to be post-Scott, and the little building is, after all, very pleasant.

Scott was of course much less active in Wales than in England — the least pronounceable parishes seemed the preserve of R. J. Withers, who at one time sought unsuccessfully to enter Scott's office — and he did no more than forty works in the Principality. One was the excellent restoration which took place in 1861-2 at St Hilary, Glamorgan. A memorial to the Rev J. M. Traherne, it was paid for by the widow who herself designed the glass for two windows. The building was underpinned and made plumb without any dismantling — note the difference from, say, Castlechurch of 1844 where the walls were taken down and rebuilt: the arcades have no capitals but a continuous moulding. Scott added the south porch: his also are the east window, flowing Decorated, and the aisle west window, three light Decorated with a straight head, simplified from the chancel south window, itself very similar to an example at Ashby Folville, Leicestershire. Internally, walls are plastered, the fittings of course are all new, and there are good iron lighting coronae. The limestone walling externally is pleasant; so is the church's setting. The only irritant is the internal woodwork. Increasingly upsetting is the manner in which all the old woodwork in such churches is swept away and the clumsy design of that which replaces it, even though perhaps in some cases an effort has been made to reproduce features of the old.

Little Horsted in Sussex is a specimen of a building which must have been so badly treated over the years that heavy restoration was inevitable. The squat battlemented Perpendicular west tower remained, acquiring a corner spirelet, but all else except a portion of the north wall containing plain Transitional arcading was rebuilt, and many details redesigned in Early English perhaps to be congruent with this, though the new east window is Decorated, and on the south wall of the nave two new windows are accompanied by a late and straight-headed window reset. So, says Murray in 1893, 'pulled down... to make way for a modern church', and Mark Antony Lower in 1870, 'recently.. restored in bad taste'.[38] But given that the church was decrepit, inconvenient, and bodged, someone in the office tried hard to make the renewals convincing.

Shalstone in Buckinghamshire is an even heavier restoration. The church had been much rebuilt in 1828 and the north aisle of this date alone remains. The rich Early English of the new work has many characteristic Scott touches — patterned bands in the tiling of the high pitched roof, the crosses on the gable copings, pierced cresting on the ridge tiles, a corbel table at the eaves, minute clerestory windows, and capitals carved with garden flowers. A pleasant village church, a bit like rich fruit cake.

At Upton Bishop, Herefordshire, a church containing work of all mediaeval periods with a fine west tower, restoration took place in 1862, quite gently. The floor level had, rather sensibly, been built up to counteract the damp: its level was reduced, it was repaved in Godwin's tiles from Lugwardine, the walls underpinned, drainage made good, and heating pipes in the floor introduced. The two side lancets of the eastern triplet, long blocked, were opened out, but the central one was not renewed: archaeologically conservationist, but artistically unfortunate. The south aisle lost its gallery: the whole was reseated. Pearson and Son did the building works for £1215 2s 4d: the architect's fee was £75 3s 9d, about 6 per cent: the clerk of works, Mr Chick from Hereford once more, got £24 15s 3d. The money was raised by small contributions, with £50 from the Incorporated Society for Building Churches.[39]

In 1863-4 Scott added a lean-to north aisle to Yarpole, Herefordshire, with square-headed windows perhaps because of the limited height, and a pleasantly striped arcade in two different stones. He rebuilt the chancel and most of the south porch, and renewed most of the nave except the walls and roof structure. But although the windows and furnishings look new, the building with its exceptional detached belfry retains a pleasant village church character. Here Smith the builder's work cost £1263 0s 9d out of £1637 0s 4d, the architect got £78 8s, nearly 5 per cent on the whole, and Chick, the clerk of works, £11 only.

By 1862 Scott had clarified his views on 'restoration', and read a paper 'On the Conservation of Ancient Architectural Monuments and Remains,[40] to the Royal Institute of British Architects. His argument and conclusions were now clear and persuasive: had practice not sometimes controverted theory, he, rather than Morris, might be hailed as the first serious preservationist.

Monuments, argued Scott, are valuable when they illustrate the rise and development of art, history and civilisation of a period. The monuments of our own race should therefore be cherished, for have we not a history as glorious and, to us at least, as interesting as that of the great nations of antiquity?

But ancient monuments are continually being lost, by decay, by wilful destruction, or by over-restoration and — probably due to atmospheric pollution — the rate of disintegration of stonework had recently increased very much. Ruins are very liable to disappear, notably by use as quarries for building materials. Ruskin is approvingly quoted as authority for looking after these ruins and keeping them in order for as long as possible, and practical steps for this are given. Also, they should be recorded by means of measured drawings.

Over-restoration of churches is deprecated, but 'we are all of us offenders in this matter'. Certain principles are to be observed: never renew unless essential; never smarten up; keep all old bits. This is very difficult without constant personal supervision.

Scott had had a set of rules and suggestions printed, and these make extraordinary reading when considered together with some of his own work: they are the very antithesis of the theory that all should become the 'early part of late middle pointed'. The structure is to be made stable; the external stonework to be repaired gradually and conservatively. Plaster is not to be stripped: whitewash must be cleaned, but not with a sharp tool and old paintings, however fragmentary, must be retained. The old roof should be retained and repaired, even if it is not of the original date or pitch: the windows should not all be altered, as they may show the church's history. Seating should not all be ripped out, but such old parts, including screens, as remain should be re-used. The floors must be levelled and freed from damp, but monumental slabs and old tiles should be left: one should not be compelled to say, 'the memorials of the dead have perished, and the works of Mr Minton (to which they have fallen victims) have scornfully ousted those of his teachers...'. And, of course, such jobs should be done 'day work' and not by contract.

Finally, he proposed that a standing committee of the RIBA be appointed to lay down a code of practice for the treatment of buildings being restored, and to promote authentic and faithful restoration and conservation of monuments and remains. In 1865, such a paper was prepared.

In Scott's new churches of this period one finds less insensitivity to local forms, at least so long as the office did not merely get out a sketch book: Northamptonshire spires are less likely to be scattered the length and breadth of the country, and details are likely to be copied from, or based on, the Cathedral of the diocese, or some out-of-the-ordinary nearby church. Three new churches of 1861 are good examples.

St Stephen, Higham, near Bury St Edmunds in Suffolk, was a comparatively rare excursion into East Anglia, usually a preserve of Teulon or Phipson or quite unknown local men. In the Geometric style, of flint with Ancaster stone dressings, it has a north nave aisle only, and a pleasing little western round tower 20 ft across crowned with a round spire and containing a rib-vaulted baptistery. The rectory here is attributed to Scott.

At Highgate in the parish of Hawkhurst, Kent, Scott designed in 1859 and built during 1860-1, a new church, All Saints, at the expense of the incumbent, the Rev H. A. Jeffreys, and his sister. *The Ecclesiologist* regarded it as 'a careful rendering of rural Church architecture of South England',[41] but it is faced in sandstone inside and out, has three gables to the west, and a shingled broach spire at the east end of the south aisle. This church, internally and externally, is an unusually well disciplined design, with slightly French detail. The interior is well-proportioned and austere, with conventionally carved capitals and a stone pulpit. The benches, as so often, do not seem to belong. The building is a good and characteristic new church of this period. St Alban's, Muswellbrook, in Australia, designed in 1863, shows many similarities. Christ Church, Wanstead, Essex, started in 1861, has a similar plan but the tower and spire attributed to J. Bressey, 1868, is over the north porch: the material is ragstone and the detail, English late Decorated, altogether different and inferior.

A much smaller building is at Edvin Loach, in a strange area of deserted villages and Revival churches in east Herefordshire. The mediaeval church being in disrepair, Scott, or his client, Edmund Higginson of Saltmarshe Court, forestalled William Morris by nearly twenty years in leaving the old church roofed but ruinous and building a new beside it about 1859. New work is always easier for the architect: here it was complained that Scott, after an initial visit, left all the work to assistants, whilst at Jarrow he spent a whole day in September 1864 directing the operations of the workmen on the site. The new church has four bays all under one roof, plate tracery in the nave, lancets in the polygonal chancel, the inevitable stained trussed purlin roof, a standard south porch and a western tower and broach spire. Externally it is of rubble: internally, whitewashed plaster. As at Ranmore, the foliage on the carved capitals is oddly large and out of scale. It is a decent little church, somehow immature.[42]

Christ Church, Southgate, Middlesex, too, was built beside the 17th-century remains of the old, from foundation stone on 9 June 1861 to consecration on 17 July 1862, at the considerable cost of £11,689 5s 9d. Its clerestoried nave sets off a tower with broach spire apparently modelled on Warmington, Northants, or Frampton, Lincs: the west doorway is said to be almost identical with, though smaller than, that at Chichester Cathedral, whilst other detail seems to derive from Salisbury. The windows have plate-tracery: the east window is a triplet with a rose over. There is a wealth of stained glass made by Morris's firm and designed by Burne-Jones and D. G. Rossetti. Contrast this with St Clement, Barnsbury, of 1864, brick outside, stone inside, with a heavily buttressed west gable flanked by the terraced cottages each side.

If Hawkhurst is the best small church of the middle period, Sherbourne, near Stratford on Avon must be the best large church, though it is not at all influenced by local forms. Externally, the west front with a north-west tower and porch and a south-west vestry is well thought out, the proportions of the parts pleasing, the windows both Early English and Decorated, the materials pleasant. The tall tower and spire has steep gables on the four sides and appears French rather than English. For once Scott has created not only good proportions but rich detail properly balanced: clustered columns of polished marble support the foliated capitals Brindley carves so well; above the nave arcade triforium-like pairs of arches before each of the circular clerestory windows are divided by shafted roof bosses resting on corbels of angels playing musical instruments. The pavement is light and simple; the benches less clumsy than usual: but the east window tracery is unusual and the reredos characteristically spiky. The carving on the chancel walls is later. The whole cost £20,000 in 1862-4 and was paid for by Miss Rylands of a Birmingham wire-drawing family. The church is well cared for, and the fine model by Salter still exists.

St James the Less, Leith, in Scotland, was designed in 1862 and built from 1863-6 for the Episcopalians and shows some original thought. The nave is wide, aisleless, and roofed with timber lattice trusses; the wide double transepts are seated as aisles. The south-east tower and spire is, alas, of Northamptonshire type with heavy buttresses at the corners, the west front, based on Dunblane Cathedral, was wished on Scott against his will, and the chancel terminates in the semi-circular apse so familiar in the mid-1850s. Indeed the church might be considered as a late development of the large cruciform class of 1848-58. The contemporary and adjacent parsonage is a stone building with very large windows and a touch of Butterfield about the chimney.

In 1864, Scott prepared designs for Christchurch Cathedral in New Zealand, in 13th-century style with details 'mainly English and part French', Speechley went out to superintend the building, and the foundation stone was laid in December. Next April the work stopped owing to lack of money, Speechley moving to Melbourne Cathedral, and then when work restarted B. W. Mountfort, a local man, who had been Scott's pupil in early days, took over and work proceeded intermittently until completion in 1904.

Two characteristic new brick churches with shingled spires may be compared: St Andrew, Hillingdon, with Christ Church, Otter-shaw. Hillingdon has the indescribably confused Victorian plan, not peculiar to Scott, for a church with a large number of seats and no galleries. It was built, mostly in stock brick, by Fassnidge, whose son at one time worked for Scott. Ottershaw had nave and apsidal chancel and was built in 1863-4 of fierce red and blue bricks, with French details; the western tower and spire was built (or rebuilt) by John Oldrid Scott in 1885. Perhaps the job was handled throughout by an assistant. The parsonage is also from Scott's office.

There were also private chapels. Peter Hoare the banker, as High Church as his partner and brother Henry was Low Church, — indeed sometimes they were not on speaking terms — inherited the Luscombe estate at Dawlish in Devon in 1849 and Kelsey Park, Beckenham, Kent, in 1851. In 1862 Scott added a chapel connected by a passage to the Nash house of 1800 at Luscombe. It did not match the house: externally a little like a small plain Early English Exeter College, with apse and high pitched roof, richly coloured polychrome stonework, and even cedarwood seats inside. A similar building in ragstone and brick was added to the Gothic Kelsey in 1869, also with an ornate interior. This was demolished in 1921 but some bits were built into the gardens of houses erected on the site.

61 Hamburg Town Hall, prizewinning competition entry, 1855. Not built.
Compare the Cloth Hall at Ypres
The Builder, xiv. 63

62 Halifax, Akroydon, 1851 on. Houses, no doubt largely by W.H.Crossland

63 Harrow, Vaughan Library, 1861-3. A small secular building displaying poly-chrome and plate tracery

64 Kelham Hall. View in 1944
National Monuments Record

65 Kelham Hall, interior of main hall, 1944
National Monuments Record

66 Kelham Hall, lodge and gate. The lodge is in the English tradition of 'cottage ornèe': the gateway has a curious effect, as of a drawing realised full size
National Monuments Record

67 Walton Hall, 1858-62. A recent view
Walton Hall Hotel

68 Westminster, Government Offices, 1862 on. Whitehall elevation
National Monuments Record

69 Leafield, 1858-60. Interior. A late example of the east end with tripled lancets and a circular window over

70 Oxford, Exeter College Chapel, 1857-9. Perhaps the summit of French mediaeval influence in the 1850s
Thomas Photos

71 Oxford, Exeter College Chapel. Polychrome and French details: possibly
Scott's finest church interior
Thomas Photos

72 Albourne, restored 1859. The archetypal village church, yet much rebuilt by Scott
Olive I. Cole

73 Englefield. Chancel restored by Scott, 1859. Possibly other work. A strangely unsatisfactory church

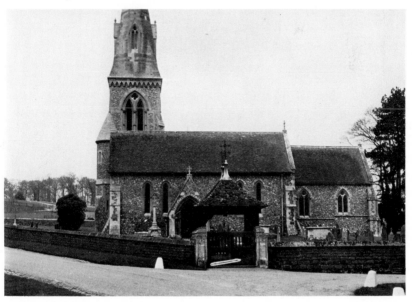

74 St Alban, Wood Street, London. Apse added 1855-6 to a Gothic Church by Wren: Scott's are also the seats. Demolished
National Monuments Record

75 Salisbury Cathedral. The choir as refitted by Wyatt, 1787-93. Looking west
Gerald Cobb

76 Salisbury Cathedral. The choir as refitted by Scott after 1866, looking west
National Monuments Record

77 Chester Cathedral. This view taken before 1868 shows how the stonework was wasted and the details defaced, despite the choir's restoration in 1844-6 and other work
National Monuments Record

78 Chester Cathedral, from the south east, after the restoration of 1868-77 showing refaced walls, new details, and parts conjecturally restored
National Monuments Record

79 Chester Cathedral, the west front and King's School shortly after Scott's elevation to the latter was completed in 1874
National Monuments Record

80 Chichester Cathedral. The interior of the crossing after the collapse of the tower and spire in 1861
Society of Antiquaries

81 Chichester Cathedral with the tower and spire rebuilt by Scott
National Monuments Record

82 Ripon Cathedral. Scott's choir seats of 1862-69

83 Pershore Abbey, restored 1861-4. The transept was rebuilt by Scott

84 Brecon Priory. Scott's vaulted roof completes the Early English design. The obtrusive reredos is by W. D. Caroe, 1927
Royal Commission on Historic Monuments in Wales

85 St Davids Cathedral, the west end as repaired by John Nash in 1789
Royal Commission on Historic Monuments in Wales

86 St Davids Cathedral. Scott's west end
Royal Commission on Historic Monuments in Wales

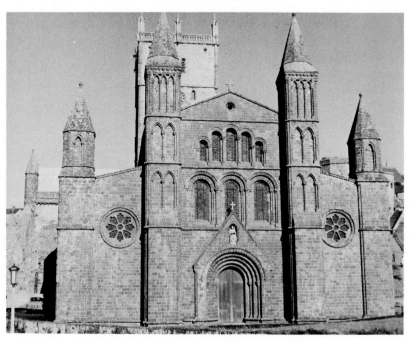

The new buildings of Wellington College in Berkshire, a new public school of the most extreme church — and — army type, were constructed to the designs of the younger John Shaw in 1859-60, in a Renaissance style strangely foreshadowing the 'Queen Anne' style made popular by his namesake Norman Shaw fifteen or twenty years later. But the Headmaster, E. W. Benson, later Archbishop of Canterbury, felt strongly that the Chapel should be Gothic, and by Scott. When Benson put his proposals before the Governors in 1860, they agreed — in spite of the Prince Consort's expressed wish to have 'Shaw to make the Chapel a precise copy of Eton, in brick, a third the size'.[43] Scott designed a high building in one space 26 x 67 ft with an eastern apse and a tall flèche to the east, in red brick and white stone to accord with Shaw's materials. The chapel is said to have been inspired by the Sainte Chapelle in Paris, but although the form is not dissimilar, the treatment is uncompromisingly the sort of Early Decorated which Scott had been using in his recent churches, such as Rugby: the carving inside is French in character, executed by Brindley, and Scott regarded it as of a very high order.

The Prince Consort was prevailed upon to lay a foundation stone in July 1861, and two years later the chapel was consecrated by Bishop Wilberforce.[44]

In 1862 Scott was again asked to enter a limited competition for a work of national interest, the memorial to the Prince Consort, who had died on 14 December 1861. A meeting to organise subscriptions for this was held at Mansion House on 14 January 1862. The sarcophagus at Windsor was composed of the largest obtainable block of granite, and the Queen was thought to favour erecting a monolithic granite obelisk 150ft high near the site of the Great Exhibition of 1851. A committee — Lord Derby, Lord Clarendon, Sir Charles Eastlake, PRA, and William Cubitt, the builder, Lord Mayor of London — was appointed to help select a design, but, the quarries of Scotland having been unsuccessfully scoured for a large enough block of granite, this committee, like the Foreign Office commission of 1856, found professional help necessary. Accordingly they asked Tite, Smirke, Scott, Pennethorne, Donaldson, P. C. Hardwick and Digby Wyatt to report. Nor surprisingly, after the Foreign Office they found it difficult to agree. The committee subsequently requested six architects — the last five plus E. M. Barry — to provide designs for a monument and for a Memorial Hall, to be built immediately to the south of Kensington Road.

The Queen wished a statue of Albert to form part of the composition, whilst General Charles Grey, the Queen's Secretary, favoured the introduction of 'various fine groups of statuary'. The submitted designs for the memorial varied a good deal but fell into two categories, statues within buildings and colossal statues alone. The feeling that the structure was unique led to some odd essays in style. Scott sent in one design for the monument and four for the hall — one, a domed 'Hall of Science' based on Sancta Sophia, with sculpture, painting, and mosaic. 'I may safely say, without being charged with self-praise, that if my design were carried out, it would, after making due allowance for dimension, material, etc. be scarcely excelled in beauty of form by any single and unbroken interior in existence.'[45]

His idea in designing the monument was to erect a ciborium to protect the Prince's statue, on the principles of those ancient shrines which he conceived as being models of imaginary buildings, jeweller's architecture; he proposed to construct one of these imaginary buildings to full size with rich enamelling and inlays of materials, which in part accounts for the extraordinary form of the structure. It seems likely that he had in mind the shrine by Orcagna in Or San Michele, Florence.[46] However, accidentally or intentionally, his design resembled very closely the similar memorial in Manchester, designed by Thomas Worthington, and illustrated in *The Builder* in November 1862.[47] It is difficult to decide which came first, for Scott prepared his design before actually being asked to do so, probably in mid-1862, having previously got up a sketch showing how an obelisk might be treated, with incised subjects on the face rather like Trajan's column and four granite lions couchant like Nelson's monument, all on a plinth.

On 28 March 1863 *The Times* revealed to a, no doubt, startled public that the monument was to consist of a monster Eleanor Cross, by Scott, nearly 300 ft in height. On 22 April, Scott was informed that the Queen, with the committee's assistance and, probably, the advice of her eldest daughter, the Crown Princess of Prussia, had indeed selected his proposal, although at the same time he was reminded of a number of criticisms and given a very strong suggestion to amend the design.

Scott by now had a reputation for expense. He admitted that his proposal might be so costly — at least £70,000 — that there would be no funds for the Hall, but in that case he felt the latter might be erected from other sources. His drawings, very ably got up and presented, were accompanied by a statement, printed in full in *The Builder*, justifying the design. 'I am so convinced that my design is just what *ought* to be erected, and that it is what the public would be satisfied with as *really* a memorial to the Prince Consort, that I would do *anything* and *everything* in my power to remove difficulties.'[48]

Indeed, the Commission considered that the cost would be twice what had been subscribed. Parliament was appealed to, and the sum of £50,000 was voted, to bring the money available to £110,000, almost by acclamation, on the motion of no other than Scott's adversary of two years before, Palmerston.

However, he did not like any of the submitted designs, but favoured an open Grecian temple containing a statue of the Prince.

There were, then, no funds for the Hall. On 18 February 1864, Henry Cole wrote to Scott to say that he had matured plans for an Albert Memorial Hall to be built by a joint stock company which he would like to ask Scott to forward on the chance of its being taken up. 'The hearing must be as perfect as science can make it.'[49]

Scott produced some elevations in 1864, but seems to have taken little further interest. In July 1866 he withdrew from the matter (perhaps he distrusted Cole after the Architectural Museum episode) but in the upshot the Albert Hall now existing was erected as a private speculation during 1867-71, designed by Captain Fowke and General Scott of the Royal Engineers. Alas, the hearing was by no means perfect until the measures taken in recent years.

John Kelk, a friend of Cole, a public works contractor who, at the age of forty-five, had already made his fortune, offered to do the building work for the memorial at cost. The Trustees and the Executive Committee accepted. Scott, resenting Cole's intrigues, was suspicious, but Kelk's work was excellent and relations between architect and builder became very good. Eminent sculptors were entrusted with the groups, statues and portrait figures. The Queen chose the Franco-Italian, Baron Carlo Marochetti[50], amid doubts not all of which were prompted by xenophobia, and he caused alarm by asking a fee of £15,000, later reduced to £10,000.

For the podium reliefs, Scott chose H. H. Armstead and John Birnie Philip, and for the virtues in the flèche, James Redfern, replaced on his death in 1864 by Philip. For the eight groups of marble statuary, the Queen named John Bell, William Theed, John

Henry Foley, RA, Patrick MacDowell, William Calder Marshall, RA, Henry Weekes, RA, Thomas Thorneycroft and John Lawlor. William Brindley was the architectural stonecarver: James Skidmore the ornamental metalworker; and Clayton and Bell did the spandrel mosaics. So many of these had worked at Scott's churches. Scott's well-tried man, Richard Coad, was appointed clerk of the works and Scott's assistants, Clayton and G. G. Scott Junior worked on the detailed designs in the office. Scott's friend Shields advised on the structural ironwork.[51]

Work started in May 1864 and proceeded slowly. Brindley and Armstead made a large scale model (now in the Victoria and Albert Museum) under Scott's direction. Scott himself seems to have gone to Ireland in 1865 in search of equipment to transport granite from quarries near Castlewellan in County Down, through the silted-up harbour at Newcastle, with predictable lack of success, and after two and a half years of struggle some of the intended Irish stone was replaced by material from Cornwall and Kirkcudbrightshire.

By early 1866 all the artists were hard at work, and Austin Layard, statesman and Assyrian scholar, who had succeeded on Eastlake's death in the special task of watching over the sculptures, regularly visited the various studios to report progress, meanwhile doing things like arranging for Marochetti to be supplied with twenty-two tons of gunmetal from old cannon for the central statue of the Prince.

Clayton made difficulties regarding delivery dates for the mosaic cartoons, but in the end Scott bound him to a contract. In 1867, Marochetti having prepared a full size model of his statue, arrangements were made to set it up in position on the site for the Queen and others to view it.

The spectators were not happy at what they saw. Neither was Scott. He had a very clear mental picture of his design, and so he wrote urgently, privately, and at length to Layard, emphasising the great size and lack of refinement of the figure and the disproportions of its lower parts — 'some very decided change is necessary'.[52] In May 1867 Layard, Marochetti and Scott met. Scott was upset to hear that Marochetti now wished the statue to be equestrian; but he got his way, at any rate on paper — the Baron agreed to reduce the size of the statue by about a tenth and to refine the draperies.

The possibility of an equestrian statue continued to harass Scott through the summer, even though the Queen had pronounced that the idea was not to be entertained. Early in August Scott and Marochetti met at the Royal Academy, and the latter invited the former to come with him afterwards to view the new figure. The meeting did not got well. The new figure was identical with the old but a tenth smaller, and when Scott attempted to discuss it he found Marochetti, as he wrote almost tearfully to Layard next morning, 'ready with the most positive asseverations of the erroneousness of what one suggests before one can get the words out of one's mouth — and seems to hold that the exaggeration of every fault which has been pointed out would do more good than its abatement!'[53] He left the matter to Layard's better management, which was, as it happened, not put to the test, because at the turn of the year the Baron most unexpectedly died, whereupon Scott wrote to Layard again, a mixture of surprise and relief, and strongly recommended Foley, though behindhand with his group, as the only man suited to the work. Scott's advice was taken, whilst John Bell bombarded Layard with suggestions that the central figure should be kneeling, in the fancy dress of a Crusader, symbolising a Christian Knight, with the graven caption 'Albert the Good'. Layard got rid of him by turning him on to Scott: there is no record of how Scott managed.

By 1869 the structure was substantially complete. Kelk, responsible for getting the whole affair finished, felt the time had come for a little yardarm-clearing. He accordingly wrote to Scott to complain that Armstead's and Philip's sculptures were already six months overdue and still showed no signs of completion. Indeed, on speaking to Armstead, he understood him to need three years more, and to say that contracts were made to be broken. Scott then had to explain Kelk to Armstead, and Armstead (who maintained that Kelk didn't see a joke) to Kelk, both at some length. Armstead concluded that it would be well if he could be left quietly at his work, and Layard was sent copies of all the correspondence.

Only in 1872 was everything complete bar the figure of the Prince, which had now been delayed by Foley's illness, contracted whilst correcting his model *in situ*. By that time Layard had long since been ambassador in Madrid, succeeded on the Committee by his friend the archaeologist, Newton, but he wrote to Scott in July 1872 to congratulate him warmly.[54] He was convinced that such a monument could not have been erected out of England. At a cost of roughly £150,000 this very complicated operation had been brought to a finish.

The structure has a profusion of elements: groups illustrating Agriculture, Manufacturers, Commerce and Engineering, 169 sculptured portrait figures of artists, musicians and literary men all round the podium, including Scott himself (inserted at the Queen's behest), eight statues of virtues in the spire, eight statues representing the greater sciences at the angles of the structure, four allegorical mosaic pictures of the fine arts in the tympana, four groups of sculpture, replete with the muscular, inadequately clothed women so dear to Victorian allegory, representing the four continents, at the corners of the plinth, the insignia of British orders of knighthood, a concrete foundation 60 ft square and 17 ft deep, 868 brick arches in the vaulting, 12,000 semi-precious stones as inlays, fifteen or more different sorts of building stone. The upper part has the typical vice of lavish ornament of an even weight covering the whole structure and in addition it appears top-heavy. It does not go well with the more restrained and sculptural plinth and steps.

The materials, and hence the textural and chromatic effect of the monument, had undergone some change, to the accompaniment of earnest discussion, some due to difficulties in the supply of stone and some to doubts as to the durability of glass mosaic and other material. Scott throughout stuck to his concept of the jewellers' shrine, and the peculiar qualities and proportions of the structure stem from this. There is nothing else quite like it, even in Manchester; each year that passes makes it more valuable as a memento of Victorian tastes and achievements. Glimpsed at the termination of one of the rides of the parks, or viewed from the top deck of an omnibus in Kensington Gore, it is a visual experience indeed.[55]

Scott was pleased with the result, but he took the criticism which was levelled at the structure as a personal affront and was at pains to correct six separate criticisms in *Recollections*. The Queen, however, was well satisfied even if all her subjects were not, with the sequel that Scott accepted, in 1872, a knighthood. Kelk, who had managed the building works with great efficiency and to everyone's satisfaction, is reputed not to have accepted the proffered knighthood: sure enough, two years later he attained a Baronetcy.

During 1863 plans were prepared for Leeds Infirmary. This building forms a refreshing contrast to much of Scott's work at this time: no pains were spared to have as convenient and up-to-date a hospital as possible, and the architect and Dr Chadwick, the chief physician, were requested to make a careful inspection of continental hospitals. Accordingly, Scott, accompanied by his wife, visited Amiens, Paris, Rheims, Brussels and Antwerp. When the plans had been drawn up, Florence Nightingale was consulted.

The site was long and narrow, rising some 20ft from the main front. This allowed the extensive out-patients department and the kitchens to be at lower ground floor level; at the centre of the site was an open court surrounded by corridors giving access to five ward blocks of two storeys each, and of the 'pavilion' type, nearly 150 ft long and with windows on both sides. Sanitary blocks were arranged askew at the outer corners of the wards. The building was Gothic, in pressed brick with steeply pitched slate roofs. The carefully composed main elevation had stone dressings; the sanitary blocks became angle turrets and quite belied their function. This was a further demonstration of what could be done with a Gothic secular building of a specialised type: indeed, *The Ecclesiologist*, more concerned with the souls than the bodies of the sick people of Leeds, expressed the hope that the new infirmary 'in proper Pointed style... will inaugurate... a new reign of art in Leeds.'[56] The

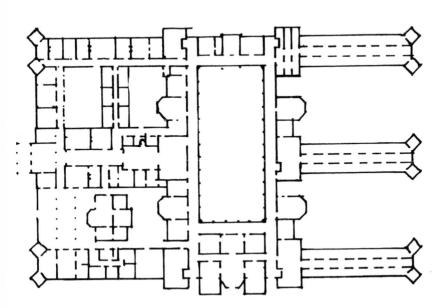

Leeds Infirmary, 1864-7. 'Plan of one pair'
Building News, iv, 461

foundation stone was laid in March 1864 and the work completed by mid-1867. Instructive comparison may be drawn with the North Staffordshire Infirmary, by Nichols and Lynam, illustrated in *The Builder* in 1866.[57]

At the same time, in Leeds, Scott was asked to prepare a design for Beckett's Bank, another Grimthorpe family interest. It was built between 1863 and 1867 of stone and hard red brick, especially made to non-standard dimensions and laid in the black north-country mortar, as much to resist the polluted atmosphere as for a brutal effect. Apart from designing the elevations, Scott took little interest; Perkin, a local man, was the resident architect and designed most of the interior.

The small and attractive public library in Lewes, Sussex, was built in 1862 in memory of Henry Fitzroy, MP. Scott put much careful thought into the plan; a two-storey block surmounted by a flèche fronted a large square toplit library space, all in red brick with detail in 'modified Italian Gothic'.[58]

In September of the same year the foundation stone of Scott's new Preston Town Hall was laid. Scott's building, of two and three storeys with a corner clock tower and spire with clusters of unbelievably elongated columns at its corners, an open arcade as part of the ground floor, and plate-traceried windows, is clearly related to his other secular Gothic buildings of the period. The *porte-cochère* and the tower are similar to those of the later St Pancras, but Scott has varied the massing and detail in all these buildings in an ingenious manner. It formed an unforgettable piece of urban townscape, facing the classic Harris library across a square, but, alas, it was burned about 1947, repaired, and demolished in 1963.

Scott exhibited in the 1862 Royal Academy a scheme for a covered market at Preston, with iron columns and semi-circular arches, perhaps to show what the 1862 exhibition building might have been like, but his design was not built.[59] Among his unusual designs of the period were one for the toll bridge supplanting the Clifton Hampden ferry, and another, unexecuted, for a livery hall for the Grocers' company.[60]

It is notable how widespread Scott's practice had now become. He had always travelled far to gain work, and in the years 1860-5 he was certainly at work in thirty-seven out of forty-two English counties (apart from Scotland, Wales and abroad), and restoring churches in thirty-four of them. Eventually he was to work in every county of

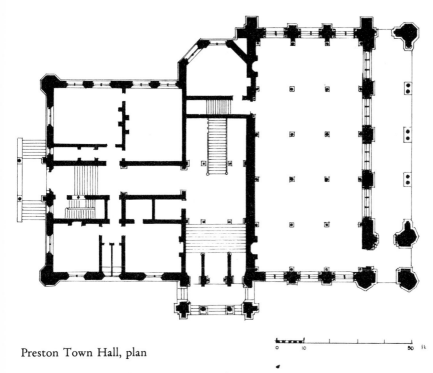

Preston Town Hall, plan

England and Wales except Cardigan. Communications were a
continual problem, and he spent an inordinate amount of time in
railway trains. He was not exceptional in his travels: for instance,
Street worked in every English county but two in a shorter period of
practice, and Butterfield in at least thirty-eight.

By 1863 Scott's ubiquity had become sufficiently noticed (indeed
The Builder sometimes credited work to him as it were naturally and
had to correct itself later) for a correspondent, sending a list of 'rare
works on architectural subjects' to *The Builder* to include — in a
series comprehending Burn on fireproof construction, Ferrey on
bridges, Hall on pulleys, Mair's stables, Shout on sound in rooms,
Tarring on fences, Tite on the British costume, and much more in
the same vein — Scott on Everything.[61]

7
Public Figure,
1864-72

During the first two months of 1864 Scott wrote the first part of
Personal and Professional Recollections, much of it in trains. He was
fifty-two, and, unsurprisingly, for the average life in the learned
professions was calculated as thirty-eight,[1] in indifferent health.
The ability to rely more and more upon new work seeking him on
account of his reputation, upon the office to run itself, and upon
John Oldrid, now twenty-three, allowed him to lift his nose a little
off the grindstone. He remarked with surprise that his life ran so
smooth a course that he didn't know what to say about it,[2] but,
insecure, he continually worried about his income though by now
he was very prosperous. The frenzied activity described by Jackson
left little time for family life, except perhaps on Sundays, for he was
a regular churchgoer. He was much away from home: apart from
continual railway journeys in England, he went abroad at least
seventeen times in twenty years, always for work or study, sometimes for considerable periods, and only once accompanied by
Caroline.

His wife led a largely independent life, making her own friends or
also away from home, often with the young children. She found
comfort in music, religion, and charitable works. Perhaps, although
possibly capable and managing, she feared her husband, who, tired
and tense after being humble, conciliatory and reasonable in his
working relationships, could too often be peevish or impatient with
her. But each year the family went to Wales, the Lakes, or the
seaside, and most often in the late 1850s to the Isle of Wight. He
joined them when he could, taking work with him, and whilst the
boys played he would work out designs to a large scale on the sand,
drawing them on paper in the evening.

Then there were the family deaths. Scott had lost his parents-in-

law in 1848 and 1857, his uncle and aunt King in 1856, and his
mother, eccentric and unbalanced and with whom he latterly had
infrequent contact, in 1854, but these were little noticed amid the
pressure of work. In January 1864 his sister Mary Jane, who had
been ill for a long time, died at Wappenham, aged 42, and he much
reproached himself for neglecting her.

Next, there was another removal. Hampstead could be cold in
the winter, and no doubt the great house tested the imperfect
heating appliances of the time: so Caroline with the two youngest
boys habitually wintered at St Leonards. During the summer of
1864 Scott, assisted by his third son, Albert, just twenty and on his
first long vacation from Exeter College, Oxford, looked for somewhere large and suitable to rent. Eventually, in September, the
family moved into the Manor House at Ham near Richmond, an
early 18th-century brick house near the Thames.

On Saturday 21 January 1865 the brothers Albert and Alwyne
rowed on the river and in the afternoon visited London. At Ham it
was clear: in London they found difficulty, groping about in dense
fog. Next day Albert felt stiff, on Monday worse, and he rowed to
get rid of it. By Wednesday evening the doctor conceded it to be
rheumatic fever. On Thursday Scott had to attend the first meeting
of the restoration committee at Salisbury. By Sunday Albert was
delirious. His father wrote an agonised and detailed description of
his illness: he died on the afternoon of the 30th, and was buried in
the churchyard at Petersham.

On 8 February, Scott's sister Euphemia, long incurably ill, also
died, followed in May by his cousin John, and in June by his younger
brother Dr Samuel King Scott, the husband of Bodley's sister.

The conjunction of diary writing and extravagant emotion with
overtones of retribution at these deaths, in a man of fifty-three,
might suggest an emotional sexual attachment. The only hint
lies in warm business letters to Mrs Dent of Sudeley Castle in
Gloucestershire, where abortive designs for rebuilding the west
range were made in 1854 and the ruined chapel restored in correct
Perpendicular in 1859-61. But in 1863 Drayton Wyatt took over the
work.

John Oldrid Scott continued to live at Ham, but his parents, after
a protracted visit to Brighton and Worthing, in 1869 rented for
three years a fine Georgian country house, 'Rooks-nest',[3] near
Godstone, nineteen miles south of London. Scott himself spent

long periods at Ham during these years, for Ham was handier for London.

In October 1870, when at Chester inspecting the cathedral works, Scott himself suffered a sudden and serious heart attack. They carried him with difficulty to the Deanery and put him to bed. He lay seriousy ill for five weeks before he could be moved, and he was not active again until the following spring: perhaps, indeed, he was never again in robust health. He became, and remained, thin. As he wrote his letters, he would start with the pain of angina, and then write on in spite of it.[4] Throughout 1871 he was conspicuously absent from public functions, and there was a perceptible drop in new commissions.

During the eight years 1865-72 the office started some eighty parish church restorations alone, mostly in English villages. These were the classic years of church restoration: to list them is a tour of England.*

Most were extensive and lengthy: it was quite usual to close the church for about a year. Many involved complete internal refitting, so that the interior after appeared very different from before. Galleries and pews, usually post-mediaeval, were removed and new open seats substituted, occasionally based on existing material, and furnishings such as screens remade on the evidence of fragments. Often there was need for more accommodation to replace that lost by removing galleries, and new aisles were built in at least thirteen instances, sometimes, as at Sarratt, with a good deal of ingenuity. The damp floors were attended to, and perhaps repaved with encaustic tiles. Sometimes a chancel was renewed, as at Ashley, where much money was expended on structural polychrome decoration and marble fittings: there, too, the upper part of the west

* Adderbury, Alford, Arksey, Asfordby, Ashley, Atherstone, Barnstaple, Berkeley, Bilton in Ainsty, Bishopsbourne, Boxgrove, Buckingham, Bushey, Bwlch y Cibau, Chesham, Chillenden, Cirencester, Cradley, Crondall, Croxton Kerrial, Croydon, Danbury, Dundee, Earsby, East Claydon, East Preston, Enville, Findon, Fleet Marston, Frankton, Fremington, Frinsted, Godstone, Grantham, Hatch Beauchamp, Holdenby, Hornsea, Houghton Conquest, Ickenham, Itchingfield, Kings Lynn, Kings Sutton, Kirby Hill, Latimer, Leeds, Leicester, Llywell, Lutterworth, **Marston Moretaine, Middle Claydon, Middleton Tyas, Milton Abbas,** Newcastle upon Tyne, North Aston, Norton, Okeford Fitzpaine, Owston, Peterstow, Pitminster, Rhuddlan, Ruislip, St Albans, Salisbury, Sarratt, Sawbridgeworth, Shilton, Spalding, Staveley, Stretton, Stroud, Tavistock, Totnes, Tydd St Giles, Upton, Uxbridge, Welton, Wilburton, Winterton, Wirksworth.

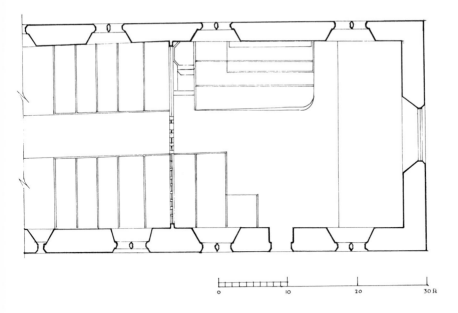

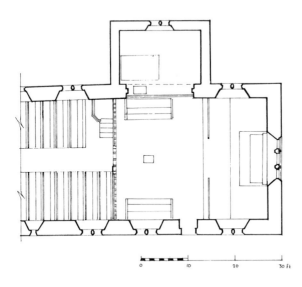

Cradley, restored 1867-8. East end, before and after restoration. The furnishings
have been made ritually acceptable

tower was strengthened by bolting through the walls into a heavy internal timber cage.

One of the most noticeable differences is to be found in roofs. Old plaster ceilings, usually 18th century, were invariably removed, and the roof structures thus exposed were usually more or less rotten. An earlier roof had often been replaced by one of Perpendicular period, low pitched and lead covered. Such roofs leak, so it was often a practical matter to substitute a pitched roof of earlier character: though at Wirksworth, Derbyshire, a rather muddled cruciform church, Scott's new clerestory and pitched roof to the nave (he left the Perpendicular west end) had its roof removed about 1949 and one of low pitch reinstated, to the benefit of the church's appearance. The almost uniform choice of red brown tiles, often from Broseley in Shropshire, in this period may be faulted, but in some cases, as at Cradley, Herefordshire, they replaced or supplemented what was already there.

The roof structure of the smaller churches would almost invariably be of the trussed rafter type: Scott must have built some hundreds of these, differing little. It has by now become another Scott hallmark. But he, and perhaps other restorers, had essentially a mason's approach to conservation. He might go to some pains to repair a Decorated window, but less often did he repair or copy a mediaeval roof structure, though for instance, at Danbury, Essex, in 1867, old roofs were 'discovered' and re-used; many mediaeval roofs had irretrievably decayed by Scott's time.

For internal fittings the same suppliers or craftsmen occur time after time. Godwin's encaustic tiles from Lugwardine, near Hereford, or Minton's from the Potteries; Farmer and Brindley of Westminster Bridge Road for carving; Skidmore for metalwork; Clayton and Bell, and Morris, are especially noticeable.

Cost varied. At Grantham, which was a very large church, £21,428 was spent over four years: at Cirencester, also large, about £12,000. The new chancel and arcades and other work at Lutterworth cost £7700. The very considerable alterations at Buckingham cost only some £4500: a modest work like Bilton in Ainsty, £1200. Perhaps, in terms of labour costs, a shilling in 1875 represents a pound in 1975, a twenty-fold increase. On this basis Grantham cost nearly half a million of present-day money: the vast majority of these churches cost over £1000 then, representing over £20,000 now. It would in many cases have been cheaper to abandon the old church and build a new one: in few was this done. At least if the major part of the church was new it was on the old site and perhaps resembled what had been there, or what Scott, always taking great care, could show might have been there at some previous time.

A few involved very little work. At St Paul, Dundee, the tower was secured and repaired, but it cost £5000. At Stroud, Gloucestershire, the reredos, carved by Geflowski, is Scott's design: at Sawbridgeworth, Essex, one window is by Scott. At North Aston, Oxfordshire, curiously huddled against the end of the Hall, the small north aisle was lengthened to form an organ chamber and one of his two new windows incorporated old bits. At Atherstone, Warwickshire, the chancel, the only mediaeval part of the church, had been alienated, and, being offered for sale by public tender (!) was bought back by the parishioners in 1869 for £260 and repaired and refitted by Scott for £750.

A careful study of the details of these eighty churches shows how the traditional picture of ruthless replacement of old features by those of an earlier period has to be greatly modified: in very many cases Scott has to a greater or less extent observed the principles he laid down in 1862. His report of 29 January 1864 on Barnstaple, Devon, shows how he would propose to deal with such churches:

Gentlemen,

Having made a careful survey of your Church, first personally, and afterwards by my practical Assistant, I beg to report the result.

The Church appears to have been originally erected early in the Fourteenth Century, and to have been a simple cross in plan — consisting of nave, chancel, north transept, and a tower occupying the position of the south transept. During (probably) the Fifteenth Century this simple plan was extended by the addition of aisles, both to the nave and chancel. Subsequently to this the Church, no doubt, went through the usual course of injurious and ill-judged repairs which was the common lot of churches; but it was reserved to the present century to inflict upon it the final indignity of removing all its pillars and arcades, and substituting columns, something in the Egyptian style, without arches. The Church is, of course, disfigured with pews and galleries in the usual manner, and some parts, especially the wall of the south aisle of the nave, are in a defective state; though, as a whole, I see no difficulty in preserving the structure, and I earnestly recommend this course, even though it were nearly as expensive as building a modern church (which it is not), for the loss of the ancient Church of an old historical town like Barnstaple would be a public misfortune.

The course I suggest is to replace the lost pillars and arches according to the best evidence which we can obtain, and thoroughly to repair and restore the ancient structure, subject to a few alterations suggested by necessity.

It is, of course, a great object to get rid of the galleries from the ancient parts of the structure; but to do this additional room must be found somewhere. I propose to effect this as follows; firstly, by slightly widening the south aisle, the wall of which requires to be rebuilt: and, secondly, by adding an aisle in the irregular space on the north side, in which new aisle I would erect a gallery, a sacrifice of feeling for the purpose of divesting the old aisles of these disfigurements. I would, however, construct this new aisle expressly for this arrangement, so as to reduce the objection to a *minimum*.

The whole Church must be fitted up in a substantial and suitable manner, and, I hope, in oak.

I was somewhat surprised to find that a feeling existed in favour of destroying the present steeple. My own impressions are strongly in its favour. Though making no great pretensions to elegance, it is a most interesting and remarkable structure, and gives much character and quaint antiquity to the aspect of the Church; I therefore recommend its retention and careful reparation.

He estimated for new work, £1700: for roofs, £550; for repairs £1770 and for refitting, £2200; total £6220.

St John, Leeds is a special case. In 1865 it was intended to demolish the church, a Perpendicular style building of 1632 with splendid and unique woodwork. Norman Shaw, visiting Leeds, heard of this, complained, and Scott was asked to report. He came down in favour of repair and restoration, 'retaining jealously every old feature and disturbing nothing unnecessarily. You will thus be handing down to many future generations a rare and beautiful specimen of the church art of the Reformed English Church erected at a period of which the specimens are more scarce than any other'.[5] The decision was made to repair and Shaw did the work: the church was however de-galleried. J. T. Micklethwaite complained that the choir arrangements had been altered, but Scott said that all was retained except the pew doors.

Godstone, a mile from Rooks-nest, on a hill a little distance from the town, perhaps received special care. The north aisle was of 1845: the chancel had recently been restored when in 1871 Scott demolished a south transept, added a south aisle with nicely differentiated late Decorated windows and a timber porch, degalleried and refitted the nave and north aisle, opened up the nave roof, restored two Norman doorways and the west window 'according to the remains found', and restored the tower, adding 16 ft to the little

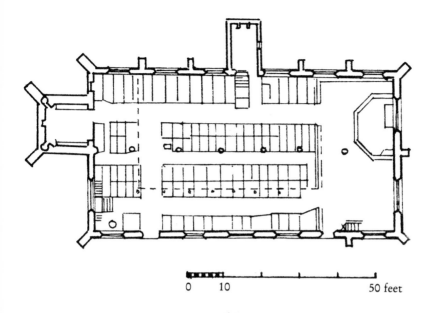

St John, Leeds. Plan prior to the alterations of 1868

Sarratt, restored 1866 Plan. Scott added or altered the hatched portions

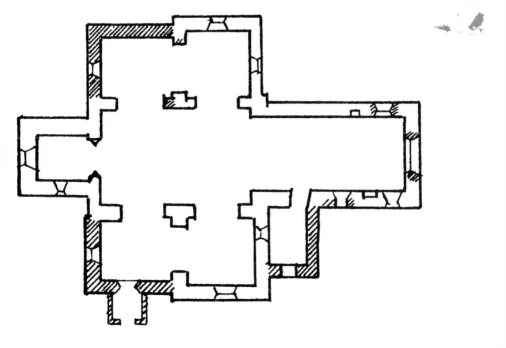

shingled spire. Stone from local quarries, which had provided material for Henry VII's chapel at Westminster Abbey, was used.

Sarratt in Hertfordshire, a very small cruciform church of flint and stone with a west tower, had to be enlarged as well as restored. In 1865 the galleries were removed and more accommodation provided by filling in the western corners of the cross and tacking on a vestry and porch. The new transept arches and arcades matched the chancel arch: the north transept fell in during the work. The timbers of the old roof were retained: each element had a pitched roof, the new was of similar trussed rafter construction to the old and the whole was retiled uniform. Probably all the windows were renewed except those of the upper tower: the two new west windows followed the character of that existing, itself stated to resemble one at Westminster Abbey. The Tudor tower top with its pitched roof remained. The new open seats were modelled on those existing: the pulpit was only moved. Wall painting was discovered but could not be conserved due to the nature of the walls. Thus there is now a decent little church with an individual character.

At Boxgrove Priory in Sussex a careful restoration of this splendid Early English fragment took place in 1864-5 under Scott in succession to William White. Scott rebuilt the west wall and the flying buttresses, underpinned the other walls, paved, drained, and reseated, provided pulpit and reredos, and did other work. White's reredos, says Chapple, was so ugly that Scott was asked to supply a new one, and the old was deposited on the rubbish dump. Scott left in place the wooden galleries or ceilings in the transepts, the very late transept windows, and the mid-16th century de la Warr chantry. All of these would, fifteen years earlier, almost inevitably have been ripped out.[6]

At St Wolfran, Grantham, one of the finest and largest English parish churches, an exceptionally expensive restoration was effected. In October 1864 a numerous and influential meeting heard Scott's report. The stonework needed careful repair and the interior required cleansing of whitewash. The south-east angle must be underpinned, the foundations examined and repaired, two porches and the top of the spire restored, the interior refitted. All roofs had been replaced and were decayed, requiring renewal and 'restoration to their proper pitch', in oak and lead. They were dealt with first, in 1865 — that in the south aisle may have been partly re-used, the rest is all new — and in 1869 the church was reopened, with its open chancel screen, new pulpit, lectern, and so on. Other fittings are from later hands. As at Newark, this was a successful work in making a major historical building safe and weathertight, and arranging fittings with what was regarded as propriety.

The mediaeval church in Scott's home parish of Buckingham had been allowed to get into such disrepair by the late 18th century that when the central tower swayed in the wind it caused certain cracks to open and shut so conveniently that boys are said to have cracked nuts in them. In the end it fell and destroyed the church. The replacement, on a different site and almost certainly by Hiorn of Warwick, dated from 1777-81, and was neither in appearance nor arrangement to Victorian taste, whilst it also had fallen into disrepair. After 1862 Scott, much to his satisfaction, began to reconstruct it in an early Decorated style perhaps more appropriate in its detail to Salisbury Cathedral than to a middling town church. It took over twenty years, probably because money had to be raised locally. By then the nave and its aisles had been reconstructed and re-roofed and the windows and external features replaced and (the first work) a new chancel added. The timber ceiling, in the style of a vault, together with the peculiar arrangement of one large aisle window surmounting two small ones, there being no clerestory, makes a pleasant though eccentric interior: the outside with its heavy buttresses and narrow window bays is quite successful. No doubt these un-Gothic proportions and eccentricities are accounted for by the work being done within the dimensions and framework of the Classical building.[7]

Norton (1868), Scott's only work in Radnorshire, is an example where local critics speak of 'ruthless rebuilding' or 'drastic restoration'. Noting the foul weathering propensities of some of the local stone and the wet climate, it is hardly surprising. One transept is new, but in all respects similar to the other: most of the stonework at the east end looks new but may indeed only have been 'dressed down and repointed'. All the tracery except that in two windows has been renewed. The buttresses have been rebuilt or repaired. The timber belfry and rood screen were taken to bits and reassembled, retaining any serviceable old work but renewing much. The roof was altered — certainly retiled, no doubt deceiled. Internally, the 1834 gallery was removed, and pulpit, lectern, seats, and tile floors are all new, thus giving the interior a wholly Victorian appearance.

At St Michael, St Albans, we may once more study Scott and

Grimthorpe together. In March 1865 Scott reported and by May 1866 it was restored, with emphasis on the connection with Lord Chancellor Bacon. The ceilings were removed, the chancel reroofed, the east wall rebuilt, a porch added, and some walls underpinned and repaired. The interior was gutted. It is said to have had a west gallery with good 17th-century woodwork supported on Corinthian columns from the chapel at Gorhambury: this went, and the local antiquary, Peter Cunningham, wished that Scott's 'reverence for antiquity and "associations" was more reverential than it is, and his hand more sparing . . .'.[8] Scott, when taken to task in 1877, was at pains to point out that the 'Elizabethan roof' of the chancel was, according to the clerk of works, quite rotten and propped up by a ceiling of 1808 formed under it. The pews Scott demonstrated to have been of the 19th century; the 'Elizabethan porch' to have an entrance of re-used Portland stone, not known in the London neighbourhood before 1620. He says nothing about the west gallery. Grimthorpe did worse. After 1890 he pulled down the tower and built a new one at the north-west corner, extended the nave westward over the site of the old tower, built a vestry on the site of the destroyed south aisle, and designed a clock. The building now looks very odd, and Scott is sometimes blamed for it all.

In 1841, when uncle King was curate at Latimer, it was to Blore, then rebuilding the mansion, rather than to Scott the architect of Flaunden, that the commission for a new church went. Blore's building, red brick with a shallow pentagonal chancel and short transepts in a sort of Perpendicular, was by the standards even of that time old-fashioned. By 1867 it was said that its 'architectural pretensions . . . were not of the highest order'.[9] That year Lord Chesham called in Scott, who perhaps lengthened the transepts on the same pattern as the original, and certainly added something at the west end, a north-east vestry, and a jolly round-ended apse at the east, adding an attractive interplay of spaces to a dull building.

Scott's major restoration feat during this period was undoubtedly Westminster Chapter House, which did not in fact come within his purview as Surveyor to the Abbey. Building by 1250, at the dissolution of the monastery in 1540 it passed to the Crown and was used as a depository for state papers. A wooden floor and galleries were inserted, and the six large windows blocked up; the old roof, iron framed but ruinous, was taken off in 1740. Scott, soon after 1849, got into the building, poked around, measured, and drew. He agitated for its restoration, exhibited a design at the Paris exhibition of 1855, and by 1865 the state papers, more for their benefit than the building's, for they lay around in much disorder exposed to damp and vermin, had been removed to Pennethorne's new Public Record Office in Chancery Lane. On 2 December 1864 the President of the Society of Antiquaries called a meeting, influentially attended, to hear Dean Stanley on its history and Scott on its architecture, and to such effect that by May the Civil Service estimates included a vote of £7000 for repair of the building. Scott recovered the window tracery from one of the seven which, against a wall and blind, had remained in its original condition, strengthened the central column, uncovered the wall painting, repaired the stonework, and re-made the roof, the drawings for which show the use of iron. It was completely finished by July 1871. Scott said, 'I know of no parts which are conjecturally restored but the following — the external parapet, the pinnacles, the gables of the buttresses, and the roof'.[10] One is grateful to him for this work.

Scott thought Bangor Cathedral once contained nothing worth seeing but three buttresses: it had been, predictably, burned by Owain Glyndwr about 1400, and rebuilt a century later. There was early 19th-century work by Lewis Wyatt and limited restoration, including a new choir roof, took place in 1857 under Henry Kennedy. Scott, perhaps at Dean Vincent's instance, reported in March 1866. He gave the Chapter a choice: thorough repair, refitting, and decoration or restoration of the eastern part in the style of the fragment of the south transept, including the buttresses, dating from before 1400. 'It is a question between redeeming the church of its mean character and infringing in some degree on its authentic architectural history'.[11] The restoration committee preferred the second alternative, so from 1868-73 the transepts were substantially rebuilt, the choir restored, and the former vestry rebuilt as an organ chamber. Considerable fragments of the pre-1400 building were found re-used in the walls, so Scott was able convincingly to reconstruct the windows and to recover large portions of other detail in the transepts. The choir was more conservatively treated but the buttresses and corbel table are his. The destroyed south choir aisle was not, as intended, rebuilt. Between April 1879 and May 1880 the nave was repaired, refitted, receiled, and refloored, and the vestry and chapter house rebuilt at the north-east by John Oldrid Scott to his father's design. A central tower and spire was built no higher than the new roofs when subsidence due to poor soil was observed.[12]

St Asaph, smallest of the old cathedrals, was, said Scott, a minor and uninteresting work, though it cost £12,000. He removed Lewis Wyatt's 1822 plaster ceiling under the clerestoried nave and aisles in 1865, and four years later restored and refitted the choir, which had been externally renewed, except for the east window, in 'costly stone but horrid architecture' earlier in the century. He prepared a design from old prints, and wanted to take down the modern work to search for details of the old before rebuilding. This the Dean and Chapter refused to allow because it would disturb the cathedral for too long. Details found in the walling showed the original form of the windows to have been different from Scott's design, and consequently the two western windows, triplets of lancets, are based on the evidences which were found, and the other four (pairs) are of Scott's original design, 'monuments of weak compliance, and beacons to warn others against such foolish conduct. There ought to be a brass plate set up recording our shame and our repentance'.[13] He also groined the crossing in oak and did some tile repaving. The stalls had been arranged in the choir in 1809-10 and copies placed in the crossing: he put the originals back in the crossing and, unwillingly, reseated the choir. The reredos, executed by Earp, was erected in 1871.

At Oxford, James Billings did some refitting in 1856 but H. G.

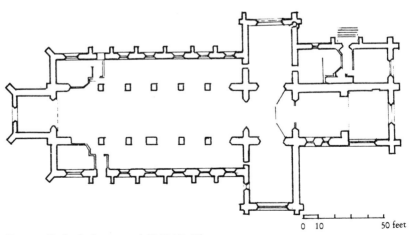

0   10   50 feet

Bangor Cathedral, restored 1865-73. Plan

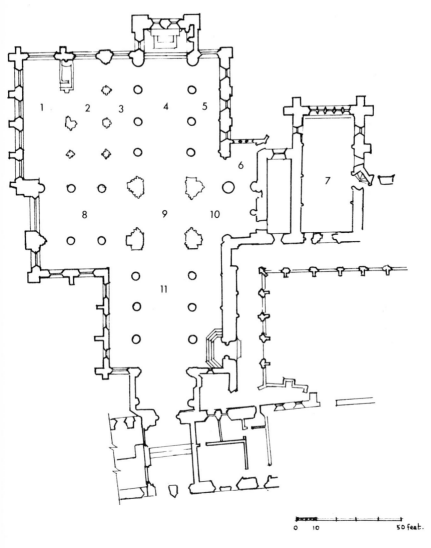

1. Latin Chapel
2. Lady Chapel
3. N. Aisle
4. Presbytery
5. S. Aisle
6. St. Lucy's Chapel
7. Chapter House
8. N. Transept
9. Crossing
10. S. Transept
11. Nave

Oxford Cathedral, restored 1870-6. Plan

Liddell, Dean of Christ Church called upon Scott in 1869. In 1870-2 Scott rebuilt the entrance and the first bay of the nave, did much repair, cleaning and refitting, and replaced the east end, where the window had been installed as recently as 1854, by one of a late 12th-century design in keeping with the rest of the presbytery, a bold act which has often been the subject of comment but which seems entirely successful. Other Perpendicular windows were repaired, but not altered. The strange Bishop's Throne, a monument to Samuel Wilberforce, is of 1876. The rebuilt bell-tower at the corner of the great quadrangle is to Bodley's design.[14]

At both New College and Merton College, Oxford, the halls had been worked upon by James Wyatt; Scott replaced the roof at New College in 1865 and much renewed Merton in 1872, reintroducing 14th-century details of a type removed by Wyatt. These were characteristic of a number of works at both Oxford and Cambridge.

Scott's restoration practice was already under fire from more than one direction. For some time he and the Ecclesiological Society had been nagging that Lincoln Cathedral was being 'skinned'. The architect involved was J. C. Buckler of Oxford, once in trouble at St Mary the Virgin there. More recently, in 1862, he had started work on restoring Headington, for which Scott had prepared plans in 1848, and it seems Scott later supplanted him. At Lincoln Scott had in 1863 designed an oak pulpit and canopy, finely complementing the rich, spiky choir stalls. Buckler was not going to be supplanted here if he could help it. In 1866 he turned on his critics, fiercely attacking Scott in terms which were to become familiar over the next twelve years.

Mr G. G. Scott is not the right sort of friend to ancient Churches; their walls groan under his prescriptions and his operations; death and destruction to antiquities follow his footsteps in many more instances than can be enumerated on the present occasion. He is not unaware of the fact, and while he is lecturing youth upon the sin of injuring a "bemossed" stone, rushing from place to place, writing up the value of fifteenth century scraps of architecture, and telling "The Times" of his zeal, his prowess and his power, he meditates havoc among the Churches in other quarters, and shall be proved by his sign manual.[15]

But Buckler was hypercritical. Scott in 1865 restored Winchester City Cross, of which the top had disappeared and the statues of the Bishops were missing or defaced. Buckler complained that William of Wykeham now held his pastoral staff in the wrong hand. At

Cirencester Scott was spending £12,000, and Buckler said he was doing it badly. But this is a church where Victorian restoration might not be suspected, except for reseating and even this is said to have been copied from a surviving mediaeval pew, and the great mid-16th-century nave remained 'unimproved'. At Heston, Middlesex, in the same year, it was proposed to rebuild the old church. Scott advised the retention of as much as possible, but it was destroyed except for the tower, and a new building by the little-known T. Bellamy took its place. Scott was annoyed and wrote to *The Times* in protest, but Buckler accused him of its destruction.

Meanwhile Bruce Allen, once connected with the Architectural Museum, cropped up again, hanging ideas on the peg of a talk on the 'Future of Architecture' by Burges, and revealing himself as an early Socialist. He was worried about two things: restoration and the lack of recognition of the actual artist. He was worried in particular about the restoration of the north cloister of Westminster Abbey, and roundly denounced Scott. 'Mr Scott fancies *Gothic* to consist in *ornament*, cusps, finials, spikes, and so on. Of the real nature and foundation of Gothic, Mr Scott has not the remotest idea.'[16] He even used the word 'capitalist' in a derogatory sense.

The Architectural Museum, of which Scott had remained Treasurer, prepared to leave South Kensington for a new building in Bowling Street near Deans Yard,[17] built in 1868 at a cost of nearly £3000, raised by voluntary contributions and Scott's efforts. It was opened the next September and the disputed material from South Kensington, together with 200 classic and mediaeval casts formerly exhibited at the RIBA, was arranged. Mr Wallis was installed as curator, and the prefix 'Royal' was granted on the Queen's becoming patron. Beresford Hope spoke at the inauguration to remind the audience that after eighteen years the Museum had its own building, having parted from South Kensington 'in the spirit of the most perfect friendship and goodwill'. They were a school of technical education, the oldest in England.

Scott still considered sketching an important part of the architect's craft. Accordingly the Spring Gardens Sketching Club was founded, one of a number of such bodies active at the time. Its membership included a large number of present and past pupils and assistants — a notable omission was Drayton Wyatt — but included among the fifty-eight members such names as Edward Akroyd, MP, Armstead, Skidmore, Dean Stanley and the Rev J. L. Petit. It published folio volumes of reproductions of sketches by its membership, perhaps for the education of workmen. The first volume came out in 1866 with neither prefatory nor explanatory matter, save a list of members. The subjects were all architectural, almost all Gothic, and with details emphasised. One imagines their use in offices rather as published collections of working details are used now. The variety of draughtsmanship is interesting, and includes examples of the slapdash pen-and-ink technique associated particularly with the later years of the century as well as the more careful work of earlier years. There seem to have been seven collections published up to 1882, after which the idea was taken up by the Architectural Association and annual volumes of the *AA Sketch Book* appeared for some years.

Scott's other activity in architectural education was to lecture at the Royal Academy schools, first as a stopgap, but from 1868 regularly, and as Professor. He took a great deal of trouble, especially in preparing drawings to illustrate his talks. His own ideas on architectural education are outlined in a talk entitled 'Thoughts and Suggestions on the artistic education of Architects' given at the Architectural Association in March 1864, a curious mixture of good sense and confusion.

Only twenty-one new churches appear to have been started during this period of nine years, reflecting a national trend and underlining the preponderance of restoration work in the practice. They were nearly all Early English verging upon Decorated, or the French equivalent, but otherwise varied, though the larger fell into some sort of pattern.

Of the smaller, at Glasynfryn, Underriver, and Ludlow rather similar two-celled churches were started in 1870, the latter two replacing buildings too far gone to save. St Leonard at Ludlow, where the stones of the old church were used to build a bridge, is of pink sandstone, rockfaced and a little aggressive, and red tiles from Broseley. There is a central gable, lancet windows, and a wheel over a triplet at the east — a throwback to an earlier type of small church. It seated 200 and cost £2228. St Denys, Southampton is of bright red brick with Bath stone dressings, always an unfortunate combination. Nave and chancel are under one roof, with a bellcote. It seated 700 on deal seats under a stained wood roof: the south aisle of 1889 is by another hand. It is uninspiring, but adequate for the masses. Busbridge, near Godalming only fifty miles away, is very different, a small and atypical church of 1865, in the pleasant Bargate stone with a small shingled central spire and, a throwback perhaps to Scott's first half dozen churches, gabled transepts without projection. This is as inspiring as St Denys is dull; it has been supposed that George Gilbert Scott Junior worked upon it. Internally all is well-mannered except the 1899 rood screen by the young Edwin Lutyens, about which there must be two opinions.

Of the larger churches, St Andrew, Walcot, Bath, and a very prosperous church, All Saints, Ryde, Isle of Wight, were buildings of the type having separate pitched roofs over nave and aisles, built in 1872-3 and 1869-71 respectively. At Bath, strangely, west porches flanked the west tower, which with its fine and original broach spire, permissible in this limestone country, gave strange views together with the ordered classic squares. It was demolished after war damage. Ryde, its foundation stone laid by Princess Christian, was, exceptionally, pure Decorated, clearly articulated with large windows between buttresses and a pierced parapet over. Internally there were naturalistic capitals and Clayton and Bell wall paintings. The north-east tower has a pinnacled parapet and a spire.

The remaining twelve have much in common. They are relatively large, costing from £6000 — the smallest (Hanley Swan), to £20,000. They are clerestoried, usually with the characteristic west end following the section of the clerestoried nave and containing the familiar triplet with a roundel over — this motif often occurs also at the east. They were designed with tower and spire, usually a broach. Roofs are high pitched, open, and timber. Style and detail are usually academic and correct. The fashion for an apsidal chancel affected Seedley, Shackleford, Derby and Edensor. Five — Shackleford, Highclere, Kensington, Glasgow, and Lewisham — had transepts, the latter a double transept on the south side only. The tower positions varied: at Chester, Glasgow, Kensington and Leicester, south-east, at Highclere, Hanley Swan, and Lewisham, north-east, at Mirfield, Seedley and Edensor, west, at Shackleford, central, and at Derby, north-west. Three were completed by John Oldrid Scott — Kensington in 1879, Derby in 1881, Glasgow 1893. Those intended at Leicester, Chester and Lewisham were not built.

Shackleford, near Godalming, is perhaps the odd one of the dozen: cruciform, apsidal, central tower with shingled spire and stair turret, its Bargate stone contrasting with the surrounding pines, with naturalistic garden flowers and foliage carved on the

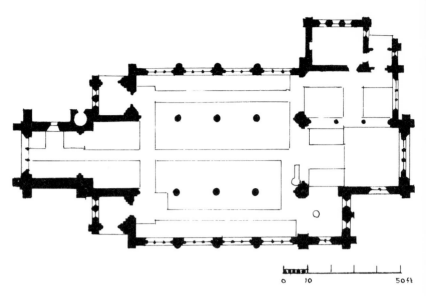

St Andrew, Bath. A large town church providing a great many sittings. The arrangement of porches at the west side is unusual

capitals and elsewhere, one of Scott's happiest and most endearing foibles. It contrasts with Lewisham which is built of Kentish rag and has the stump of a north-east tower. On the south it has a double transept on the Leith pattern, a well-proportioned interior and Early English details in notably French style; the leafage of the nave pillars is after the later 12th-century churches in the Oise valley.[18] Derby, also French in its detail, with an oddly thin tower and spire almost recalling Pugin, was built when brother Melville was incumbent.

The most characteristic and lavish of the group, St Mary Abbots, Kensington, occupies a prominent corner site, and stands up to the competition of out-of-scale later structures. The old church, incompetently built around 1700, had partially collapsed four times in the early 19th century alone. In 1869 G. M. Hills pronounced it in an advanced state of decay. But already in 1866 appeals for money had been made, and in April 1868 a committee was formed which obtained a design from Scott to cost £35,000.

Scott reported, neatly catching the mood of the vicar, Archdeacon Sinclair, 'I have aimed at giving to the church a degree of dignity proportioned to the important rank and position of the parish for which it is intended'. Indeed, the area was prosperous,

Shackleford, capitals showing conventional foliage not of a mediaeval character

due partly to the influence of Kensington Palace and of Holland House, and indeed the Queen subscribed £200. Scott's new urban churches tended to be in working class areas, and no doubt he welcomed a chance to be a little more expansive. A first contract was let to Dove Bros in 1869, a second in 1870, and the major part was consecrated on 14 May 1872 at a cost of £25,000. Building of the tower and spire continued predictably under John Oldrid Scott and was completed in November 1879. The charming curved arcaded approach from the High Street, which does so much to relate the church to its surroundings, is by Scott's pupils Micklethwaite and G. Somers Clarke in 1889-93.

The church seats 1800, the greatest number accommodated in a church without galleries in the diocese. The tower and spire are, at 278 ft, said to be the eighth tallest in England. The extreme length is 279 ft, the extreme width 109 ft, giving the proportions of one of the smaller cathedrals such as Oxford or Manchester.

The plan is wide, almost rectangular, characteristic of the Victorian town church and of some late Decorated churches. Somewhat confused at the east end, it therefore has a little of the mystery and intricacy which some of the straightforward new churches — Halifax, Leafield — lack. There is a high-pitched clerestoried nave with steeply roofed aisles and properly developed clerestory windows, a pair to each bay, a lower chancel, chancel aisles, the north double, double transepts, and a north-east tower. The walls are of stock brick faced externally with Kentish rag and internally with Bath stone: the external dressings are of Bath stone from a different quarry. There are Irish marble columns in the chancel, the roofing is of Whitland Abbey slates, and Godwin's tiles

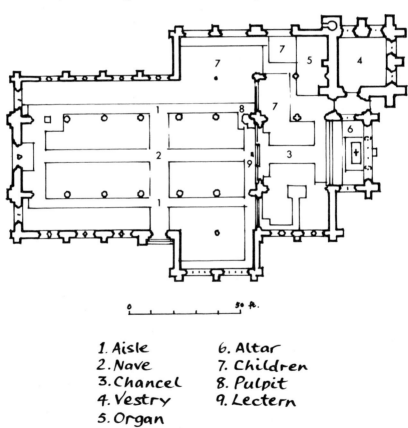

0 ————————— 50 ft.

1. Aisle
2. Nave
3. Chancel
4. Vestry
5. Organ
6. Altar
7. Children
8. Pulpit
9. Lectern

Kensington, St Mary Abbots, 1870-2. Plan
The Builder, xxviii, 9

are used in the pavements. The reredos and altar are Scott's, as are, unusually, the communion vessels, based on 13th-century examples from Rheims, illustrated many times. One might spend a great deal of time looking for precedents for parts of the design. The west front, as at Leith, is supposed to be influenced by Dunblane Cathedral, the nave by Paisley Abbey; the tower and spire bear passing resemblances to St Mary the Virgin, Oxford but perhaps derive more directly from Scott's own church at Ryde; the spire has been likened to St Mary Redcliffe, Bristol. The calling in aid of Scottish precedents is not so illogical as it seems: the practice had by now worked through its French period but Scottish mediaeval architecture was much influenced by France.

These years were very important for Scott's secular Gothic works. A few works show marked, perhaps aberrant, originality, and some buildings are in the mainstream of the development of secular Gothic based on 14th-century prototypes.

In 1872 Scott was at work on St Mary's Homes, adjoining Godstone church, a one-off building most unlike his other work. George Devey in particular exploited such 'old English' forms as heavy oak framing with plastered infill and scratched decoration, tiled roofs and moulded brick chimneys, but here is a grouping which, however unfamiliar, is totally authoritative and successful; indeed it might not be out of place as a *tour de force* of the 1930s. The building is artistically asymmetrical, as is Kelham. The centre block has two gables of unequal size as so commonly seen in the parsonages. At the north end there is a little chapel complete with crypt, bellcote, flèche, and a stone Norman chancel, Scott's first Norman design for a new building for nearly thirty years. It is all illogical: it must always be summer, when the alms people, apple-cheeked old women, have nothing to do but tend their garden.

In a similar idiom was the new 'cottage hospital' of 1871 at Savernake, near Marlborough, with moulded chimney stacks and half-timbered oversailing gable at the front and carefully considered arrangements: but it has been so altered that its original form is not apparent. A third, orthodox, hospital work was in 1869-71, when Buckeridge, with Scott as consultant, added fever wards and two sanitary blocks to the Radcliffe Infirmary in Oxford.

At Ashley, Scott designed a school for Richard Pultenay, rector and squire, in 1858. He was back in 1865 to do the schoolmaster's house and remodel the parsonage, possibly with help from Law.

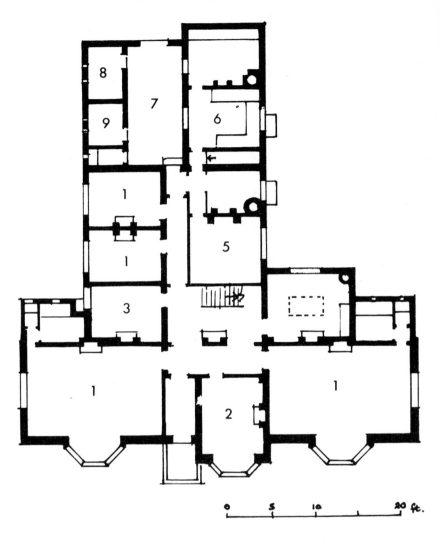

1. Ward
2. Board Room
3. Nurses' Room
4. Operating Room
5. Kitchen

6. Laundry
7. Yard
8. Mortuary
9. Coals

Savernake Hospital. Plan
The Builder, xxxi, 186

87 Worcester Cathedral. Choir as refitted by Scott after 1863
National Monuments Record

88 Stoke Talmage, restored 1861. Another small country church, rescued by
Scott from decrepitude

89 St Hilary, restored about 1861-2. The west window is of Scott's design

90 Hawkhurst, 1859-61. Detail of south aisle. A design of unusual purity, possibly the best of Scott's small churches

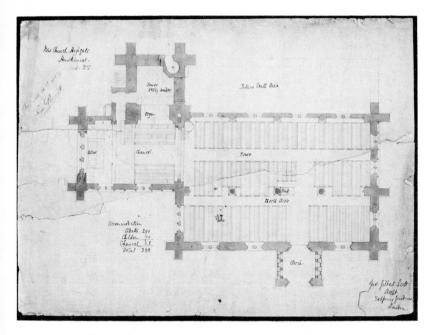

91 Hawkhurst, plan. One of a set of contract drawings dated 1859
Victoria and Albert Museum

92 Hawkhurst. A plain interior with unplastered dressed stone walls

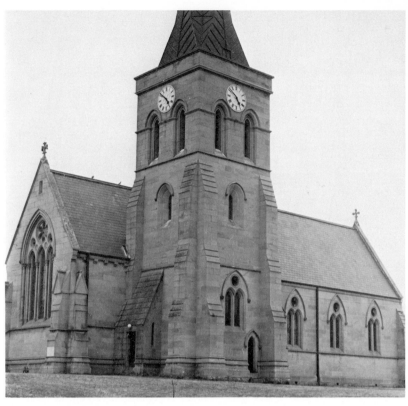

93   Muswellbrook, 1863-9. Plate tracery effectively exported to Australia
Rev. P. Ashley Brown

94 Muswellbrook, interior looking east
Rev. P. Ashley Brown

95 Edvin Loach, 1859. A small country church exhibits plate tracery, lancets, a standard porch, apse and broach spire

96 Sherbourne, south elevation. The addition at the east is by J. O. Scott

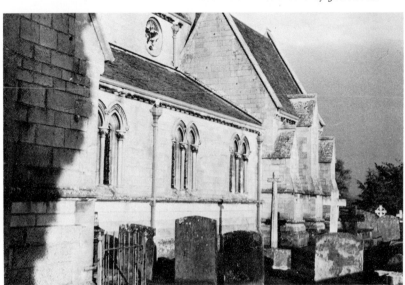

97 Sherbourne, 1862-4. The tower does not seem to be paralleled in Scott's other work: the north porch is unusual

98 Sherbourne, interior. A rich and well balanced composition; money was
plentiful

99 Leith, 1862-6.
View from east. Note
apse, buttressed tower
with broach spire,
transept, and tran-
sitional windows

100 Leith parsonage
about 1862. A plain
Scottish house scarcely
recognisable as Gothic

101 Kensington, Albert Memorial, 1864-71
Allan Miles

102 Leeds Infirmary, in 1895
National Monuments Record

103   Preston Town Hall, 1862-7. Demolished
The Builder, xx, 621

104 Godstone, restored about 1872. Detail of window. Polygonal masonry, flowing
Decorated tracery, grotesque beast labels

105 St John, Leeds. Interior after Norman Shaw's alterations
National Monuments Record

106 Sarratt, view from west. The gables each side of the tower are Scott
additions

107 Fleet Marston, restored 1868-9. View from south west. A small church to a deserted village, carefully repaired by Scott

108 Buckingham, restored 1860-7. View from the south east

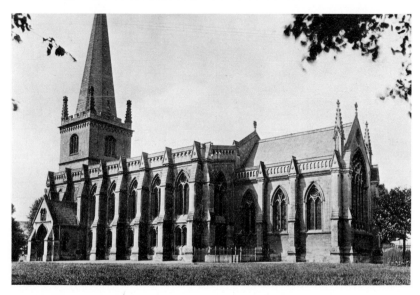

109 Norton, restored about 1868

110 Latimer, Church by Blore. Additions, including apse, by Scott, 1867

111 Westminster Abbey, Chapter House. Interior before restoration *Gleanings from Westminster Abbey*, 2nd edn, p 32

112 Westminster Abbey and Chapter House prior to 1864 showing the exterior of the Chapter House in its final unrepaired condition
Gerald Cobb

113 Westminster Abbey, Chapter House, as restored in 1864-5
Gleanings from Westminster Abbey, 2nd edn, plate xiii

The squire of a parish was having his house rebuilt, at a heavy cost, by that leading architect whom I will designate as Mr. Boss. Schools had been erected in the parish a year or two before, and required something to be done to them: so the vicar on one occasion waylaid Mr. Boss, and asked him to look at the buildings. On getting sight of it, Mr. Boss exclaimed, "Ah, neat little work; who was the architect?" To which the astonished vicar replied, "Yourself".'

Could Ashley be the original of this story?

Scott designed a number of orthodox Gothic schools, but the school-cum-chapel at Burcot, Oxfordshire, built in 1869 at a cost of only £700, was unusual. with red brick walls, tiled roof, carved barge-boards, apse, shingled west flèche and rectangular windows with small panes, unless these are an alteration. It could almost be by W. E. Nesfield or Norman Shaw.

In 1823 Lamprell's baths were built near the Brighton seafront, a circular domed building and in 1862 Charles Brill, Lamprell's nephew and successor, opened a new sea-water swimming bath for ladies which prospered exceedingly. It was roughly elliptical with a domed roof, (possibly influenced by Porden's nearby stables), polychrome in bricks, limestone, granite, and Portland stone, with Maw's encaustic tiles and Skidmore's gasoliers. The architect does not seem to be recorded. Scott was quite certainly involved in the extension designed in May 1866 and said to be in building during 1866-9 — contemporary accounts are a little confusing. This circular bath was 60 ft in diameter, covered by an iron dome with a lantern and surrounded by two tiers of Gothic arcading of a vaguely Venetian character, the lower having twisted barley sugar columns between pairs of four-panelled doors, a most unusual building. It was a great success when new, but later became very run down and disfigured by advertisements.

Gothic for public buildings attained its high water mark in the late 1860s when Scott produced five major designs — St Pancras Station, the Law Courts, Glasgow University, the Albert Institute at Dundee, and Berlin Parliament House.

In 1865 the thrusting, well-managed Midland Railway, finding it no longer tolerable to reach London by running over Great Northern tracks into Kings Cross, built its own line from Bedford to a London terminus on the site of the Agar Town rookery. That year it invited eleven architects, E. M. Barry, G. Somers Clarke, F. P. Cockerell, Darbishire, Hine (of Nottingham), Owen Jones, Lloyd, Lockwood and Mawson (of Huddersfield), Scott, Sorby and

Walters, to compete for the design of a new station and hotel. Early in 1866 the placings were released — 1st Scott, 2nd Clarke, 3rd Barry, 4th Sorby.

The railway crossed the Regent's Canal and the Fleet River to terminate north of Euston Road at high level. This permitted a vast Burton beer warehouse beneath the passenger station, leading in turn to Barlow's great roof spanning the 240 ft width of the passenger station with the then largest arches in the world, tied together by the basement roof. Barlow and Allport, the general manager, had worked out block plans and circulation for the building to the south of the great roof. The site gave scope for the commanding building Scott realised. He alone gave two floors extra to the competition requirements, and thus his entry was estimated to cost £316,000, much more than the others, which ranged from £135,000 to £255,000. In the event, his scheme was chosen both because it was commanding and on account of its careful planning.

The company speedily started work, although the financial crisis following the Overend and Gurney bank failure in 1866 made it seriously consider curtailment. The building was opened in three stages, the last in 1877, and the hotel remained magnificent and popular until the end of the century; 'the appointments leave nothing to be desired by the wealthiest and most refined'.

Scott designed with loving care and his own hand: he disposed towers and flèches, he drew out elevations and thoughtfully related the openings in the walls and he applied the riches of fifty sketch books to ornament the construction, inside and out, with eclectic 14th-century Gothic detail, supplemented by the painted frescoes of Frederick Sang. The marriage with mechanical services was achieved, 'the ventilation of the kitchen is conducted up a "service" staircase and shaft, being completely separated from the establishment generally; a dust shaft runs from the top floor to the bottom, provided with a closed mouth on each floor for the reception of dust, and terminating in a fireproof cistern; apparatus for the prevention and extraction of fires is provided in all parts of the hotel, speaking tubes and electric bells run in all necessary directions giving the maximum accommodation with the minimum of noise'.[19]

The completed building resembles no English mediaeval work: perhaps it is most similar to a Flemish *hôtel de ville*. Contemporaries were unenthusiastic. The houses in Broad Sanctuary repeated (not so); the design for the Foreign Office *rechauffée* (untrue); 'a monument of confectionery'. But the result of Scott's careful design, looked at in the perspective of a hundred years, is a building which, were it his only major work, would at once place him among the first half dozen of Victorian architects.

1866, at the height of the building boom, was a year of great activity as regards large public buildings: an opportunity for Secular Gothic to show what it could achieve; the year of the competition for the Law Courts.

As early as 1840 the widely scattered premises used for the administration of justice were considered both insufficient, and incapable of enlargement. Sir Charles Barry was consulted on their removal and concentration: he proposed the centre of Lincoln's Inn Fields, but this was very properly dropped after an outcry about the loss of open space. He then suggested a slum in the Strand, which was eventually used and for this he prepared a Greek scheme. Nothing was done. In 1845 he placed before a Parliamentary committee another scheme for the Strand site, and one for enlarging the old buildings. These too were deferred, in accordance with the notions of economy then prevalent.

Twenty years later, action could be put off no longer. The Strand site was purchased and cleared, in spite of loud lamentations that the country could not afford it. At the same time proposals were afoot for a new National Gallery in Trafalgar Square. The Foreign Office affair pointed to caution: in February 1866 the most eminent architects in the country were invited to enter in limited competitions for each building. Five were selected for the National Gallery — E. M. Barry, Banks and Barry, Digby Wyatt, Scott, and Street — and six for the Law Courts — E. M. Barry, P. C. Hardwick Junior, Scott, Street, Waterhouse, and T. H. Wyatt. Scott, finding himself on both lists, withdrew from the (ultimately abortive) National Gallery competition in order to devote all the time he could spare from his practice to the Law Courts. Street, with a busy practice also, entered for both buildings.

No doubt for the same reason, Scott did not compete for Manchester Town Hall in 1867: instead John Oldrid Scott was one of eight, mostly from the north, who went forward to the second stage of that contest which was won by Waterhouse with a Gothic design which itself may be considered a fine exemplar of Scott's theories on secular Gothic architecture.

The six Law Courts competitors were to get £800 each. It was felt by some, including both Beresford Hope and Tite, that the competition should not be limited: the Government was defeated on a motion to that effect. So nine were asked to compete for the National Gallery and twelve for the Law Courts, and that list, after Digby Wyatt and Hardwick had declined, now read: Abraham, E. M. Barry, David Brandon, Burges, Deane, Garling, Gibson, Lockwood, Seddon, Scott, Street, and Waterhouse. An impractical condition requiring the successful competitor not to undertake any other work requiring his personal attention for a period of three years without Treasury consent was now withdrawn. Scott acted as chairman of the architects when dealing with the Board's officials.

The assessors were Mr Cowper, the First Commissioner; Gladstone; Sir Alexander Cockburn, Lord Chief Justice; Sir Roundell Palmer, Attorney-General; and Sir William Stirling Maxwell. As at the Foreign Office, they found professional advice necessary, and John Shaw Junior and G. Pownall were added. This body considered eleven sets of drawings, Gibson falling out: a pity, for a design by the architect of the National Provincial Bank in Old Broad Street would have been worth seeing.[20] All the entries were Gothic, except one: Garling, no doubt with the Foreign Office in mind, submitted both a Gothic and an Italian design. All the illustrated schemes had a profusion of towers. Barry's included the dome supported on a cube which his father had affected. Burges' design included his characteristic circular fairy-tale towers.

Scott laboured from April to September in 1866 getting his plan to work, then spent a month at the seaside over the architectural details. The final scheme had a four-storey block to the Strand with a higher central block having a high roof and two flanking towers, and arcading on the ground floor. The general treatment had a similarity to St Pancras Station. The plan shows a surrounding block of offices with inside it most of the twenty-four courts required, areas or light wells between them, and then a colonnade or ambulatory surrounding a space in which was an octagonal central hall surmounted by a dome — Gothic details on a plan almost symmetrical about both axes. But the minute requirements of the lawyers produced somewhat similar plans in all the schemes.

In the award, in July 1867, the technical men placed Barry first and Scott second: the legal, Scott first and Waterhouse second. As a body — there are here discrepancies between Scott's and Street's memoirs — they preferred Barry's plan but Street's architectural treatment, and so proposed, perhaps with vague recollections of how Sir Charles Barry and Pugin had worked together on the Houses of Parliament, a joint arrangement. At this, Scott protested, claiming it unfair to weigh two men's merits against one's; and indeed the judges were asked to reconsider the decision as being one which their conditions disallowed. Street protested against Scott, who, perhaps relying upon his friendship with Cowper and with Manners, agreed to accept the decision if reaffirmed. After four months, it was reaffirmed, and Scott, as he had promised, withdrew. Waterhouse, on the other hand, engaged in keen gamesmanship to influence Cowper toward his own appointment. Early in 1868 it became apparent that Waterhouse had been insufficiently, or too, insistent, and that Street alone was to have the work: whereupon a regrouping of interests took place, and strenuous but unsuccessful attempts, in the House of Commons and elsewhere, were made to unseat him. 'The chances of war and one or two good friends hoisted (Street) over the decision of the judges'.[21]

Scott considered the matter a great failure: but perhaps he had less energy for the fight than for earlier battles, or perhaps his respect for Street made him less persevering. For Street also the outcome was unhappy. The site was moved to the Embankment and back again, requiring complete replanning each time, and the location was not settled until 1870: meanwhile the architecture was criticised. George Godwin echoed Scott's view, deprecating a pure Gothic building and hoping that the Gothic adopted would such as would best admit of the developments suggested by modern views, modern requirements, modern materials, and modern modes of construction. Others were severe: Tite, who hated Gothic; Fergusson, who hated what he considered unscholarly Gothic; and Grimthorpe, who hated Street. Then the tenders exceeded the estimates of three years before, due to a general rise in prices, and economies were made. At Street's death, aged fifty-seven, in 1881, hastened by the strain of executing the scheme, the work was not quite finished. The Office of Works refused to have anything to do with competitions for major public buildings for many years, because of the unsatisfactory conduct and outcome of the two Victorian examples in which Scott played a leading part.

Glasgow University seems to show failing powers. The University, lodged in a slum in the High Street in 1846, commissioned a layout from a prominent local man, John Baird, for a site on Gilmorehill in anticipation of a sale to the Monkland Railways. The sale fell through, so the new site remained empty until after a sale was effected in 1867 to the City of Glasgow Union Railway. Scott was commissioned to design buildings to the old layout. It has been stated that he used as his model John Honeyman's unsuccessful design for the Sydney Houses of Parliament[22] and we cannot tell how much may be due to his assistant, Conradi; but it cannot be accounted a successful design. The main view is of a long, low, symmetrical building with hard and mechanical Gothic detail, punctuated by a weird translucent tower and spire containing ventilating shafts. There were thirteen professors' houses and a detached building stated to be an almost exact reproduction of the Abbott's Kitchen at Glastonbury. The major part was completed in 1870, but the Bute Hall, between the two great quadrangles, and almost certainly designed in Scott's lifetime, had its superstructure started in the summer of 1878. With its circular corner towers and vaulted undercroft it is externally much the most successful part of the building. It has affinities with the Albert Institute at Dundee, which itself is similar to the library at Lewes. Scott designed the Institute in 1864, and modified it later. He intended it to be of the best period of pointed architecture with Scottish national characteristics, the flèche and the extraordinary Frenchified staircase like

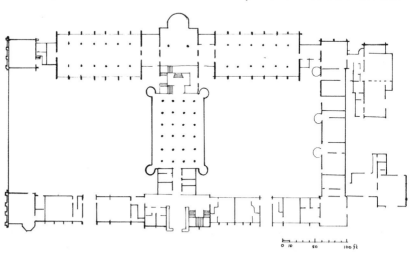

Glasgow University, 1867 on. Plan

some 17th-century castle such as Drumlanrig — a style which Scott claimed was all his own invention. The estimate 'seems to come to about £14,000', said Scott, 'I fear that the cost . . . will be in excess of your funds. Nor do I see my way to rendering it otherwise'.[23] He was usually more courteous: but it was built, and is undoubtedly one of his most attractive buildings.

Scott's penultimate design for a major Gothic public building was his entry, with John Oldrid Scott, for the Berlin Parliament House competition in 1872. The Crown Princess of Prussia, who had wanted him to design the Albert Memorial, influenced his invitation to compete. Germans gained the first four premia, the Scotts the fifth. The style, in the mainstream of Scott's theories, was again an invention, an exercise in historical might-have-been. 'The Germans, at the commencement of the thirteenth century, were on the high road to a noble form of Gothic architecture wholly their own, but were disturbed by the importation of French architecture. My object has been to imagine this interruption to be non-existent . . . .' The building used modern systems of construction and modern appearances as far as tenable, and it had a cupola ' in some degree like that of St. Peter's would be if translated into early German style'.[24] We may sense an appeal to Prussian Chauvinism, but feel that architectural style had almost become a game.

The artists and tradesmen who collaborated with, and worked for, Scott were not always successful. The Morris firm, which supplied much stained glass for his churches, was an artistic, but not a commercial, success. One remembers particularly the sculptors Redfern and Philip, both dying in poverty in 1875-6. Early in 1872 Skidmore, the ornamental metal worker of Coventry, went into liquidation and his works, built in 1857 and extended to cover three-quarters of an acre, were sold that June. The list of buildings with which he had been involved reads like that of Scott's; including nine cathedrals, 283 churches, the Albert Memorial, the Government Offices, St Pancras, Warwick Castle, and Lambeth Palace. His failure is another signpost to the end of the Revival as a growing and developing force.

Scott had hardly recovered from his own illness, when his wife Caroline died at Rooks-nest on 24 February 1872: all that winter she had suffered from the heart trouble endemic in the family.

Scott was upset and self-reproaching. He had a great regard for her character, 'a person of very strong and clear intellect; of quiet and decided perception of the right thing to do, under any emergency; ... gifted with that decision and courage in which I was myself naturally deficient'.[25] He designed at Tandridge a tomb of restrained Italian Renaissance character belied only by the Gothic lettering.

On 9 August 1872 Scott was knighted for his part in the Albert Memorial, taking for arms a device bearing three Catherine Wheels. His description of the ceremony is curiously unworldly.

I have had a very agreeable day. I was summoned to Osborne to the Council, and was invited to go down by the special train at nine o'clock. At the station I met Lord Ripon, Mr Cardwell, Mr Childers, the Lord Advocate of Scotland, and Sir Arthur Helps. We went down together to Gosport, where we adjourned to a large man-of-war's boat of twelve oars, and were rowed, under the command of an officer, to the mouth of the harbour. Here we embarked on a fine steamer, and proceeded towards the Isle of Wight. After a little time our attention was called by an officer to a mass of smoke far ahead. It was the American fleet, which had been for some time lying in the Southampton water, saluting the Queen in passing Osborne. We presently met them, one after another, five vessels. On coming off at Osborne, we were landed in the ship's boat, and found carriages in waiting to take us up to the house ... the Prince of Wales passed through the staircase. He shook hands with and congratulated me.

Presently Lord Ripon came out and told me that my business would come on last: then the council were called in, but their business did not occupy more than a few minutes, and, at length, I was summoned. Having made my bows, the sword was handed to the Queen. She touched both my shoulders and said in a familiar gentle way, "Sir Gilbert". Then she held out her hand, I kneeled again and kissed it, and backed out, the whole taking something less than half a minute.

I thank God for the honour.[26]

This honour is the zenith of his career. He had designed his major buildings, work came in on the strength of his reputation to be executed in an office which ran itself, whilst he, a widower with grown sons and in poor health, could spend more of his time in travelling abroad, in antiquarian research, in documenting his life, and in attending learned societies. Caroline's death marks the end of *Recollections* as a coherent narrative: much of the remainder is ill-arranged, devoted to his work at various cathedrals, building by building, and to the anti-restoration movement.

Perhaps Scott would have felt with Thomas Hardy, himself ar

architect, who in this year, 1872, published his novel *Desperate Remedies*:

it is a melancholy truth for the middle classes that in proportion as they develop, by the study of poetry and art, their capacity for conjugal love of the highest kind, they limit the possibility of their being able to exercise it — the very act putting out of their power the attainment of means sufficient for marriage. The man who works up a good income has no time to learn love to its solemn extreme: the man who has learnt that has had no time to get rich.

8

Viri Probi Architecti Peritissimi, 1872-78

Early in 1873 Scott moved from Godstone back to Ham where John Oldrid and family, Alwyne and Dukinfield lived. He resigned his professorship at the Academy and was elected President of the Royal Institute of British Architects: but in the middle of the year after winning the competition for Edinburgh Cathedral, he became ill again, and, after induction as President, started on 11 July 1873 an extended continental tour with Dukinfield and his manservant, John Pavings. They travelled through Holland and Germany to Sils in Switzerland, remaining five weeks; then joined by John Oldrid, his four year old son John, and Alwyne, they travelled to Evian. Thence Scott, leaving his family, went via Avignon to Rome and spent five weeks there, much in the company of John Henry Parker, his Oxford publisher. He returned through Naples and France, reaching London on New Year's Day, 1874.

Refreshed, he regularly attended to his duties as President of the Institute. His Presidential Address on the preceding 3 November[1] was read by Eastlake in his absence; it reads in part like an old man's reflections that times aren't what they were and in part like a young man's that things are worse than they ought to be. He refers to periods in history, including the Renaissance, when men were devoted heart and soul to their art 'and with whom personal advancement, social position, or any other consideration was as dust in the balance when weighed against the perfection of the arts to which they had sworn allegiance'. Although the revived feeling for the study and resuscitation of mediaeval architecture is unparalleled since the Renaissance many bad works are being produced, whilst criticism singles out those whose heart is in their work for deprecation and the 'mere offal of our art' has not a word said against it: the public does not know good from bad. Architecture is a means of living rather than one of the noblest employments of life, and competitions are a lottery. Sadder still is the restoration of old buildings by those who have neither knowledge of, nor respect for, them. The equivocal motto *Donec templum refeceris* will perhaps prove the death knell of ecclesiastical antiquities. How different is all this from the conversion of thirty-five years before! And had he forgotten how desperately he had needed architecture as a means of living?

No doubt it was at his initiative that the Royal Gold Medal of the Institute, annually conferred on some distinguished architect or man of science or letters, was offered to John Ruskin in 1874. Ruskin, ageing and eccentric, refused it, giving his reasons fully:

1 The neglected condition of the tomb of Cardinal Brancaccio at Naples.
2 The conversion of S. Miniato, Florence, into a cemetery.
3 The destructive restoration of S. Maria della Spina at Pisa.
4 The recklessness with which the ruins of Furness Abbey were dealt with by the railway engineers.

For these (notwithstanding that three of the four instances were in Italy) he considered members of the Institute answerable, and also considered it no time to play at adjudging medals to one another.[2] Scott, piqued, and knowing Ruskin would disapprove, substituted Street's name. At the same occasion the next year, the Gold Medal went to the antiquary Edmund Thorpe,[3] to the accompaniment of much headshaking from Scott and Christian over how much the remains of abbeys had decayed in the last twenty-five years.

Scott can have done little architectural work himself in 1873, and only twelve new churches were started between then and his death, continuing the sharp down trend evident since 1865 and perhaps reflecting the depression of the early 1870s. He said at the foundation stone laying of St Michael, New Southgate in 1872, 'It is an honour to any architect to be concerned in building a house of God, and I rejoice that I have designed many, but I only wish there were more of them than there are'.[4]

The smallest is at Green Hammerton, Yorkshire, built in 1876. The heart does not warm to it, an aisleless cruciform of rockfaced stone under a red machine-made tile roof with a standard central bell gable: the early Decorated detail is modelled on that of the nearby Bilton in Ainsty. To Scott's office is also attributed the small box-like school in similar materials. St Lawrence in the Isle of Wight — Scott spent holidays in nearby Shanklin — was built during 1876-8, a tired essay in the Decorated style. Guyhirn, Cambridgeshire, where the client appears to have been Scott's brother John, of Wisbech, was a small and atypical building with lancets, in gault brick and stone. The old chapel, of 1660 and Puritan in its fittings, was allowed to remain — it was neither restored nor demolished. This is in line with advanced conservationist thinking of the time.

The remainder were larger, aisled, usually clerestoried, and sometimes with a tower. Two at New Southgate, St Michael of 1872, and St Paul of 1873, had spirelet or turret respectively. All Saints, Gloucester, in a poor part of the city, consecrated in November 1875, is possibly Scott's best late church. Its site is unpropitious: it needs a tower and spire, though perhaps this was intended on the south-east; the west end is not entirely satisfactory; but yet the refined late Decorated detail in a pleasant stone, the various square clerestory windows, and the steep tiled roofs, impress. Internally the roof is not open, but boarded and panelled. Scott's favourite suppliers are at work again: Potter, who, with Leaver, had succeeded Skidmore as Scott's favourite, for ironwork, Godwin for tiling, Clayton and Bell for glass, and so on. The interior detail and the furnishings are handled with more grace than in most of the big churches of the classic period of the mid-1850s.

There are then three churches in hard red brick. St Saviour, Leicester, started in June 1875, is atypical: cruciform, red brick inside and out, Norman west front but mostly Early English elsewhere (why should one try to give the impression of a church growing by degrees when it is in hard red modern brick?), a vaulted crossing with circular granite piers, a south-west tower, and — a throwback to the 1850s — an apsidal chancel. Scott also designed the parsonage and the school. St Peter, Fulney, near Spalding, built with its parsonage and school between 1877 and 1880 for over £20,000, is also transitional between Norman and Early English, with its internal arcading of pairs of lancets under round arches derived (why?) from Boxgrove Priory in Sussex. The tower and spire is detached, to the west.[5]

At St Giles, Newcastle under Lyme, Scott for the last time

retained and repaired a mediaeval tower and replaced the body of an old church: this one was brick, of 1721, designed by William Smith, 'the leading master builder in the West Midlands',[6]on a site sloping 7 ft from end to end, dilapidated and too small. The new church of 1872-6 is large — 150 ft long, dominant, in Scott Decorated and Blyth Marsh stone, costing £13,300.

All Souls, Blackman Lane, Leeds, a memorial to Dean Hook, is Scott's last Early English essay: it looks already more like John Oldrid's work than his father's. It went through more than one design; at one time a central tower was intended, but in the end — the foundation stone was laid in September 1876 but the latest drawings are dated June 1877 — it was a large stone church, almost rectangular in plan, with lancets, some coupled and tripled, and a large north western tower, no doubt added when money became available. The cost was in excess of £20,000.

St Michael, Stourport on Severn, was Scott's last work in his favourite Decorated. Designs were prepared, perhaps in 1875, for a large building seating 1200 and costing as much as £25,000, but in the end it fell to John Oldrid to realise a part only. Building started in 1879 and, by the consecration in 1910, the nave, aisles and porch had been built — a magnificent fragment.[7]

To Scott fell the honour of being the first to have a whole new British cathedral built to his designs — the Episcopalian Cathedral of St Mary, Edinburgh. Two sisters, Barbara and Mary Walker of Drumsheugh, willed £45,000 for the purpose, and directed that three English and three Scottish architects be asked to submit designs, and that six or eight trustees, citizens of Edinburgh, including the Bishop, the Dean, and the Provost, should make the arrangements. Accordingly, Scott, Street and Burges, together with Alex Ross, Lessels, and Peddie and Kinnear, were asked to submit designs by August 1872. Street, before agreeing, visited the Bishop, Cotterill, and understood that the trustees would not, as with the Foreign Office, attempt to make a selection without competent professional advice. The initial cost limit of £45,000, was raised to £65,000, so every one had to revise their schemes.

At submission, it was found that someone, perhaps Scott, had sent in two designs: one was returned, and so anonymity was not maintained. Next, it was supposed that the trustees nevertheless intended to make an award without professional help. Scott and Burges (Street being abroad) protested, and eventually Christian, architect to the Ecclesiastical Commissioners and a practised churchman both in construction and in attendance, was appointed as adviser. His report, after much pressure, was published: it made no outright recommendation but clearly preferred Street's design. However, Bishop Cotterill, who had come to Edinburgh earlier in 1872 from Grahamstown in South Africa, where no doubt he had known of Scott in connection with the latter's 1860 design for the alterations, not yet undertaken, to the Cathedral, supported him stoutly, and his influence was decisive in the award to Scott — his last competition success — made prior to the publication of Christian's report, late in 1872 or early in 1873. It has been stated that Scott's designing the building in Early English, incorporating parts of many Scottish churches and ecclesiastical edifices of that time was decisive, but Street and no doubt others, had done exactly this. Street felt badly used: his scheme was well spoken of, and within the cost limitation. He and others considered that he should have been selected, as he had stated positively that his scheme could be executed for his estimate of £60,500, whereas Scott, cautiously and characteristically, qualified his estimate of £75,000.

It is a magnificent building, cruciform, 262 ft long, with a central tower and spire 275 ft high and two western towers and spires 209 ft high. The nave is 71 ft high inside. It is thus one of the shorter of our

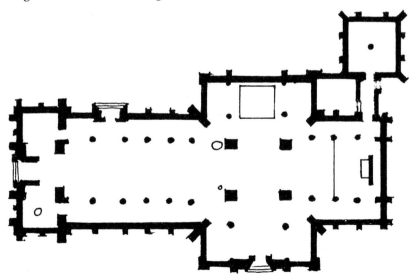

Edinburgh Cathedral, 1875, north-east view

cathedrals in length (due to its plan being adapted to congregational needs rather than monastic needs) and of nearly similar height to the generality of such buildings in England. The whole gains greatly from its stylistic homogeneity both inside and out, although the refinement and grace of its 13th-century counterpart, Salisbury, is quite missing. Perhaps the most serious criticism is of the badly proportioned detached shafts above the nave columns — a mistake of the same sort as at Doncaster twenty years previously. The choir roof alone is stone-vaulted, and the east end is groined so as to appear apsidal, but on plan it is square. Details are reproduced from the abbeys of Jedburgh, Kelso, Paisley and Holyrood; Dunblane and Elgin Cathedrals; and St Giles, Edinburgh.

Building lasted from 1874 to 1879 and cost £92,132, plus Farmer and Brindley's metalwork and the fees, but owing to rising wages it had not been possible to build the chapter house nor the western spires: the former was built in 1890 for £5000, the latter in 1915 and 1917 for £13,200, both to the original design.

Over seventy church restorations are traceable to this period. Scott's personal involvement in many was clearly slight: he was in poor health and spent periods abroad. Sometimes the office proceeded independently; in many cases he insisted on conservative principles in talking to clients or potential clients and by exhorting the office. A number were designed in his lifetime and finished, or even started, posthumously by John Oldrid Scott. There is no evidence that the latter, who seems singularly colourless, was anything other than dutiful and acquiescent in such matters, however he may have behaved after his father's death. For whatever reason, restorations of this period seem to range the whole way from the most careful conservation to radical remodelling.

For example, at Ashbourne in Derbyshire, Scott restored the chancel between 1876 and 1881, other parts of the building having been dealt with earlier by other hands. There were pairs of lancet windows, some dating only from 1861, and a Perpendicular east window, roof and parapets. He underpinned the walls without taking them down, retained the lancets, and replaced the tracery of the east window without altering its style. No attempt was made to raise the roof to a high pitch: the battlements were repaired, or even added. He was possibly responsible for producing new tiling based on patterns of remaining 14th century work. The Kempe glass dates from 1896.

At Hillesden, the church near Buckingham which Scott knew as a child and drew so competently in the mid-1820s, he had built the new vicarage in 1870 and three years later reported upon the fine Perpendicular church, for which he had made, no doubt unsolicited, proposals as far back as 1855. In 1874-5 he, probably acting without a fee, repaired the leaky roofs, restored the ceiling (which had substantially disappeared) from stored fragments and his early sketches, repaired damaged external stonework — he had kept fragments himself — replaced at his own cost the vaulted ceiling of the porch, repaired the screen, did a certain amount of refitting, retaining some old woodwork and, after a fight, a large 18th-century pew slightly altered but, true to custom, removing the Georgian gallery. Here was a labour of love.

St Nicholas, New Romney, visually an extraordinary church, was reported upon by Scott in 1875, and drawings for restoration, mostly of the Norman west end, were prepared in his lifetime though the work started in 1880. Again, old fittings, notably the pews and rails, were retained. For St John the Baptist, Halifax, where in the 1860s Scott was rebuffed by the incumbent: 'let it be, it will last my time', [8] plans for restoration had been prepared, by March 1878, and carried out by 1880. The 17th-century pews and rails were retained but the galleries removed: the only external alteration is said to have been the replacement of lost parapets. Even so, he was criticised for his supposed sweeping intention before the work began. At Orchardleigh, Somerset, a chapel on an island in a wood, a restoration of 'much tact and respect', [9] was undertaken in 1878-81 to Sir Gilbert's designs. George Gilbert Scott Junior was possibly concerned in the execution.

Hardwick, Oxfordshire, was the subject of a gentle restoration planned by Sir Gilbert in 1877 and carried out by Gilbert Scott Junior after May 1878. Here we have an isolated instance where it is recorded that as far as possible the old roof timbers were preserved: the chancel walls were hardly touched, although it was necessary largely to rebuild the nave and add new south aisle, porch, bell turret, altar, pulpit and lectern.

Stowford in North Devon, restored in 1874, is chiefly remarkable for the great profusion of carved oakwork then introduced, replicas of noted examples from Devon and the adjacent counties. At Llangurig in Central Wales, in a costly work of 1876-80, a part of the

15th-century screen removed at a harmful restoration in 1836 was found and a copy of the original installed.

In one celebrated instance, Scott's conservative principles were disregarded. At Tadcaster, Yorkshire, the church was in disrepair in 1875. Scott inspected and pronounced it safe, but the parish wished to rebuild it entirely at a higher level as it was so often flooded. When the chancel roof was touched it collapsed, whereupon the church was taken down and rebuilt.

Other works fell into the familiar pattern of so many previous works, of reseating and refitting. Cleobury Mortimer is typical: during a year in 1874-5 the west gallery and the ceilings were removed, and the church refitted with pitch pine seats and a new pulpit. Since it was said to be in poor condition — indeed it is still much out of plumb — no doubt a number of repairs took place. St John the Baptist, Coventry, and Halesowen are similar cases.

Some involved furnishings only, such as at South Weald, Essex, where screens were added in 1877 to a church restored by S.S. Teulon ten years earlier: or the monument to Dean Hook in St Peter, Leeds. Sometimes there is a simple addition in the character of the old church, as at Tandridge, Surrey, where in 1874-5 Scott added north aisle and vestry, with pitched tiled roofs and polygonal masonry matching the existing, and Decorated aisle windows. It is all unremarkable but partakes of the character of a Kent church.

Occasionally Scott had a second or third quite separate go at a church previously restored by him. At Olney, where Scott had restored the chancel in 1869, in 1873 work on the nave was proposed: that was done probably during 1877-8 and certainly included removing the west gallery and refitting, but since it cost £4000 probably involved a good deal more, perhaps of repair work. Farnborough, Warwickshire, is similar. In 1858 Scott had restored the chancel, and now in 1875 he reroofed the nave and supplied a new north aisle and spire. St Mary of Charity, Faversham, Kent had had its 1754 nave Gothicised and its 1799 tower recased by Scott in 1853 or thereabouts, but by 1873 further repairs were found necessary and by February 1875 the nave had been reseated and heated by Scott, whilst the chancel had been inexpensively restored by Christian. At Danbury, Essex, the pulpit of 1878 was added to the church which Scott restored in 1866.

In other cases he added to a Victorian church. The example of

Farncombe, Surrey, has already been noted. At Brereton, Stafford-shire, a small cruciform church in Early English style, of grey limestone, competently designed by Thomas Trubshaw and built in 1837, in 1876-78 aisles were were added, the east end altered, and some refitting undertaken. The octagonal tower, crowned by some-thing between a spirelet and a spire, seems to have been part of the original design but was altered in 1887. The style and material of the old building has been matched by Scott, and a low pitched and warm interior has resulted from the enlargements and the somewhat involved structure: there is a cosiness and mystery completely foreign to an unsatisfactory early church like St Mark, Swindon or a better middle church like Leafield. And Scott's details, shafted window jambs and all, are much more polished than Trubshaw's. This is one of Scott's most human and endearing works of its kind, and indeed, it is said, his likeness watches over it from the corbel at the junction of the first arch of the north aisle and the second arch of the nave.

In many cases over the years, Scott has been blamed for destruc-tion for which he was not responsible. A case in point is Bledlow, just north of the Chilterns. Whilst it is suggested that the church had been altered and 'much stone removed from the interior and used as roadstone',[10] Scott's contribution was only a limited in-volvement with the chancel in 1877, when he removed an 18th-century reredos, reinstating it in the south aisle rather than throwing it out and perhaps blocking a doorway. Again, if one looks at the small church at Dyserth, Flintshire, externally there seems to be little altertion attributable to Scott's restoration except that some of the windows have obviously been renewed and, as so often, the roof re-slated: yet it is stated that all the windows except two were renewed, that the north transept aisle was added, and that the building was largely or entirely rebuilt.

On the other hand, there are instances of works not wholly conservative, where substantial alterations or conjectural restora-tion, often involving the removal of 'debased' modern work, were made. St Andrew, Plymouth, was a large Perpendicular church of the West of England three-nave pattern, with short secondary aisles and a west tower. It had already come under the improving hand of the classical John Foulston, 'the leading architect of the neighbour-hood'.[11] He is said to have, in refitting and altering the church in 1826, removed screens and oak fittings, which were auctioned for

£134 15s. Scott in 1875 removed Georgian galleries, partitions and fittings, which may not have been of very good quality, provided a new screen, replaced the east window in Perpendicular, did much work to the roofs and provided benches, reredos and font: £5000 was spent.[12]

Godalming, Surrey, poorly restored by J. Perry, a local man, in 1840, came under Scott's care in 1877.[13] This meant that he had been involved with all four churches in the old parish — Godalming, Farncombe, Busbridge and Shackleford.

Artistically the church is pleasant but its enlargement has meant that almost all the external walls of the aisles, west end and north transept are Scott, and all the windows, once Perpendicular, have been rebuilt in characteristic Scott Decorated, the north aisle of earlier detail than the rest. It seems to follow that the roofs were renewed. The low tower arches much impeded vision from nave to chancel: that on the west, said to be Saxon, was removed, and built into the tower's west wall, being replaced by an Early English arch, and the Norman arch at the east was ingeniously raised up 5 ft. On the other hand, Norman fragments were discovered and exposed, wall paintings uncovered, and the Elizabethan pulpit retained.

There was a similar problem at St Margaret, King's Lynn, Norfolk. Refitting had been talked of since at least 1867, and in 1872 Scott prepared plans for work executed in 1875, including removal of galleries, which had cut off the chancel entirely, re-seating, and rebuilding or repairing the interior of the nave and adjoining parts, rebuilt in inadequate Gothic by Matthew Brettingham Senior in 1742-6, after the fall of the south-west spire in a storm. On the one hand Scott has been thought to be too thorough in demolishing and rebuilding: on the other, not thorough enough in ameliorating Brettingham's grotty Gothic. Scott did nothing to the chancel, once again restored by Christian.

St Chad, Stafford, was in 1873 the remains of a Norman church, with the nave exterior destroyed in the 18th century and recased in brick and the chancel restored in 1854. Scott in 1875 provided a new Norman west facade and some Norman aisles as well as repairing the nave. The church must now be artistically more satisfactory than in its previous condition. At Kirkby Moorside on Earl Feversham's Yorkshire estates is another example of an entirely rebuilt chancel. What was wrong with that existing before 1874 is not clear, but Scott's new limb has reset in it a genuine Norman window and 14th-century sedilia. At Kirtlington, Oxfordshire, Benjamin Ferrey in 1852-4 had provided a Norman tower, a genuine conjectural restoration, for its predecessor had disappeared at least eighty years before, and undertaken other work: Scott in 1877 rebuilt the chancel, replacing the battlemented, flat pitch roof by a tiled roof of steep pitch, copying the odd details, re-using a 13th-century piscina, and reproducing faithfully the east window, a simple unfashionable four-light affair with intersecting tracery.

Histon, Cambridgeshire, is a classic example of replacing the work of a previous style. The chancel was first Norman, then restored in the 13th century in Early English, then again around 1600 in late Perpendicular. Scott, in 1874, removed the plaster from the walls, discovering two lancets: it was also established that the chancel had been truncated, Norman mouldings were found built into the wall, and at the same time the proprietor of nearby Madingley Hall was pulling down the gallery there, outwardly of red brick, when 'inside was found the clunch that had been removed from the church in 1600, with the rich moulding and colour as fresh in some parts.as though the work had been executed only a short time since'.[14] The chancel ended up with thirteen lancets, and was faced with recovered stone from Madingley.

At St Nicholas, Newcastle-on-Tyne, during 1871-9, Scott made the tower safe, but he removed a good chancel interior of 1793. Lastly, there is to be noted the extensive restoration of St Nicholas, Colchester, Essex, so greatly altered and extended, at a cost of some £11,000, as to appear almost new.

Of the three ruined abbeys the work on two was abortive. Kirkstall, near Leeds, was owned by Lord Cardigan, the mad hero of the Crimea, and he wanted to sell it. There was a proposal to restore it as an Anglican church in 1873, and Scott's office was asked to do it; but it was probably just as well nothing came of the suggestion. Rievaulx was promoted by Earl Feversham, and in August 1877 Scott was sketching and noting: a design for restoration of choir and transepts was prepared, but as a result either of Scott's death or the fire at Duncombe Park in 1879 when some internal work by Scott was consumed, nothing was done and Scott's fee was never paid. At Jedburgh, Scott had little involvement, and merely confirmed the architect Anderson's ideas of the conservation of the ruin.

After 1872 Secular Revived Gothic had passed its apogee. A set of rooms at New College, Oxford, and three blocks of chambers at Lincoln's Inn in London, have something in common: the plans are not dissimilar. The Oxford building of 1873 is faced in Milton stone; that in London, the better to withstand the soot-laden atmosphere, is in hard red East Malling brick with blue diaper, Ancaster stone dressings, pea green slates, square headed windows, and plain Tudor gables — a strange echo as Scott neared the end of his life of the style of some early workhouses, though it follows that of existing buildings there. The first block was started in 1873 and was followed by two more, the third completed in 1880 under John Oldrid Scott. This may have been undertaken at the behest of Lord Grimthorpe, who was certainly involved with Scott's work of 1871-3 enlarging the library by three bays copying P. C. Hardwick's work of 1843, and with Scott's design for adding to the chapel, eventually realised by Samuel Salter in 1881-3.

However, Scott had not lost faith in his secular Gothic. Whilst visiting Newcastle-on-Tyne he heard that new Assize Courts were proposed. After discussion with the chairman of the Building Committee he did much work in preparing a design, submitting in April 1876 an elaborate set of drawings with the proviso: no charge unless he should be appointed, but he would not engage in competition. The Committee liked the scheme, but local architects got up a successful opposition to the interloper and head-shaking items appeared in the technical press. Unfortunately no details of the design seem to be known.

Two of his last, and posthumous, works were of the Eleanor Cross type, like the Martyrs' Memorial at Oxford. In the memorial to Thomas Clarkson the anti-slavery propagandist in his native Wisbech, the upper stages were open not solid, and a statue was placed within the structure. It was designed by May 1876 and completed under John Oldrid Scott in 1882. The other, at Ashby de la Zouch, Leicestershire, commemorates the Countess of Loudoun, and probably cost over £3500, more than twice as much as that at Wisbech.

Of the remaining cathedral and abbey restorations, Manchester and Winchester were minor works, the former including the organ case, the latter only the screen. At Exeter, work for some time proceeded under Robert Cornish, 'a very kindly and excellent old gentleman, and a thoroughly practical man',[15] who had consulted Scott occasionally and later, apparently, without any professional advice. In 1870 Scott was appointed to deal with the internal restoration and a merry time was had by all. In his report he favoured, in line with his principles, retaining the close screen with the organ over between nave and choir. The local architectural society, led by P. B. Hayward, son of James Hayward the foremost local architect, and by Archdeacon Freeman, the antiquary, stated that the nave was a fashionable lounge, that the screen was not of 1320 but much more recent, and supported a scheme of James Hayward's put about in 1858, for moving the screen to the west end of the nave to form a narthex, in which presumably the fashionable might lounge, and its replacement by a more open structure. Otherwise, it was argued, the restoration would not be conservative as it would involve reseating the choir for congregational use. Scott had recommended chairs in the choir aisles and piercing the screen at the backs of the choir stalls. It was the usual controversy over the proper way of opening up a cathedral to embrace congregational use, as had happened for example at Ely or Salisbury. The screen was kept: the choir stalls and the screens behind them replaced. Almost the only old works which could be retained were the 13th-century misericords re-used in the later stalls, and the fine early 14th-century Bishop's Throne.

Next there was the new reredos. Scott did a very bad design for a sculptured triptych, and when it was erected, in June 1873, Archdeacon Phillpotts, Diocesan Chancellor and a doctrinaire low-churchman, petitioned Bishop Temple, claiming it was unauthorised, illegal and idolatrous.

The Bishop acted in the prescribed form, and on 18 April 1874 read to a packed Chapter House the opinion of Justice Keating that it was indeed illegal, and that it must be replaced by a stone screen without images and bearing the ten commandments. At once all restoration work was stopped and the workmen paid off. It soon started again: the Chapter retained the reredos, arguing that the injunctions against imagery were only directed against those used for superstitious purposes, for which the new sculpture was not intended. In July 1876 the choir was finished and opened: the interior work had cost £20,000. The nave was then cleaned and repaired; noticeable is the pulpit, a memorial to Bishop Patteson of Melanesia, murdered in 1871. In October 1877 the whole was reopened: £50,000 had been spent in seven years, most of this, despite the amount of heat generated, conservatively.

St Albans, too, involved much controversy and untold writing, and brings in, for the last time and in full flight, Lord Grimthorpe, though Scott took only a small part. The Abbey church was sold to the town in 1539, and was by now in great disrepair, despite attention from L. N. Cottingham in 1832-3; a public footpath ran through it to the east of the altar, and east of this it was used as a grammar school. In 1856 there was a movement to restore the Abbey as a cathedral; Scott was selected as architect and reported on its state. Any action, like most subscriptions, being contingent on the formation of a see, nothing was done until 1870, when the rector, after examining a crushed pier of the central tower, sent for Scott, who advised shoring the eastern tower arch and rebuilding the crushed pier. As work proceeded it was found that openings in the presbytery wall, the removal in parts of the flint and Roman brick outer skin of the tower and a 5 ft diameter hole under the south-east pier which was strutted up and filled with rubbish, as if an attempt at mining had been made, had weakened it very much and all the tower arches had to be shored and bricked up. Scott himself was ill, but he told his eldest son, who told the office manager Wood, who told Chapple, the clerk of works, what to do. By Christmas 1871 all was safe, the hole filled up with brickwork, the faulty stone replaced and the whole held together with iron bolts; the external plastering was removed, or perhaps fell off, during the operations.

Bells were hung and pealed for the first time for many years, but in February 1882 the 'new chimes' fell just before afternoon service, fragments of ceiling injuring two people. In 1872 tons of earth, which had piled up against the building sometimes up to 10 ft deep, were removed, and levels were reduced internally; in so doing portions of the 14th-century shrine of St Alban were recovered and when the blocked arches at the east end were opened more were found, and 2000 fragments were eventually pieced together and restored. The presbytery and Ramryge chapel were repaired, the exterior stonework of the Lady Chapel restored and part of the south-aisle re-roofed. The five leaning bays at the western end were righted only a short while before Scott's death and the clerestory windows partly restored. The Abbey gatehouse was repaired and the grammar school moved into it. Scott was assailed on one side by an ill-informed and stupid amateur, J. G. Loftie, who complained with a wealth of inaccurate instances that terrible things were done, whilst Grimthorpe on the other hand wanted sweeping action. When

Gilbert Scott died and John Oldrid Scott carried on everyone — Street, Christian, Blomfield, Morris, Grimthorpe, Earl Cowper, Neale, Chapple, White, Lord Caenarvon, Loftie — had an opinion on what ought or ought not to be done, and mostly in respect of the pitch of the nave roof: John Oldrid and Street had a splendid quarrel in print over this, and Chapple and White another over a corbel table, but in November 1879, the funds of the restoration committee being overspent, it was found that Grimthorpe had applied for a faculty to continue the work himself, and this, despite opposition, he obtained. He paid off the debt of over £3000, and himself spent a quarter of a million — literally a fortune — on restoration to his own design, noticeably the west front, which is almost entirely his. He had, as William Morris put it in 1890, 'bought the people who ought to have taken care of the building and put them in his pocket'.

At Rochester Cathedral, Cottingham undertook a restoration in 1825-30, Lewis Vulliamy work in 1845, Scott (previously consulted on minor matters) another restoration in 1871, Sedding the stalls, and Pearson's west front followed in 1892. Lastly, in 1905 Scott's one-time pupil, C. H. Fowler, took down and rebuilt Cottingham's central tower. Scott, with £40,000 in hand, restored the mutilated north side and east end of the choir and presbytery; the east end had three lancets below with later tracery (perhaps Cottingham's work) and a Perpendicular window above, which was replaced by lancets, and the gables of choir and east transepts were raised to their former height: the roofs have however never been raised to match. The choir and presbytery floors were restored to their original levels and paved with tiles based in design on old tiles then recovered. The clerestory and triforium of the nave were strengthened, and the nave walls underpinned. The screen remained, but the removal of some woodwork (perhaps, again, Cottingham's) in the choir revealed wall paintings representing a diaper with lions and fleurs-de-lys. Scott concluded that such decoration had once covered the whole of the side walls behind the stalls and reproduced it up to the string course: garish but no doubt correct. The exterior works were completed at the end of 1873, the interior later. Reredos, throne, and organ case (of 1878) followed. The lack of contemporary reference suggests that controversy was avoided.

Colonel Akroyd of Halifax took an interest in Selby Abbey and in 1865 he and Scott inspected it. The building was in a graceless, neglected state: the collapsed central tower had been rebuilt in 1702, the nave, unused, was divided from the choir by a blocked chancel arch and had a flat roof, the east end was largely a Gothick rebuild, unscholarly but not without charm, all the walls were well buried in earth. Scott thought that the insecure and heavily buttressed nave south wall, the central tower and the west end with its two towers, should be rebuilt, the missing south transept re-created, and the west end rebuilt with two new towers. The cost was put at over £50,000, so not surprisingly nothing was done. Scott was once more approached late in 1871 and during the subsequent two years he took off the flat roof and underpinned the south wall of the nave, lifting it back into place hydraulically as in so many other instances and removing the unsightly buttresses. In these he found pieces of the south aisle vaulting. The nave and aisle roofs were remade to high pitch and re-ceiled. The triforium and north porch were much rebuilt. Floors and the ground outside were lowered. This completed the first phase of the work: Ruskin was unimpressed and wrote 'all be-Scottified'. (Yet Ruskin must still have had some regard for Scott: as recently as 1872 he had consulted him over a proposed fountain on one of the greens at Carshalton in Surrey.)

The church remained under the care of the Scott family until 1951: first John Oldrid Scott, then Charles Marriott Oldrid Scott his son. In 1889-90 the former was at work south of the crossing. On 19 October 1906 a serious fire occurred, obliterating much of Sir Gilbert's work. In 1907 the nave was repaired, in 1909 the choir restored and the upper stages of the plain central tower rebuilt in the Gothic style, in 1912 the south transept was rebuilt on the same lines as the north and probably to Sir Gilbert Scott's design. In 1935, the upper stage of the western tower was completed.

Canterbury was under the care of George Austin and his son, H. G. Austin, for many years from 1820. Scott stated in 1860 that he had been engaged in works to the upper part of Becket's chapel, but in 1877 that he had done no structural work at all. After being retained in 1875 he, perhaps at the instance of Beresford Hope, but to the disquiet of others, replaced Archbishop Tenison's choir stalls executed by John Smallwell in 1704 by a restoration, albeit on very slight evidence, of Prior Eastry's stalls of 1304, executed by Farmer and Brindley for £6000 in 1878-9.

At Durham, in 1859, restoration of the central tower had been put in hand by Walton and Robson with Scott watching over all.

E. R. Robson, a local man, recently a pupil in Scott's office, was now architect to the Dean and Chapter. Scott says he did not work here on his own until in 1875 he rearranged the choir — indeed, the Chapter was so anxious to have him do the work that they waited for him to come back from Italy. In 1845 Bishop Cosin's mid-17th-century screen had been removed, and the choir stall canopies were chopped into lengths and pushed back between the columns, thus opening up the length of the Cathedral — a somewhat early example. Scott did not, or could not, recover the Cosin bits, but repositioned the side stalls and canopies and, considering that no cathedral suffered so much for want of a chancel screen, designed a light open marble screen, not without opposition from a few Canons. He also designed the variegated marble chancel paving, lectern, pulpit (a rich affair in alabaster supported on the backs of small lions and costing over £1000) and replaced a sculptured altar front dating from 1845 by needlework: both screen and pulpit are out of sympathy with the Norman work; the lectern is 'laboriously ornate and highly dangerous to the reader's shins'.[16]

The organ case and repairs to the stalls were done at the same time by C. Hodgson Fowler, another old Scott pupil, now chapter architect. But when the Bishop was asked to preach at the reopening of the church in October 1876 he declined. He thought the money would be better spent in new churches than in work which he disliked and thought expensive and wasteful.

The last year of Scott's life was saddened by a storm about 'restoration'. It started with William Morris. One could not expect that Morris and Scott should understand each other. Morris, securely cushioned by an adequate private income, yet profitably using his wealth and time to study many arts and contribute something to all of them; the anarchist who supported in Trafalgar Square his belief that ultimately the state would wither away; whose prose and verse romances unfold a weird and brutal vision of the middle ages; who is supposed to have pronounced, 'If a chap can't compose an epic poem while he's weaving tapestry he'd better shut up, he'll never do any good at all'. Morris stands contrasted with Scott, painfully conscious of his position as a self-made man, with his clerical family connections and noble business connections; who had spoken of 'the quaint absurdities of old Cobbett' and whose silent politics were those of the country conservatives who call themselves 'Independent'; who had studious and antiquarian tastes, yet forced himself to relax by dining in the terrifying company of Bishops. But now Morris, forgetting how many churches bore his firm's stained glass in Scott's windows, exploded intemperately into print in *The Athenaeum*, which had, as a change from being wittily sarcastic about three-volume novels badly written by anonymous ladies, been taking side-kicks at the restorers.

My eye just now caught the word "restoration" in the morning paper, and, on looking closer, I saw that this time it is nothing less than the Minster of Tewkesbury that is to be destroyed by Sir Gilbert Scott. Is it altogether too late to do something to save it — it and whatever else of beautiful and historical is still left us on the sites of the ancient buildings we were once so famous for? Would it not be of some use once for all, and with the least delay possible, to set on foot an association for the purpose of watching over and protecting those relics which, scanty as they are now become, are still wonderful treasures, all the more priceless in this age of the world, when the newly-invented study of living history is the chief joy of so many of our lives?... our ancient buildings are not mere ecclesiastical toys, but sacred monuments of the nation's growth and hope.[17]

Not a sentiment to bring the clergy flocking in thousands to the banner of the infant Society for the Protection of Ancient Buildings, which was the outcome of Morris's endeavour in the early part of 1877. It gave Morris and Webb opportunity to dash up and down the country being rude to clergymen (occasionally, indeed, not without reason) in the same way, but for the opposite reason, as the equally militant members of the Cambridge Camden Society used nearly forty years previously. The church at Inglesham, Wiltshire, retaining an accretion of furnishings, some of doubtful artistic value, is an example of Morris's philosophy in action.

Sir Edmund Lechmere, chairman of the Tewkesbury Abbey Restoration Committee, fearing its effect on funds, showed Scott the letter. He replied saying how he was in favour of conservative restoration. Sir Edmund then wrote that others might have sinned, but the Tewkesbury restoration would be very conservative. Morris, excited, retorted that it could never be put back in its former state: indeed under Scott's care restoration would not turn out to have been 'conservative' at all. The building in its present state hurt no-one: the works should be put off until architecture recovered from its present wholly experimental condition.

But what exactly happened? Typically, the chancel of the great abbey church had been cut off by a screen bearing an organ, adapting it for congregational use. The interior stone was damaged and whitewashed, the great east window an insertion of 1686, the nave and transept roofs of 1820, the pews and transept galleries of 1795. Scott wished to fit up the nave temporarily for service, clean and repair the stonework, do some reflooring, remove galleries, choir stalls and screen, move the organ to a transept, replace stalls, fronts and canopies, screen and seats, provide a new lectern and pulpit and add to the reredos.

In 1872 Thomas Collins, the local builder much employed by Scott, offered to do substantially that work, except for the screen and pulpit, within the sum of £3000 which had been promised. It seems that little was done at this time; a contract with Collins for £2285 was finally dated 22 February 1875, and completed in a little over a year. It included repairing the roof and cleaning and colouring the interior but no exterior work, nor the rearrangement of the choir, for the manner in which this was to be undertaken was still being discussed in June 1876. This was all that was done in Scott's lifetime. So Morris was being at once hasty and laggard in 1877. The next contract was dated April 1878, and £6300 was spent in 1877-78 completing the work, so that when decayed stone and roofs required £25,000 spending in 1956 it was possible to speak of the Scotts' work as contributing to its 'present excellent state'.[18]

J. J. Stevenson, Scott's former pupil, then took a hand in the row. He had already, on 2 February 1875, read a paper before the Architectural Association on the 'Queen Anne Style'.[19] Gothic, he said, was all right for churches, but there were difficulties in adapting Gothic forms to 19th-century houses and those who loved old Gothic had abandoned it for Renaissance in domestic work. 'The free classic styles were the vernacular architecture with a touch of life added.' Scott's last entry in *Recollections*, early in 1878, was a note on 'Queen Anne', suggesting that it started from the difficulty of accommodating sash windows to Gothic, but now no detail was too antique for this new style.

So on 28 May 1877, Stevenson, on behalf of the Society, rent his former master at the Royal Institute of British Architects in a paper entitled 'Architectural Restoration: its Principles and Practice'.[20]

For many years I have felt that restorations, as usually conducted, were a mistake; that they were destroying the old art, and obliterating the history of the country. But it seemed useless to say anything, and the few whom I knew to hold similar views were equally hopeless. The mass of the architectural profession was against us; the clergy, who had the chief say with regard to churches, the most numerous and important of our old buildings, considered it a duty to art and to religion to restore them, giving liberally their exertions and their money, and exhorting all upon whom they could influence to aid in the good work. The tide in favour of restoration was so strong, that it seemed hopeless to oppose it — the only result injuring oneself, and offending friends, for it was useless to speak without giving examples of the harm and destruction we believed were being done...

To illustrate the present practice of restoration, I have taken my instances from the practice of Sir Gilbert Scott, Mr Street, and others, whose standing and eminence are a guarantee that their work is a favourable example of the system.

I take a paper of advice to the promoters of restorations, issued by the Institute of British Architects, as a fair exponent of the present system. It is entitled "Conservation of Ancient Monuments". It seems to me to consist mainly of commendations for their destruction. This paper bears the date March 1865. It was, I believe, the result of an admirable address on the evils of restoration read by Sir Gilbert Scott to this Institute in 1862. It is difficult after reading this address to believe that any more old churches would be destroyed by restoration. Yet the progress has been going steadily on, approved by clergy and architects, the press, and the public (as holy work).

He referred to the formation of the Society, and deplored the tacit assumption that the Reformation was a mistake and that everything later should be destroyed, such as the choir screen at Canterbury, or indeed that any Perpendicular additions should be swept away also; instancing the tracery in the aisle windows at Durham, the chapel at Chester which Scott had been criticised for replacing, or the flat roof at Jarrow which Scott exchanged for a steeply pitched affair, to the ruination of the tower. Indeed, no period was safe. At Canterbury a Norman west tower had been pulled down and rebuilt as a copy of its late fellow. Nor was the practice of stripping plaster off wholesale commended: the tower at St Albans, the interiors at Burford (by Street) and at Heckington, were bad examples. The architect was a forger using stone carefully selected to be indistinguishable from the old. Yet perhaps a few churches might still be left untouched, as authentic and continuous records of the past?

Beresford Hope rose to the occasion in the discussion which followed. 'A gospel of despair and death', said he, 'Everything that was bad in English church architecture, every bit of stinting and scamping by the village carpenter in league with the insolvent bricklayer under the pastoral superintendence of Parson Trulliver

— all and everything was to be sacred.' He jibed at 'laborious imitations of Queen Anne work'. He pointed out that the Canterbury tower had been taken down forty-five years before, in the 1830s; 'the wanton destruction of the tower was received with indignation, and it was that indignation which was one of the first rallying cries of that ecclesiological movement which Mr Stevenson deprecated' and maintained that there was no intention of destroying the screen.

Scott was no doubt taken aback. The meeting, or at least, Ferrey, expected him to speak — and he said wittily and temperately, that he hardly knew what to say. Stevenson had the advantage of never having restored a church: he was not only incapable of committing sin, but had never experienced temptation. Scott admitted his ability might not be equal to the task, his judgement might be wrong, but he advanced himself to be neither inconsistent nor critical of others to benefit himself. At Canterbury it was a question of whether two very interesting features should be shown, or one be hidden by the other: at Chester, the Perpendicular chapel had been quite rotten; it had taken him five years to trace out the details of its predecessor, which had been rebuilt mostly with its own material (a statement which *The Builder* regarded as 'a somewhat courageous one'): at St Albans the plaster was not removed but fell off.

The discussion was adjourned to Monday the 11th, and *The Builder*[21] pointed out how the mediaeval church builders removed the work of their predecessors without the slightest compunction. 'The war cry of a new sect of architects and amateurs, who wish to make their voices heard in some way or other...the teaching of common sense in this matter is, as we have long endeavoured to show, — touch all old buildings and monuments with reverence, but prevent the necessity for wholesale renovation hereafter by careful maintenance and repairs in time.'

On the 11th, Scott read a long paper which he had written in the interim.[22] He recalled how 'When Napoleon III was told that a prophetic authority had pronounced him to be Anti-Christ, he replied, "He does me too much honour!". Much the same is the honour intended to be conferred on me'. He welcomed the Society as recruits to the expression of sentiments which he himself had reiterated for thirty-six years, but warned it against over-enthusiasm. He, himself, was used to being misunderstood. He quoted correspondence of 1841 with J.L. Petit over Stafford; his paper 'On the Faithful Restoration of our Ancient Churches' of 1848, urging the most conservative treatment; Ruskin's *Seven Lamps of Architecture*, precursor of Stevenson's plea against all restoration; his paper of 1862, followed by the Institute's handout of 1865; his Presidential address eight years later, that of 1874 when Ruskin refused the Royal Gold Medal, 'the ominous words, so sadly realised, *Donec templum refeceris*'; and that of the next year. He referred, in the way of practice as opposed to theory, his part in enabling Norman Shaw to repair the Jacobean fittings at St John, Leeds; to Llandaff Cathedral, where Mr Wood had turned part of the ruined interior into a double of one of the public halls at Bath and where Pritchard and Seddon had 'rooted out the barbarism of the eighteenth century and reinstated the beauty of the thirteenth'; to St Davids, where he saved the structure from collapse, made it watertight, and only altered one window from Perpendicular to Early English; to Chesterfield, carved up with galleries; to another church where 'a noble family held an octagonal glazed pew, hung like a bird-cage from the chancel arch, and so well contrived that, by facing about east or west, his lordship could attend either the nave or chancel service'; to Buckingham; and to Hillesden. Stevenson must have been uncomfortable.

The anti-party turned to the irrepressible Loftie, who wrote a long article on 'Thorough Restoration'[23] castigating Scott for ruining St Michael's, St Albans by pulling out Bacon's pew. Scott proved that what he had destroyed was of no age to be Bacon's pew. Loftie complained that the plaster had been stripped from the tower of St Albans abbey and the interior gutted, and that Canterbury choir had been ruined. Scott gave him short shift in a long-winded letter.[24]

There was a need for such a society as Morris's: there is even more a need for such societies today, when even some of Scott's own best buildings are in danger. But Scott, as church architects went, was conscientious and knowledgeable: his real enemy was the size of his practice, so that for each work of conservative restoration he could point to, his honesty compelled him to admit to another where theory and practice had not met.

At the end of his life, particularly, some restorations were being undertaken on very conservative principles. For these we have no doubt to thank such assistants as W. S. Weatherley, whose restoration of Shere, Surrey about 1895 is generally considered a model, or

H. Thackeray Turner, whose work in the Guildford area bears comparison with Webb, or indeed the influence of G. G. Scott Junior.

Morris's unrepentant view is enshrined in his 1889 'judgement' on Bradford on Avon church; 'scraped to death by G. Scott the (happily) dead dog'.[25] Curiously, it wasn't a Scott restoration.

Scott was now worried that his practice dwindled off, and at the costliness of his mode of living: perhaps less money was being made because more care was being taken, though in 1878 his fee income was in excess of £7000, equivalent to at least £140,000 at present values. As Ham was expensive and John Oldrid and Mary Ann did not much care for it, in early 1875 he purchased, surprisingly, Courtfield House, a large new four-storeyed, classical, house in Courtfield Gardens, Kensington, just off the Cromwell Road.[26]

On 18 September 1876 he wrote a letter of complaint to the Kensington Vestry and followed with another to *The Times*. He had purchased Courtfield House, yet the Vestry had neglected for two years to pave the Cromwell Road beyond its intersection with Gloucester Road; as a result houses in Cromwell Road remained unlet — he himself owned several such. It appears that he also owned property in Kensington Church Street. Publicity had its effect: during the winter the road was made up, and late in 1876 the family removed from Ham to Courtfield House, not without misgivings on Scott's part.

Early 1878, when they had been there over a year, was a dismal time; apart from the cold winter weather, Lord Derby had resigned, trade was greatly depressed, there was famine in India, trouble in Ireland, war in the Balkans, and the 'anti-scrape' controversy at home. And in March, in the high, darkly furnished, gaslit rooms at Courtfield Gardens, Scott became unwell again. He had long suffered from varicose veins in the left leg and on 19 March he was, in much discomfort, ordered to bed by his doctor. He suffered also from 'Rheumatism situated ... in the muscles between the ribs'. On the 25th he felt better, and met, and lunched with, Dr Allan Thomson and his companion in connection with the Bute Hall of Glasgow University. Next day he recounted to his manservant, John Pavings, 'a quaint dream which he had had, over which they had a good laugh together. "In the course of it ... I saw my dear wife: I never saw her more plainly in my life"'. That evening he wrote out a cheque in favour of 'a Roman Catholic architect who had had great misfortunes and was lying ill'. Later, says George Gilbert Scott Junior.

114 St Asaph Cathedral, choir, largely rebuilt by Scott, 1866-9. The right hand windows are of Scott's original design, the left hand triplet is based on evidence found during the work

115 Lincoln Cathedral, choir. Scott's 1863 pulpit, at the right, is in keeping with the mediaeval woodwork

116 St Leonard, Ludlow, 1870-1. A late version of the two-celled chapel

117 Mirfield, 1869-71. Longitudinal section, one of a set of coloured contract drawings on cartridge paper
Victoria and Albert Museum

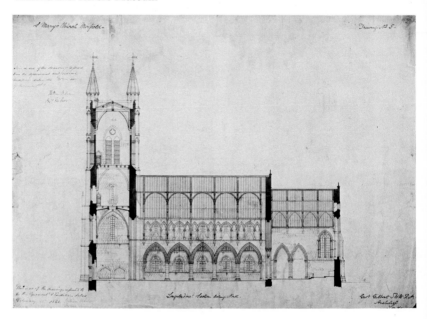

118 Kensington, St Mary Abbots, 1870-2. View
The Builder xxviii. 11

119 St Mary's Homes, Godstone. View from road

120 Savernake hospital, 1871-2. A development from Scott's schools, with 'old English' elements introduced
The Builder xxxi. 186

121 Brill's Baths, Brighton, about 1874. Rotunda immediately prior to demolition in 1929
The Chief Librarian, East Sussex County Council

122 St Pancras Station, 1866-76. A 19th-century view
National Monuments Record

123 St Pancras Station. Interior of coffee room
British Railways Board

124 St Pancras Station. Detail of stair
National Monuments Record

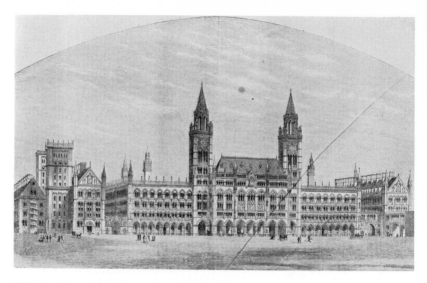

125 Law Courts, Holborn, 1867. Competition entry, view
The Builder, xxv, 225

126 Dundee, Albert Institute. 1865-9

127 Glasgow University, view
The Builder xxvii. 967

128 Berlin,
Parliament House, a
detail of the competi-
tion entry with J.O.
Scott, 1872

129 All Saints, Gloucester, 1875. North-east view

130 Bombay University, hall, 1876. Perhaps Scott's last secular Gothic design: a characteristic importation of Gothic forms into a foreign country
The Builder xxxiv. 15

131 Edinburgh Cathedral, interior
The Builder xxxi. 167

132 London, Lincoln's Inn Buildings, 1875

133 Clarkson Monument, Wisbech, 1879. A late development of the Eleanor
Cross or the Albert Memorial

134 Exeter Cathedral, restored 1869-77. East end of choir, showing Scott's controversial reredos

135 Rochester Cathedral, restored. West side of north transept: one of a set of contract drawings for restoration about 1872. Such drawings were made in ink and wash on cartridge paper and copies traced
The Dean and Chapter of Rochester Cathedral

136 Tewkesbury Abbey before restoration
National Monuments Record

137 Tewkesbury Abbey after restoration
National Monuments Record

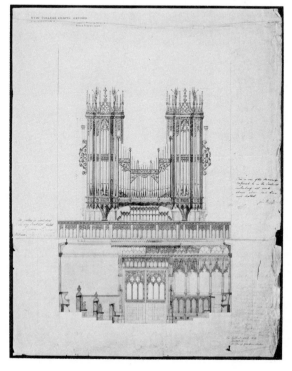

138 Oxford, New
College Chapel, con-
tract drawing of organ
case and returned
stalls, about 1877
Victoria and Albert
Museum

He talked cheerfully until about eleven p.m., when his man handed him his Bible and hymn-book, and left him for a little. He returned for a few minutes. "It is pleasant," said my father, "to see your fat face. Goodnight. Schlafen Sie wohl".

About four o'clock in the morning his bell rang. Pavings finding him coughing violently gave him some brandy, and at Sir Gilbert's request prepared a poultice. While thus engaged, my father said to him, "You had better make up a bed on the sofa; for if you leave me, you will find me gone in the morning". The instant the poultice was placed over the region of the heart, my father called out, "Oh, it is come again! Lift me up". My brother John was summoned at once, but my father never recovered consciousness, and died some twenty minutes afterwards. A little before he died he opened his eyes, and lifted them upwards, as though in prayer. This was the last gesture he made: the eyelids fell, and after a few heavy moans all was over.[27]

The funeral pomp on Saturday, 6 April, almost surpassed that of Royalty. How the Kensington Vestry must have congratulated itself on its perspicacity! Along the newly metalled Cromwell Road ran the cortege with its thirty-eight carriages, one of them Royal, filled with relations, notables and men from the office, on its way to Westminster Abbey, for Dean Stanley, forestalling an approach from the Royal Institute of British Architects, intimated his wish that the body should lie within those walls, which Scott loved, besides Scott's own great nave pulpit.

A vast concourse of people of all classes of society crowded round the grave and filled to overflowing the great Abbey, as if homage was due not only to the eminent architect but also to the self-made man, although many of them could not have well appreciated his life's work. Mitford, of the Office of Works: Lord John Manners, MP, the Postmaster General: Redgrave from the Royal Academy: Charles Barry Junior, the President of the Royal Institute of British Architects: Frederic Ouvry, the President of the Society of Antiquaries: and Beresford Hope, MP, President of the Council of the Architectural Museum and Scott's unfailing supporter in ecclesiology for nearly forty years, acted as pall bearers. Deputations of members of many societies connected with architecture, archaeology, art and learning also attended. The next day Dean Stanley preached a splendid funeral sermon, on the text 'I was glad when they said unto me, let us go into the house of the Lord', which was printed as an appendix to *Recollections* and should be read in its entirety.[28] The tombstone was designed by Street: the coffin bears the legend, *Viri probi architecti peritissimi.*

Epilogue

Scott's will was dated November 1876 and proved at under £130,000; in present day terms he was a millionaire. Probably every penny of this had been made out of his practice. He left £200 to his servant Pavings, £3000 to his youngest son, and released his brother William from a mortgage. He then provided for George Gilbert Junior and John Oldrid to share his architectural books and his sketch books (of these the former took the even numbers and the latter the odd), and for them jointly to have an option on the office if they went into partnership within twelve months. If not, John Oldrid was to have it. They were, together, or separately and taking what they would, to finish the outstanding jobs: if neither wanted a job, the executors were to appoint someone. All the papers referring to the practice were to be kept together for at least five years, when the four sons were each to have equal shares in them.

But after the funeral was over and the emotion had died down the effect on the office was perhaps less than one might have expected. Life went on, and there were sixty or more works in progress. Abbeys, cathedrals, minsters, churches, chapels and monuments, even a castle, a hall, a court, a university — all were there. This work was being handled, it appears, by an office of only eighteen.[1]

Though his will provided for two of his sons to continue, in the event arrangements were made for John Oldrid to do so alone. Even though some of the faithful left the office, like Arthur Baker who set up on his own in 1878, and Irvine who joined Pearson, he must have carried on much as usual, for he had had a responsible position for many years, although the volume of work quickly fell. A mature family man approaching forty, he lived at Oxted in Surrey, with a comfortable income. His son Charles Marriott Oldrid Scott continued a small practice until his death in 1954. There are 222 known works for the period 1878-1913.

Scott's lectures and drawings, many by W. S. Weatherley, for his
Royal Academy lectures were assembled and corrected for publication in two volumes by John Murray in 1879, entitled *Lectures on the
rise and development of Mediaeval Architecture delivered at the
Royal Academy.*

After the five years stipulated by the will, there was a great office
turnout. The accumulation of forty years must have been formidable. It is said that Irvine subsequently bought two tons of
drawings from a waste paper merchant and much ended up at the
Bodleian Library in Oxford. During the war years of the 1940s, they
were disposed of as waste. Not even a record of the content can be
found.[2] Other material is thought to have disappeared when Sir
Giles Scott's office suffered war damage. Even so, it is fortunate
that a large number of drawings and John Oldrid Scott's half of the
sketch books are among a sizeable amount of surviving material.

Scott's eldest son's later career was tragic. Shortly after his father's
death he astonished his friends and relations by joining the Roman
church. He edited *Recollections* for publication in a spirit of filial
piety, pruning a long manuscript by omitting much of personal
interest and of personalities. Then in July 1883 as a result of
overwork and drink — he was not a methodical worker — he
suffered a breakdown, imagining he had been shot at on the rifle
range on Wimbledon Common, and that the police conspired
against him. Dukinfield Scott discussed with his wife his 'immoral
relations' with other women. He was sent to Bethlem Hospital on
20 July 1883: eight weeks later he escaped, and on 19 November was
arrested, after threatening a servant at his parents-in-law's house in
Eastbourne with a knife, and subsequently sent to an asylum at
West Malling. He escaped again on 11 December and went to
Rouen, no doubt to be with the "French lady" who figures in the
story, returning the next month. Dukinfield then applied to have
him restrained under the Lunacy Act of 1862. The hearing, before
Mr Justice Dearman and a special jury of 23, terminated by his
sending the Judge a postcard in verse containing his opinion about
lawyers generally. He was found of unsound mind in England, but
declared sane in France and carried on his English practice from
Rouen. He gradually withdrew from practice, allowing John Oldrid
to finish his work, and, dropsical, died on 6 May 1897 in his father's
St Pancras Hotel, aged 57. *The Builder* belatedly published a notice
saying there had been difficulty in getting anyone to write his

obituary and summed up his work 'among those ... attracted by ... later English Gothic and early Renaissance styles which had been neglected and ... despised during the rage after everything early and foreign'. His works at Pembroke College, Cambridge and the demolished St Agnes, Kennington may be instanced as outstandingly successful examples of his architecture.[3] His second son, Giles Gilbert Scott, born in 1880, and his third, Adrian Gilbert Scott, born in 1882, both took architecture as a profession. Giles was articled to Temple Moore, himself a pupil of the young man's father, and, although a Roman Catholic, won an open competition for Liverpool Cathedral in 1902, when he was twenty-two. This set him up in practice — indeed, the job went on for the rest of his long life — and thereafter his career strangely paralleled that of his grandfather, in its amalgam of major works, successes, controversies, criticisms, and honours. His practice continues under his son, Richard Gilbert Scott. There have been other architects in the family.

The two remaining sons of Sir Gilbert's were not architects. Alwyne, a barrister, died in November 1878, aged twenty-nine. Dukinfield, who studied classics, then engineering, then botany, held academic appointments in London and after 1889 had a notable career as a pioneer palaeobotanist, working on the traces of plants to be found in coal. He married a student, had three sons who all died young and four daughters, and lived comfortably on independent means until his death in 1935 at East Woodhay, Hampshire.[4]

Notes

1

[1] Here he knew the poet Cowper and the gloomy cleric John Newton.

[2] See J. Scott, *Life of the Rev Thomas Scott*, 1822, 682, for a revealing account of the death of his four-year-old daughter Anne in 1780.

[3] G. G. Scott, *Personal and Professional Recollections*, 27. Hereinafter cited as *Recollections*.

[4] *Recollections*, 10-11.

[5] Nathaniel Gilbert and Melville Horne were the names of the ministers who had led the emigration of 1000 to Sierra Leone sponsored by the Church Missionary Society.

[6] *Recollections*, 26.

[7] Sir William Chambers (1723-96), the foremost official architect after 1760, published a *Treatise on Civil Architecture* in 1759 and subsequently. James Stuart (1713-88) and Nicholas Revett (1720-1804) measured and drew all the principal monuments of antiquity in Athens for publication as *The Antiquities of Athens* in four volumes from 1762-1830.

[8] *Recollections*, 31.

[9] ibid, 55.

[10] ibid, 58.

[11] Peter Nicholson (1765-1844), a cabinet maker by trade but later County Surveyor of Cumberland, devoted his life to the application of scientific methods in building and to writing at least twenty-eight books on building and mathematical matters. It is not clear to which of these Scott refers: the most likely seems *Principles of Architecture*.

[12] *Recollections*, 58.

[13] Sketch book No 7.

[14] ibid.

[15] The Market was demolished with the building of Charing Cross Station in 1862.

[16] These drawings are still extant in the RIBA collection.

[17] *Recollections*, 73. Colvin, *Biographical Dictionary of English Architects 1660-1840*, 504.

[18] *Recollections*, 75.

[19] ibid, 76.

[20] In the catalogue it is incorrectly indexed.

[21] According to *Architectural History*, xix, 55, Voysey, Kempthorne's master and grandfather of C. F. A. Voysey, did so: according to Mozley, *Reminiscences*, 130-1, Scott did so himself. See also J. Brandon-Jones, 'C. F. A. Voysey 1857-1941', *Arch. Ass. Jnl.*, lxxii, 241.

[22] *Recollections*, 74.

[23] *Architectural History*, xix, 55: Colvin, op cit, 338.

[24] Probably Thomas Frankland Lewis, possibly George Nicholls.

[25] *Recollections*, 77.

2

[1] *Recollections*, 79.

[2] ibid, 79.

[3] *The Builder*, vii, 452.

[4] Sketch Book No 67.

[5] As many as forty can be more or less reliably identified.
   Moffatt. Amesbury (1836).
   Scott in the area from London through the East Midlands to Cheshire: Amersham (1838), Belper (1836), Buckingham (1836), Lichfield (1838), Loughborough (1837), Lutterworth (1839), Macclesfield (1843), Newcastle under Lyme (1838), Northampton (1836), Oundle (1836), Rushden, Towcester (1836), Uttoxeter, Winslow (1835).
   Moffatt in the West of England with Scott's assistance: Bideford (1837), Bodmin, Clutton, Flax Bourton (1837), Gloucester, Liskeard (1837), Mere (1838), Newton Abbot (1837), Penzance (1838), Redruth (1838), St Austell, St Columb (1838), Tavistock (1837), Tiverton (1836), Totnes (1836), Truro, Williton (1836).
   Eastern England: Boston (1837), Hundleby (1837), Louth.
   East of London: Billericay (1839), Dunmow (1838), Edmonton (1839).
   West of London: Guildford (1836), Windsor (1839).
   I am much indebted to Mrs Anna Dickens for help in this connection.

[6] *Recollections*, 82-83.

[7] As, for example, Latimer.

[8] It is amusing to note that part has suffered the introduction of bogus half-timbered work.

[9] Sketch Book No 19.

[10] The house was demolished on the building of the Admiralty Arch in 1911.

[11] Why, one wonders, were no children in residence at the time of the census in May 1841?

[12] Number 246: now in the RIBA collection.

[13] *Architectural History*, xix, 56.

[14] It survives, with little external alteration, as Snaresbrook Crown Court.

[15] The previous building by R. F. Brettingham was only about forty years old, but perhaps it was too small.

[16] *The Builder*, vi, 190.

[17] All have sustained extensive alterations and additions.

[18] A further restoration took place in 1897.

[19] The warden's house, a semi-circular front added to the sham Gothic castle built as a gaol in 1758 at the north end of Buckingham Market place and known as 'Lord Cobham's Castle', has been dubiously attributed to Scott.

[20] See Clark, K., *The Gothic Revival*, 1950, 171.

[21] *Recollections*, 90-91. Buckland, Reader in Mineralogy at the University and later Dean of Westminster, was a learned, radical, and greatly respected geologist.

[22] There was then a stone roof. Its replacement by slates, and the repewing, were undertaken by the local practitioner Wilkinson in 1875.

[23] *Recollections*, 86.

[24] This interior is similar to that of J.H.Newman's church at Littlemore, near Oxford, as designed by A.J.Underwood about the same time.

[25] The north aisle and chancel were added to the designs of C.Hodgson Fowler, in 1909.

[26] These churches were later identified by G.G.Scott Junior in his editing of *Recollections*.

[27] Probably all the first six had chancels added later: Hanwell in 1897 by a high church local man, William Pywell, who copied Scott's work faithfully; Norbiton by Rushforth and Luck possibly in 1868; Turnham Green by James Brooks, himself a noted church architect, in 1887. Shaftesbury, for which Scott prepared chancel plans several years after building, waited until 1908. Frogmore is, rather oddly, of perfect apsidal basilican form, and, if indeed the attribution to Scott is certain, one wonders from where he got his inspiration.

[28] *Recollections*, 86.

[29] ibid 155. Sketch Book 7.

[30] The church was eventually built to designs by the Maidstone architect John Whichcord Senior.

[31] It was thus an earlier Minton connection than Penkhull.

[32] Edward Blore (1787-1879), an architect with a large practice 1816-49. See Colvin op cit 78-82.

[33] So called from the publications *Tracts for The Times* in which they propagated their views.

[34] *Recollections*, 88.

[35] ibid, 89.

[36] ibid, 88.

[37] ibid, 87.

[38] *The Ecclesiologist*, iii, 56.

[39] This was Cox of Oxford, who possibly did other carving here as well.

[40] The attribution of Wall is uncertain. It seems there was a competition in 1839, when Scott and Moffatt advertised for tenders. The building consecrated in 1843 is unlikely to be Scott's, as the style is unusual: indeed, it would be his only entirely new Perpendicular church. The large stones meticulously laid, with picked face and worked margins, are totally at variance with any other Scott church.

⁴¹ The two-celled church at Greenstead Green had a moulded brick spire, apparently an innovation, above another tower with an octagonal upper stage. The school and clergy house may also be by Scott.

⁴² Zeals, as built, is different from plans prepared in 1843, which showed a scheme with well-developed transepts. Its tower is octagonal, with a spire of 1876. The school seems of about the same time, and may possibly be by Scott.

⁴³ The parsonage is of the same date. The north aisle is of 1859, and the south aisle is of 1900. The 1935 vestry is rather different.

⁴⁴ Built on an insecure clay hillside, it had long been shored up by 1862. Plans were prepared for rebuilding on a larger scale and a design by Henry Curzon was accepted 'because it was so pretty' (*Tottenham and Edmonton Weekly Herald*, 21 March 1863). If this is the Henry Curzon who did work in Shropshire at this time, 'pretty' is an odd word, as he was a forceful and unconventional designer. At the end of 1865 a new nave and aisle had been attached to the old chancel, and the porch rebuilt. In 1869 the chancel was renewed. In 1873-4 a tower and spire more elaborate than originally proposed was erected. It is not clear whether the architect was Curzon, as his original design has been described as 'eccentric'. After further subsidence extensive engineering works were undertaken in 1953-4.

⁴⁵ Pevsner, N., *The Buildings of England: Warwickshire*, 1966, 469-70.

⁴⁶ Norbiton, Woking, Hanwell, Turnham Green, Shaftesbury, Birmingham, Bridlington, Zeals, and Wimbledon.

⁴⁷ *The Ecclesiologist*, iii, 56. The reference is to Hartshill.

⁴⁸ Donington Wood is a not very graceful hybrid, with short transepts, a nave, two bays of a chancel. Here, possibly for the first time, one notes alternate bands of square-ended and round-ended machine-made red tiles on the roof. The Duke of Sutherland paid for this church, as also for Holy Evangelists, Longton, of 1847.

⁴⁹ It is not clear whether this should be treated as new or restored. The mediaeval church had been largely rebuilt by John Johnson of Leicester in 1788. Its square nave with a curved bay and porch attached to the west end was not very pretty, and not to the mid-Victorian taste. The nave was rebuilt by Scott and Moffatt in 1843, in a rather gawky Perpendicular, perhaps to match the remains of the old chancel, with aisles, a western tower with parapets and spire, a high south porch, and internal galleries, the whole faced in flint with stone dressings. The chancel was also rebuilt, supposedly by Scott in 1860. The resultant building is well-situated but dull in detail.

⁵⁰ The church was originally designed, about 1844, as a small cruciform building with a south-western tower/porch. It was built, in 1846-8, as a large cruciform church with aisles, a curious bell gable, roundel windows in the clerestory, and flowing Decorated tracery.

⁵¹ At a cost of 3½d each.

⁵² Pevsner stated that the exterior had been 'over-restored', but the interior, containing items of the 16th and 17th centuries, does not seem to have been touched. This job came through Stevens, whose first wife came from this village.

⁵³ Scott recased the red sandstone church of 1736, introduced middle pointed windows, a south aisle, new roofs, a western timber bell turret and spirelit, and a

long chancel, and refitted it except for communion rail and pulpit. The glass in his east window, installed perhaps in 1852, is stated to be A. W. N. Pugin's last design.

⁵⁴ Drawings exist at the RIBA for the rebuilding of Barnes church (Surrey?), signed Scott and Moffatt. There is no evidence of the work having been done, and the church was much altered in 1904-8 and later.

⁵⁵ Also at the RIBA is a single Scott and Moffatt drawing for refitting Debenham, Suffolk.

⁵⁶ *Recollections*, 96.

⁵⁷ It was moved into the north transept when the 1898 reredos by Temple Moore was installed.

⁵⁸ *The Architects' Journal*, 17 January 1923, article by L. T. Moore.

⁵⁹ *The Ecclesiologist*, xxvii, 297-8.

⁶⁰ Now concealed by a ceiling of 1928-31.

⁶¹ In 1873 he provided an (unexecuted) design for a reredos and also a monument to John Charrington in the chancel.

⁶² Unpublished correspondence of the Oxford Architectural Society, 205. Further alterations were made in 1864-7 by Buckeridge, who had been Scott's pupil, with Scott as consultant. The north aisle was enlarged, reusing an Early English window. Organ chamber, vestry, and chancel stalls were added, and the old pulpit and screen (itself of the 1844 restoration) replaced.

⁶³ Possibly James Stanger, the benefactor of the restoration, had family connections in Scott's area of the East Midlands.

⁶⁴ That now in place was built in 1889 following the type of the west window. At the same time the present reredos was introduced, the architect for both being Ferguson, another former pupil of Scott's.

⁶⁵ Bodley's father was a Hull surgeon, friendly with the Hull Scotts; he retired to Brighton. G. F. Bodley's sister Georgiana married Scott's brother, Samuel.

⁶⁶ Richard Coad of Cornwall (perhaps a Moffatt connection) stayed for a long time. Edward Rumsey was another son of the Chesham doctor. H. E. B. Coe, later in practice with H. B. Garling, was a man of unfulfilled promise. Of C. Hynam, R. Lamprell, C. W. Orford, and E. Oliver nothing is ascertainable.

⁶⁷ He later changed his name to Cheaike and emigrated to Canada.

3

¹ *Recollections*, 116.

² George Edmund Street (1824-81) — see Street, A. E., *Memoir of G. E. Street*: Clarke, B. F. L., *Church Builders of the Nineteenth Century*, 146 et seq.

³ *Recollections*, 127.

⁴ The Clerk of Works was at first Mortimer, who was killed in an accident on the site. Scott, always an emotional and intemperate mourner, assisted his family and designed a memorial window at Witham, Essex. The Clerk of Works for the tower was Little, but the slightly sinister J. T. Chapple, who appears frequently in Scott's practice, was also involved. Burlison worked as chief assistant, spent some time in Hamburg, and even learned German, as did Scott to a limited extent.

[5] *The Ecclesiologist*, iv, 199.

[6] The letter is printed in full in *Recollections*, 135.

[7] *Recollections*, 130.

[8] *The Ecclesiologist*, xiv, 199.

[9] The stone carving, including the reredos of 1879, is by Edward Geflowski, a Pole much favoured by Scott.

[10] *The Ecclesiologist*, viii, 54.

[11] In 1892 there was a fire, and the rebuilding was undertaken by G. G. Scott, Junior and J. O. Scott. Further additions in the first decade of the present century were by Giles Gilbert Scott, the son of G. G. Scott, Junior.

[12] This is either L. N. Cottingham, by now a sick and elderly man, but perhaps the most careful restoring architect of the first half of the century, or his son N. J. Cottingham. See Colvin, op cit, 153-54.

[13] The work of Hiorn of Warwick.

[14] At Bradfield, Scott had already built the church of Sts Simon and Jude, a chapel of ease on a site given by Stevens adjoining the workhouse, which Scott and Moffatt may also possibly have designed in 1835.

[15] Scott was engaged on the extensive rebuilding of the nave and aisles at Mansfield Woodhouse about this time.

[16] This is perhaps based on examples at Hillingdon and Harmondsworth in Middlesex, which he had sketched in 1847.

[17] The latter kept up the connection, later designing buildings, becoming a school governor in 1883, and in 1868 marrying Mary Ann Stevens, a daughter of the Founder.

[18] *Recollections*, 156. See also Blackie, *Bradfield 1850-1975*, 1976, passim.

[19] The galleries in the north aisle and in the lower part of the tower were reserved to the school, and were not removed until 1887, the scholars having meantime moved into their new chapel nearby, also by Scott.

[20] The vestry of 1909 is by Sir Aston Webb.

[21] As the Bridgewater family gave £3500 of the £8000 it eventually cost, Ellesmere was no doubt a consequence of Worsley, started three years earlier. Charles Kynaston Mainwaring was another benefactor.

[22] It is stated that the vestry is by Scott (1866). When the churchyard was closed to interments in 1864, Scott designed the chapel, caretaker's house, walls, and gates of the new cemetery at Swan Hill.

[23] *The Ecclesiologist*, viii, 118.

[24] One can compare the present church with the careful description of the building in its previous state in *The Ecclesiologist*, v, 75.

[25] *Recollections*, 149-50.

[26] The tracery of the old window remains as an ornament in the garden of a house in Aylesbury.

[27] This is one of the restorations to which there are many contemporary references, eg *The Builder*, viii, 21, 264; xxiii, 301, 577; xxiv, 52, 729; xxvi, 417; *The Ecclesiologist*, ii, 59, 168; ix, 391, 401; x, 231.

[28] *The Builder*, vii, 581.

[29] The present altar rails are not his; the reredos is by A. W. Blomfield in 1875. Scott's contractor was G. Wyatt.

[30] Indeed, as a result of this address, the rood loft at Wing was demolished, against Scott's wish.

[31] Scott, G. G., *A Plea for the Faithful Restoration of our Ancient Churches.*

[32] James Essex (1822-84), see Colvin, op cit, 197-200.

[33] *Recollections*, 146.

[34] Its design was in the Royal Academy Exhibition in 1863.

[35] Seventy windows were treated up to 1866, involving the artists Gerente, Wailes, Warrington, Howes, N. J. Cottingham, Hardman, Lusson, Moore, Clutterbuck, and Wilmshurst.

[36] Designs had been made some years previously.

[37] Henry L'E. S. L'Estrange (1815-62), an amateur decorative painter, had also worked for Butterfield at St Andrew's, Holborn. See *The Ecclesiologist*, xxiv, 103: *Dictionary of National Biography*, xi, 996.

[38] Thomas Gambier Parry (1816-88), another moneyed dilettante, painted frescoes also at Gloucester Cathedral and Tewkesbury Abbey, and in his own church at Highnam, designed by Woodyer. See *Dictionary of National Biography*, xv, 386.

[39] John Birnie Philip (1824-75), see *Dictionary of National Biography*, xv, 1044.

[40] *The Ecclesiologist*, ix, 334.

[41] Samuel Cundy, the Abbey mason, gave material and financial aid.

[42] Hunt, H., *Pre-Raphaelitism and the Pre-Raphaelite Brotherhood*, 1905, 180.

[43] In 1877 he says, 'I, who am no investigator of antiquarian documents...' *Archaeological Journal*, xxxiv, 323.

[44] Some garish stained glass had already been obtained. This was replaced in 1902 by other glass in which Bodley had a hand.

[45] The Scott pulpit was removed in 1935 and replaced by the 17th-century pulpit which had been taken out in 1781. Scott also designed a marble pulpit for the nave, which was installed in 1862, removed for the coronation of Edward VII, and later presented to St Ann's Cathedral in Belfast.

[46] H. H. Armstead carved the figures and Salviati, who had recently revived the glass factories of Murano, near Venice, executed the mosaic 'last supper' designed by J. R. Clayton.

[47] This was replaced by a conjectural restoration of the previous Renaissance style altar in 1930.

[48] The doorways are by Gilbert Scott, possibly with the help of John Oldrid Scott, but the remainder is by J. L. Pearson, Scott's successor as Surveyor, one of the two finest designers of churches in revived Gothic, but insensitive and non-conservative as a restorer. Note also his work at Peterborough and his intended work at Lincoln and Hereford. See Clarke, B. F. L., *Church Builders of the Nineteenth Century*, 1938, 196-209; Fawcett, J. (ed), *Seven Victorian Architects*, 1974.

[49] *The Builder*, vii, 185.

[50] After which T.G.Jackson designed six boarding houses and the big school room.

4

[1] Benjamin Ferrey (1810-1880), articled to the older Pugin, and a designer of numerous unremarkable churches.

[2] *Recollections*, 157; Sketch Book No 17; Bradley, *Ruskin's Letters from Venice 1851-2*, 43.

[3] *The Builder*, ix, 104.

[4] *Recollections*, 167.

[5] ibid, 168.

[6] This church ought not to be confused with the earlier Holy Evangelists.

[7] It was enlarged to the west in 1863 following Scott's original plans, in 1873 from the designs of a Mr. Lynam, again in 1903, and 'renovated' in 1927-30.

[8] Scott's structure replaced an older church, and was given by the sisters Anna Maria and Frances Mainwaring.

[9] The vestry is later; the chancel fittings of 1901 and 1936 are out of character.

[10] The tiles were by Godwin of Lugwardine near Hereford, chancel seats by Rattee and Kett, the Cambridge woodcarvers, brasswork was by Skidmore, and other carving by Farmer.

[11] The capitals were by Farmer; the glass by Wailes.

[12] It was later rendered insignificant by the building of the cathedral of the Roman church nearby. About the time of its centenary it was demolished and replaced by an undistinguished office.

[13] Weeton, the first of many works by Scott in this part of Yorkshire, was built under the superintendence of Mr. Parsons, Lord Harewood's agent.

[14] *Architectural Review*, cxxxvi, 88.

[15] The builder was Beanland, from Bradford.

[16] *Recollections*, 176.

[17] The whole building, severely war damaged, was demolished in 1956.

[18] These were done in 1877 and 1884. The choir seating and reredos are by John Oldrid Scott.

[19] The reredos of 1879 by John Oldrid Scott does not look altogether comfortable.

[20] Designs were made for new chancel seats in 1878 but no work seems to have been carried out on these.

[21] It has been stated that Scott worked at Gawsworth, Cheshire, in 1851, where the Puritan incumbent, Edward Massie, had the church soundly scraped. There is no contemporary evidence, and this may be a case where a destructive restoration has been attributed to Scott.

[22] The metal screen is an early work by Skidmore.

[23] A final oddity is Scott's membership of the Ilam Anastatic Drawing Society, which published an annual volume of amateur pen and ink sketches.

[24] *Recollections*, 172. For example, Denison disliked Scott's font and insisted that

it was 3 in shorter and its supporting pillars 1½ in nearer the centre. Bodley would not be put about so: when in 1879 additions were proposed to St Martin, Scarborough, Denison, as Chancellor of the Diocese of York, returned Bodley's plans with marginal notes. Bodley sent back the plans with the notes rubbed out. Scott was incapable of such a gesture.

[25] *The Ecclesiologist*, xxi, 145-52.

[26] The sanctuary decorations were added only in 1868, by an unknown hand. The major and minor prophets peering out of porthole medallions in the nave arcade spandrels are by J. B. Philip: they are too high to be appreciated and contribute to the bad scale. The similar features at Halifax about the same time are more successful. The font is the best thing in the building, a good and unusual design in green marble, placed centrally in the south chancel aisle. The pulpit is an unremarkable design by Denison. Scott castigated the Clerk of Works, G. S. Cleverley, as despicable and untrustworthy. He was assisted by the fourteen year old J. F. Bentley.

[27] Redpath, a clerk employed by the Great Northern Railway, had swindled a great deal of money out of the company by an ingenious share transfer fraud.

[28] This large work brought others in its train, including the work at Christ Church, Doncaster, extensive work in 1855 on the Perpendicular nave of Loversal, succeeding G. G. Place, and the new church at Cadeby.

[29] *The Builder*, xxii, 549.

[30] It was Denison's ideal of a modern church: the turret was rebuilt by a Mr Teale to Denison's directions.

[31] The screen was made at a low price as Skidmore was keen to display something large at the International Exhibition of 1862. It has been removed, and lies in pieces in Coventry. The decoration of the North Transept was by Octavius Hudson.

[32] *Recollections*, 291.

[33] The clerk of works was Chick, who acted also for Scott at church restorations nearby — Upton Bishop in 1862, Aconbury in 1863, and Peterstow in 1865. The builders, Ruddle and Thompson of Peterborough, did much similar work. The west front and nave triforium were not rebuilt until 1904-8, by John Oldrid Scott, not in Norman but in late Decorated.

[34] *Recollections*, 292.

[35] Smirke designed a reredos for the chancel, which was exhibited at the Royal Academy in 1857, but it was not liked. *The Ecclesiologist* derided the design as a meaningless row of bristling niches in bad Perpendicular, destitute alike of beauty and convenience (xviii, 178) — though how could a reredos be convenient? Scott also made a design for this reredos, and for the throne, stalls, and pavement. Street did two tombs for members of the Hodson family and William Slater executed the font. The woodwork was carved by Evans of Ellaston and Skidmore did the gas lighting fittings.

[36] Scott died before the work, initiated by Dean Bickersteth, was far advanced. John Oldrid Scott carried on, apparently with assistance from Pearson, until 1908, and then worked on the Chapter House, central spire, and other parts of the

structure: he even wished to remove the roofs and rebuild them to a higher pitch. The building works from 1877-81 alone cost £165,000.

[37] It is noteworthy that Pevsner does not even mention him in 'The Buildings of England' description of Peterborough Cathedral.

[38] The decrepit central tower was taken down by Pearson in 1884. Rebuilding was attended by the activities of Lord Grimthorpe and members of the Society for the Protection of Ancient Buildings.

[39] Correspondence in Dorset County Record Office.

[40] Jackson, B., *Recollections of Thomas Graham Jackson*, 1950, 55.

5

[1] Though there is no mention of the word 'Gothic' in the title, the spine is marked *On Gothic Architecture, Secular and Domestic*.

[2] A. J. B. Beresford-Hope (1820-87), see *Dictionary of National Biography*, ix, 1203.

[3] This is exactly the same argument advanced by the Georgian revivalists of the 1920s. Scott, *On Gothic Architecture*, 1857, viii.

[4] *On Gothic Architecture*, 6.

[5] ibid, 7.

[6] ibid, 221. This remark led to misunderstanding.

[7] Tentatively identified as Dinton, Buckinghamshire.

[8] His early church at Turnham Green had iron columns; Westminster Abbey Chapter House, Woolwich Dockyard Chapel, and Brill's Brighton Baths are other examples of his enterprising use of iron.

[9] Two of these fireplaces have been removed to the Bedford County Museum.

[10] The whole building is now used as the offices of the Mole Valley District Council.

[11] For instance Arthington House, Yorks; Pendell Court, Surrey; Polwhele, Cornwall.

[12] A further competition was held in 1876 and John Oldrid Scott entered unsuccessfully, but by that time the joy had gone out of secular Gothic.

[13] Comprising the Duke of Buccleuch, William Burn, Lord Eversley, Lord Stanhope, David Roberts, I. K. Brunel, and Mr Stirling. They found it necessary to co-opt two more architects, Samuel Angell and George Pownall.

[14] The work was completed by his son E. M. Barry. Sir Charles Barry had wished, perhaps with ministerial encouragement, to record his own views on the replanning of the Whitehall area, and in 1857 drew up plans for a frightening 'concentration of government offices', involving almost the whole area from the Horse Guards to Great George Street as well as outlying sites. Road improvements would have resulted in a nine acre close north of the Abbey. The offices themselves had bay upon bay of Classical elevation, a big dome in the middle, and smaller domes elsewhere.

[15] *Hansard* (Commons) iii ser 152, cols 270-3.

[16] *Recollections*, 191.

[17] *Hansard* (Commons) iii ser 155, cols 918-41.

18 *Recollections*, 191.

19 ibid, 195.

20 ibid, 197.

21 *Hansard* (Commons) iii ser 164, cols 507-40.

22 Jackson, G., *Recollections of Thomas Graham Jackson*, 73.

23 Blomfield, R., *Richard Norman Shaw, RA*, 1940, 56.

24 The spandrel groups are by Philip and by Armstead.

25 The south porch is an addition of 1868. The vestry of 1885 is by John Oldrid Scott.

26 In 1933 the whole was moved to a site in Rochester Way, Woolwich.

27 In Cannon, J., *Oxfordshire*, 1952, 44.

28 *The Ecclesiologist*, xxi, 152.

29 Much has been undone, and at present the interior displays much white and gold, more to current taste. Scott's collaborators were at different times, W. H. Mason, Herbert Williams, and H. J. Williams.

30 The shell of the church was flattened to make way for a bulky police station in 1962. At St Olave, Hart Street, nothing of Scott's work remains visible.

31 See Lethaby, W. R., *Philip Webb and his work*, 1935, 66. J. C. Birkinshaw was consulting engineer, Buckeridge the Clerk of Works. T. G. Jackson rebuilt the top 48 ft of the spire in 1892-6.

32 Jackson, B., *Recollections of T. G. Jackson*, 50.

33 Jackson, B., op cit, 59.

34 Lethaby, W. R., op cit, 66.

6

1 Durham, Salisbury, Chester, Bath, Chichester, Ripon, Pershore, Dorchester, Bury St Edmunds, Brecon, St Davids, Worcester, Gloucester and the two chapels at Windsor.

2 Due to further failures which Scott could not have foreseen, more work was done to the tower in 1898.

3 *Recollections*, 303.

4 Jebb, J., *The Choral Service of the United Church of England and Ireland*, 1843.

5 The 17th-century font, considered out of character, was allegedly given to a church at Yankalilla, South Australia.

6 The whole cathedral was now repaired, except for the north porch, which Street restored in 1880.

7 Hussey was responsible for the side windows, Scott for those at the east.

8 Frater was Clerk of Works. He was succeeded in 1875 by Osborn. Haswell, a local man, was the builder. Later Thompson of Peterborough, associated with Scott in many such works, took over in the nave.

9 *Recollections*, 332.

10 Lighting was by Skidmore, heating by Haden, stained glass mostly by Clayton and Bell. The old glass was retained and placed in clerestory and west windows. The reseating was by Brock in 1870.

[11] Scott's pupil T. G. Jackson did more work to the west end in 1895 and later renewed flying buttresses, fitted the memorial chapel, and designed the organ case and vestry.

[12] Dean Hook is credited with having initiated seventy-one buildings in or around Leeds.

[13] Scott engaged Marshall as Clerk of Works, Bushby was to do the foundations, and Beanland of Bradford the upper parts.

[14] *Recollections*, 311.

[15] More recently, the latter has been brought out of retirement to supplant the Bodley structure, which is too light for present tastes.

[16] Jabez Bignall assisted.

[17] The painted decoration is of 1949.

[18] J. D. Wyatt looked after the work, with Mr Darkin of Bury as 'general Superintendent of the Works'.

[19] The church attained cathedral status in 1914, and the aisleless chancel is considered too small and parochial. Plans for a larger eastern end and extensions to the north have been prepared.

[20] The rebuilding of the vaulted south-east St Lawrence chapel is not by Scott, but rather by W. D. Caroë in 1929-30.

[21] *The Builder*, xxv, 414.

[22] By now Clear had been succeeded by C. R. Baker King, a great tower of strength in Scott's later practice.

[23] It is strange that the Royal Commission on Historical Monuments mentions no 19th-century work whatever here.

[24] *The Ecclesiologist*, xviii, 355-7; xxiii, 224.

[25] Parts of the former stalls and organ case have been made into a screen at Sutton Coldfield, Warwickshire.

[26] *The Builder*, xxx, 122.

[27] ibid, xxv, 454.

[28] *The Ecclesiologist*; xxiv, 107. Pevsner thinks it 'dull'. *Berkshire*, 1966, 272.

[29] The glass mosaic is by Salviati. The marble walls derive from the exhibition at Paris in 1867 of 'marble inlay scriptural panels' by Baron H. de Triqueti of Conflans, bought by the Royal family. Triqueti was also sculptor of Prince Albert's monument and of the reredos.

[30] It is often difficult, in the absence of practice accounts, to establish the date of a fresh commission: and work was often spread over long periods — twenty years at Aylesbury, eight years at St Sepulchre, Northampton, forty years at intervals at Melton Mowbray, for example.

[31] The statement that Scott worked here in the 1840s is incorrect, so the Bursar tells me.

[32] His Clerk of Works was the invaluable Irvine. A. W. Blomfield recased the Lady Chapel and the tower in 1889-91.

[33] Much work was done later, in 1886, 1891, 1923, 1933 and 1950.

[34] His views on Parochial Church Councils are interesting: 'Worse than useless. Turns every member into an aggrieved parishioner unless the particular hymn tune he likes is sung, breeds discontent, ἀνομέα, communism, and leads rapidly to disestablishment of church and state'. Kirk-Smith, *William Thomson* 73.

[35] This work went to T. G. Jackson in 1863, he being a local man, from Stamford.

[36] Although externally the building now looks a trifle odd, the device of adding the major part of a new church to the east has meant that the round can be more effectively preserved as an architectural relic.

[37] *Victoria County History, Oxfordshire*, viii, 209.

[38] Murray, *Sussex*, 1893, 58, and Lower, M. A., *History of Sussex*, 1870, i, 250.

[39] The polygonal vestry of 1880 is not by Scott.

[40] *Trans RIBA*, 1 ser, xxii.

[41] *The Ecclesiologist*, xxiii, 54.

[42] One ought to compare it with its twin, nearby Tedstone Wafre, paid for by the same Higginson at the same date. Tedstone Wafre was designed by Edward Haycock Junior of Shrewsbury. See Pevsner, *Herefordshire*, 1963, 299.

[43] Newsome, *A History of Wellington College*, 105.

[44] The north transept was added by A. W. Blomfield in 1896; the south aisle of 1899 is a memorial to Benson.

[45] See *Survey of London*, xxxviii 1975, 179-81.

[46] I am grateful to Mr Julian Litten for this idea.

[47] *The Builder*, xx, 305.

[48] ibid, xxi, 267-77.

[49] Letter at RIBA.

[50] See *Dictionary of National Biography*, xii, 1078.

[51] To get the memorial built, four trustees — Lord Torrington, Mr Cubitt, Sir Charles Phipps, the Keeper of the Privy Purse, and Sir Alexander Spearman, the Comptroller of the National Debt Office — were appointed to manage the funds and an executive committee was set up to look after the works, consisting originally of the last two trustees together with General Grey (as Chairman), Sir Charles Eastlake, PRA and Sir Thomas Biddulph, Master of the Household. Mr Doyne C. Bell of the Privy Purse Office acted as their secretary.

[52] B.M. Add MSS 388994, 61.

[53] ibid, 251.

[54] *Recollections*, 269-70.

[55] It is fortunate that the design of a Mr Bedborough of Southampton, who in 1877 wished to enclose the whole structure in a Gothic glass case 340 ft high flanked by two enormous greenhouses (see *The Builder*, xxv, 384, 452) was not proceeded with.

[56] *The Ecclesiologist*, xxiv, 136. The original drawings, by Drayton Wyatt, were destroyed comparatively recently.

[57] *The Builder*, xxiv, 485-87.

[58] It ceased to be used as a library in 1955 and has been altered. It is now used as a dwelling.

[59] The architect of the structure which was erected, at the considerable cost of £6000, was a local man, Garlick. There was a lot of trouble with the instability of the roof.

[60] The present building is the work of H. Cowell Boys in 1889-93.

[61] *The Builder*, xxi, 263.

7

[1] *The Builder*, xxi, 530.

[2] *Recollections*, 134.

[3] Designed about 1816 by John Shaw the elder; now known as Owborough.

[4] Scott, M. H., *The Force of Love*, 1899, 298.

[5] Report quoted in *The Builder*, xxiii, 932.

[6] It is perhaps significant that the authors of the Sussex volume of the *Buildings of England* do not mention Scott in four pages of description.

[7] All Saints' Great Marlow, which underwent a similar transformation after 1875, is entirely the work of John Oldrid Scott.

[8] *The Builder*, xxiii, 762.

[9] *The Builder*, xvii, 50.

[10] *Recollections*, 285.

[11] Quoted in Clarke, *Bangor Cathedral*, 1969, 32, a model of a descriptive pamphlet on such buildings.

[12] A proposal to add first a tower, then a spire in 1950 came to nothing. In 1967 Caroe finished off the stump with battlements and a pyramidal cap.

[13] *Recollections*, 319.

[14] Liddell and Robert Scott (no relation) compiled a comprehensive Greek lexicon. A timber hoarding had previously covered the vault, which prompted a splendid lampoon from Lewis Carroll, who maintained that it had been designed as a gigantic copy of a lexicon, in order to commemorate the name of the Dean and the architect.

[15] Buckler, *A Description and Defence of the Restoration of the Exterior of Lincoln Cathedral*, 1866. See also *The Ecclesiologist*, xxii, 223; xxv, 245; xxvii, 280, 291.

[16] *The Builder*, xxv, 413-14.

[17] Designed by Joseph Clarke and Ewan Christian, now demolished.

[18] Bumpus, T. E., *London Churches Ancient and Modern*, 1908, ii, 295ff.

[19] See Simmonds, J., *St Pancras Station*, 1968.

[20] *The Builder* published illustrations of those by Barry, Brandon, Burges, Lockwood, Scott, Street and Waterhouse, and descriptions of all.

[21] *The Builder*, xxx, 237.

[22] Howarth, C. R. *Mackintosh*, 1953, 57.

[23] *The Builder*, xxii, 619.

²⁴ ibid, xxiii, 224ff.

²⁵ *Recollections*, 248.

²⁶ ibid, 327-8.

8

¹ *The Builder*, xxxi, 882-5.

² ibid, xxxii, 941.

³ ibid, xxxiii, 521.

⁴ ibid, xxx, 864.

⁵ Pulpit, font, nave seats, and some screens, are certainly by John Oldrid Scott. It should not be confused with the smaller St Peter, Spalding, another red brick church of 1875.

⁶ Colvin, op cit, 555.

⁷ In 1979 it is proposed to raze almost the whole to plinth level.

⁸ *The Builder*, xxiv, 907.

⁹ Pevsner, *North Somerset and Bristol*, 1958, 240. He credits the work to G.G. Scott Junior but the latter disliked Bath stone, which was used here, and documents do not support this.

¹⁰ Victoria County History, *Buckinghamshire*, ii, 250.

¹¹ See Colvin, op cit, 213-14.

¹² The church was gutted in 1940 by enemy action and it seems all Scott's work is now lost.

¹³ Scott was associated with Ralph Nevill, a local antiquary — see *Collns. Surrey Archaeological Society*, vii, 277.

¹⁴ *The Builder*, xxxiii, 650.

¹⁵ *Recollections*, 445.

¹⁶ Pevsner, *Durham*, 1953, 109.

¹⁷ *The Athenaeum*, 5 March 1877. For the SPAB manifesto, ibid, 2591, 807.

¹⁸ *The Times*, 20 February 1956.

¹⁹ *The Builder*, xxxiii, 179.

²⁰ ibid, xxv, 552.

²¹ ibid, xxv, 572.

²² ibid, xxxv, 601; *Recollections*, 398.

²³ *Macmillan's Magazine*, June 1877.

²⁴ *The Athenaeum*, 2593, 22.

²⁵ Henderson (ed), *Letters of William Morris*, 1950, 314.

²⁶ *Recollections*, 330.

²⁷ ibid, 330.

²⁸ *Recollections*, 387. Obituaries: *Proceedings of the Society of Antiquaries*, 2 ser vii, 381 — 'Reserved in manner, equable in temperament, plain and even hesitating in speech'; *The Times* 8 April 1878; *Journal RIBA* 1878, 305; *The Athenaeum*, 2631, 419.

Epilogue

[1] *The Builder*, xxxvi, 383. There were George Wood, described as 'Chief practical assistant and private secretary'; Jabez Bignall, chief draughtsman; C.R. Baker King; John Swanwick Lee, Surveyor; John Bignell, Arthur Baker, J. Medland, Tonge, Jones and Thackeray Turner, in charge of jobs; Barker, W. S. Weatherley, Norton and Perkins, draughtsmen; Butters and Monkton, the pupils; two office clerks; and twelve clerks of works, Godfrey, Irvine, Chapple, Morgan, the Roomes, Hannaford, Saville, Kaberry, Sheffield, Prosser and Snelgrove.

[2] So Mr Julian Litten informs me.

[3] *Building News*, xlvi, 537, 577, 616, 776; lxxii, 699.

[4] *Dictionary of National Biography*, 1931-40, 796.

Appendix 1
Sources

1 DOCUMENTARY MATERIAL

a Drawings
i) A major collection at the RIBA of which a catalogue is now in in preparation.
ii) Victoria and Albert Museum.
iii) Public Record Office.
iv) Society of Antiquaries of Scotland.
v) Many odd drawings at museums, county archive collections, libraries, etc.

b Sketch books
About sixty, with the drawings collection of the RIBA.

c Practice accounts
A new set of books, including work in progress or unsettled, was started at Scott's death and continued by J. O. Scott and C. M. O. Scott. They are at the RIBA: vols 1 and 2 are relevant. Earlier accounts have disappeared except for a few sketch book entries.

d Correspondence
There are collections at the British Museum and at the Victoria and Albert Museum.
Many letters exist in parish records, county archive collections, and houses.

e Faculties

In County Record Offices, Diocesan Registries, or parochial collections.

f Letter

From C.R.Baker King to G.G.Scott Junior dated 27 May 1879, a list of 541 works executed by Sir Gilbert Scott.

g Card index

Of church restorations compiled by H.S.Goodhart Rendel.

2 PRINTED MATERIAL

a Books by G.G.Scott

A plea for the faithful restoration of our ancient churches, Parker, 1850.

Remarks on Secular and Domestic Architecture, Murray, 1857; 2nd edition, 1858.

Gleanings from Westminster Abbey, with others, 1st edition, Parker, 1861; 2nd edition, enlarged, 1863.

Personal and professional recollections, edited by G.G.Scott Junior, Sampson Law and Co, 1879.

Lectures on the Rise and Development of Mediaeval Architecture, 2 vols, Murray, 1879.

b Pamphlets

About forty printed pamphlets and reports are known.

c Contemporary periodicals

The contemporary technical press contains a large number of articles, letters, and reports of lectures and papers, as well as many thousands of individual references to buildings. The most useful are:

> *The Builder*, v. i (1843) on.
> *The Ecclesiologist*, v. i-xxix (1840-68).

Others are:

> *The Building News*

The British Architect
The Civil Engineer's and Architect's Journal
The Illustrated London News
The Times
Transactions of the (Royal) Institute of British Architects
Country Life

Important items thus printed include:

'On the conservation of ancient architectural monuments and remains' (1862), *Trans RIBA*, 1 ser, xxii.

'Reply to J.J.Stevenson's paper...' *ibid*, 1 ser, xxvii.

There are often useful references in local newspapers.

d General works

Architectural Publication Society, *Dictionary of Architecture*, 11 v, 1852-92.

Clarke, B.F.L., *Church Builders of the Nineteenth Century*, 1938.

Ferriday, P., *Lord Grimthorpe*, 1957.
                ed, *Victorian Architecture*, 1963.

Jackson, B., ed, *Recollections of Thomas Graham Jackson*, 1950.

Pevsner, Sir Nikolaus, *The Buildings of England*, 46 v, 1951-74.
                Some Architectural Historians of the Nineteenth Century, 1972.

Physick, J. and Darby, M., *Marble Halls*, 1973.

Royal Commission on Historic Monuments, inventories, many v, various dates (in progress).

Sir Gilbert Scott (1811-1878) – Architect of the Gothic Revival, 1978, catalogue of the exhibition at the Victoria and Albert Museum.

Scott, J., *Memoir of the Rev. Thomas Scott*, 1822.

Scott, Melville Hey, *The Force of Love*, 1899.

Street, A.E., *Memoir of G.E. Street, R.A.*

Victoria History of the Counties of England, many v, various dates (in progress)

e Local guides and pamphlets dealing with individual buildings

There exist some hundreds, varying very much in value.

f County works on churches

The two most useful are Cranage, *Churches of Shropshire*, and R.M.Robbins' admirable *Middlesex Parish Churches*.

f Articles

Dickens, A., 'The Architect and the Workhouse', *Architectural Review*, clx, 345.

Ferriday, P., 'The Church Restorers', *Architectural Review*, cxxxiv, 87.

Stamp, G., 'Sir Gilbert Scott's Recollections', *Architectural History*, xix, 54.

Briggs, M.S., 'Sir Gilbert Scott', *Architectural Review*, xxiv, 92, 147, 180, 290.

Cole, D., 'Some early works of George Gilbert Scott', *Architectural Association Journal*, lxvi, 98.
This should not be relied upon in the light of later discoveries.

Appendix 2
Architectural Works

There is no authentic list of Scott's works. Their total number remains in doubt and the following list of 879 entries is not definitive. Certain authorities for the entries are keyed as follows:

1 C.R.Baker King's letter dated 27 May 1879.
2 H.S.Goodhart Rendel's card index.
3 *Personal and Professional Recollections.*
4 Contemporary reference in *The Builder.*
5 Contemporary reference in *The Ecclesiologist.*
6 Sketch books.
7 Account books.
8 Drawings.
9 *The Builder,* xxxvi, 360. (This contains many errors.)

No list by date is given, as designs were frequently prepared years before work started, the actual date of starting work is often not ascertainable, and work might go on over many years, or in stages.

A number of monumental works, some unidentifiable, are omitted.

Aberdeen, Angus, St Machar. Survey and report, 1867.	6, 9
Abergavenny, Monmouth, St Mary. Restoration (?) by 1881.	7, 9
Abergwili, Carmarthen, St David. New, 1843.	1, 9
Abingdon, Berkshire, St Helen. Reports on tower, 1858, 1875.	4
Abingdon, Berkshire, St Michael. New, 1864-7.	2, 4
Aconbury, Hereford, St John Baptist. Restoration 1863.	4, 9
Adderbury, Oxford, St Mary. Internal alterations 1867-71, 1877.	1, 4, 9
Albourne, Sussex, St Bartholomew. Restoration 1859.	
Alderney, Channel Islands, St Anne. New c 1850.	1, 3, 5, 9
Alford, Lincoln, St Wilfrid. Restoration 1865-8.	1, 4, 7, 9

Algarkirk, Lincoln, Schools and masters' houses. New, c 1857.   5

Alton, Derbyshire, Manor House. (Unidentified.)   1, 9

Ambleside, Westmorland, St Mary. New, 1850-4.   1, 4, 5, 8, 9

Amersham, Buckingham, Poor Law Institution. New, 1838.   3

Amesbury, Wiltshire, Poor Law Institution. New, 1836, demolished.   3

Ampney St Peter, Gloucester, St Peter. Addition 1878.

Anstey, Warwick, St James. Tower and spire, 1856, restoration 1876. 1, 5, 7, 9

Antrobus, Cheshire, St Mark. New, 1847-8.

Arksey, West Yorkshire, All Saints. Restoration 1867-70.   1, 4, 9

Arthington, West Yorkshire, St Peter. Restoration 1864.

Arthington, West Yorkshire, Hall. Altered c 1848-55.   3, 8

Arundel, Sussex, St Nicholas. Restoration 1871-4.   1, 6, 9

Ascot, Berkshire, Hospital of the Holy Trinity. New, 1864 with
  C. Buckeridge.   5

Asfordby, Leicester, All Saints. Restoration 1866-9.   1, 4, 9

Ashbourne, Derby, St Oswald. Restoration 1876-81.   1, 4, 7, 9

Ashby de la Zouch, Leicester, Loudoun Memorial. New, 1877-9.   1, 7, 9

Ashley, Northampton, St Mary. Restoration c 1867.   1, 8, 9

Ashley, Northampton, Schools. New, 1858.   9

Ashley, Northampton, Schoolmaster's house. New 1865.

Ashley, Northampton, Parsonage. New or altered. c 1858.   9

Astbury, Cheshire, St Mary. Reredos, 1862.

Astbury, Cheshire, School. c 1850-2.

Aston Sandford, Buckingham, St Michael. Windows, 1877-8.   9

Aston Sandford, Buckingham, House. New.

Atherstone, Warwick, St Mary. Restoration of chancel. c 1869.   1, 5, 9

Audley, Stafford, St James. Restoration 1847.   5, 6

Aylesbury, Buckingham, St Mary. Restoration 1850-1, 1865-9.   1, 3, 4, 5, 8, 9

Bangor, Caernarvon, Cathedral. Restoration 1868-73.   1, 3, 4, 9

Barnes, Surrey, St Mary the Virgin. Design for restoration. c 1835-46.   8

Barnet, Hertford, Christ Church. New, 1845, addition 1855.   5

Barnet, Hertford, Christ Church parsonage. c 1845.   5

Barnet, Hertford, Christ Church schools. c 1845.   5

Barnstaple, Devon, St Peter. Restoration 1864-82.   1, 4, 5, 9

Barnwell, Northampton, St Andrew. Restoration 1851.   4, 5

Bath, Somerset, Abbey. Restoration 1860-77.   1, 4, 5, 9

Bath, Somerset, St Andrew. New, 1870-3, 1879-80.   1, 2, 4, 7, 8, 9

Bath, Somerset, Partis College Chapel. Alteration.   1, 3, 9

Batsford, Gloucester, St Mary, Mitford Memorial, 1867.

Battlefield, Shropshire, St Mary. Restoration 1861-2 with
  S. Pountney Smith.   4

Beckenham, Kent, St Agatha's Chapel. New, 1869, demolished 1921.   1, 9

Bedworth, Warwick, Poor Law Institution. New, possibly
  unexecuted, 1839.   6

Beeston, Nottingham, St John Baptist. Restoration 1844.   2

Belgrave, Leicester, St Peter. Restoration 1877.   1, 7, 9

Belper, Derby, Poor Law Institution. New, 1838, ? later additions. 1, 3, 9
Belton, Lincoln, Sts Peter and Paul. Tomb, c 1851.
Berkeley, Gloucester, St Mary. Restoration 1864-6. 1, 4, 5, 6, 9
Berlin, Germany, Parliament House. Competition entry 1872
 with J. O. Scott. 4
Betley, Stafford, St Margaret. Restoration 1842.
Beverley, East Yorkshire, Minster of St John. Screens 1844,
 1877: Restoration 1866-8. 1, 3, 5, 7, 8, 9
Beverley, East Yorkshire, St Mary. Restoration 1863-7. 1, 4, 8, 9
Bibury, Gloucester, St Mary. Restoration 1863. 1, 4
Bidborough, Kent, St Lawrence. Restoration (?). 1
Bideford, Devon, Poor Law Institution. New, 1837.
Billericay, Essex, Poor Law Institution. New, 1839, ? later
 additions. 1, 3, 6, 9
Bilton, West Yorkshire, St John. New 1855. 2, 3, 9
Bilton in Ainsty, West Yorkshire, St Helen. Restoration 1868-70. 4, 6
Bingham, Nottingham, St Michael. Restoration c 1848. 1, 4, 9
Birmingham, Warwick, St Mark. New, 1840. Demolished. 2, 3, 5
Birmingham, Warwick, Grammar School. Competition entry 1832. 3
Bishop Auckland, Durham, Castle chapel. (? report.) 9
Birstall, Leicester, St James. Restoration 1869. 1, 4, 9
Bishopsbourne, Kent, St Mary. Restoration c 1872. 1, 4, 9
Black Bourton, Oxford, school. New, 1865.
Blakesley, Northampton, parsonage. New, 1839. - 6
Bledlow, Buckingham, Holy Trinity. Restoration 1876. 1, 7, 9
Bletchingley, Surrey, Pendell Court. Alterations 1877. 7, 8, 9
Bodmin, Cornwall, Poor Law Institution. New, 1838. 1
Bombay, India, fountain. New, 1865. 4, 9
Bombay, India, University Hall. New, 1875. 1, 4, 9
Boston, Lincoln, Poor Law Institution. New, 1837. 6
Boston, Lincoln, St Botolph. Restoration 1843-6; 1851-4 with
 G. G. Place; 1873. 1, 4, 5
Bottesford, Leicester, St Mary. Restoration 1865. 1, 9
Bourne, Kent, church. Restoration, unidentified. 1, 9
Bourton, church. Restoration, unidentified. 1
Boxgrove, Sussex, Priory of Sts Mary and Blaize. Restoration
 1864-7. 4, 5, 8
Brabourne, Kent, St Mary. Restoration 1874. 4
Bradfield, Berkshire, St Andrew. Restoration 1847-8. 2, 3, 5
Bradfield, Berkshire, Sts Simon and Jude. New, 1845.
Bradfield, Berkshire, St Andrew's College. New, 1853-66. 3
Bradford, West Yorkshire, Town Hall. Competition entry, c 1858. 5
Bradford on Avon, Wiltshire, Christ Church. Addition 1878. 1, 2, 7, 9
Branston, Lincoln, All Saints. Restoration 1876, altered. 1, 4, 7 8, 9
Brecon, Brecon, Priory of St John Evangelist. Restoration 1860-2,
 1872-5. 1, 4, 9
Brereton, Stafford, St Michael. Alteration 1876-8. 1, 4, 7, 9

Bridge, Kent, St Peter. Restoration 1858-61.   9
Bridge, Kent, parsonage. New, c 1859.   9
Bridlington, East Yorkshire, Christ Church. New, 1840-1.   1, 2, 3, 4,
Bridlington, East Yorkshire, Priory. Restoration 1875-80.   1, 4, 7, 8, 9
Brighton, Sussex, College. New, 1848-63.   1, 4, 9
Brighton, Sussex, Brill's Baths, Pool Valley. New, 1866-9,
    Demolished 1929.   1, 4, 9
Bristol, Gloucester, Cathedral. Report 1859.   5
Bristol, Gloucester, St James. Survey 1863.   4
Bromborough, Cheshire, St Barnabas. New, 1862-4, 1878.   1, 2, 4, 7, 9
Bromsgrove, Worcester, St John Baptist. Restoration 1858.
Broughton, Oxford, St Mary. Restoration 1868, 1876-8 with
    G. G. Scott Junior.   1, 7, 9
Broughton, Oxford, Castle. Restoration 1867.   1, 9
Broughty Ferry, Angus, church. New, c 1858.   2, 5
Brownsover, Warwick, Hall. New.   1
Brownsover, Warwick, St Michael. Restoration 1875-6.   1, 2, 4, 7, 9
Buckingham, Buckingham, gaol. Addition c 1839.
Buckingham, Buckingham, Poor Law Institution. New, 1836,
    demolished.
Buckingham, Buckingham, Chantry chapel or latin school.
    Restoration 1875.
Buckingham, Buckingham, Sts Peter and Paul. Restoration
    1860-7.   1, 2, 3, 4, 7, 8, 9
Burcott, Oxford, St Mary. New, 1869.   1, 9
Burgh next Aylsham, Norfolk, St Mary. Restoration 1876-8 with
    R. M. Phipson.   6
Bury St Edmunds, Suffolk, St Mary. Restoration (?).   1
Bury St Edmunds, Suffolk, St James. Restoration 1863-4, 1867-9.   5
Busbridge, Surrey, St James. New, 1865.   4, 9
Bushey, Hertford, St James. Restoration 1870-1.   1, 2, 4, 8, 9
Bushley, Worcester, St Peter. Addition of chancel c 1858.   1, 2, 5
Bwlch y Cibau, Montgomery, Christ Church. Restoration c 1864.   1, 2, 9
Bylchau, Denbigh, St James. New, 1857.   2

Cadeby, West Yorkshire, St John Evangelist. New, 1856.   1
Calcutta, India, monument to Lady Canning.   1, 4
Calcutta, India, Cathedral, Elgin monument.   4, 9
Calcutta, India, St James. Design, 1861, unexecuted.   1, 5, 9
Camberwell, London, St Giles. New, 1842-4.   1, 2, 3, 4, 5, 9
Camberwell, London, Camden Chapel. Addition of chancel 1854,
    demolished 1956.   4, 5, 9
Cambridge, cemetery chapel, Mill Road. New, 1853, demolished.   1, 4, 5, 9
Cambridge, Christ's College Hall. Restoration 1875.
Cambridge, Jesus College. Survey of tower 1864.
Cambridge, King's College Chapel. Restoration 1859-63, 1875.   1, 3, 9
Cambridge, King's College, Chetwynd buildings. New, 1871.   8, 9

Cambridge, King's College, Great Court, Competition entry 1877.
Cambridge, Peterhouse, Combination Room and Hall. Restoration
   1868-70.   1, 5
Cambridge, St John's College, Chapel. New, 1863-9.   1, 3, 4, 5, 8, 9
Cambridge, St John's College, Master's house. New 1863.   1, 9
Cambridge, University buildings. Restoration 1863-7.   5
Cambridge, St Edward Confessor. Restoration east end, 1858.   5
Cambridge, St Mary Major. Restoration 1851, 1862-5.   1, 4, 5, 9
Cambridge, St Mary Minor. Restoration 1858.   5, 9
Cambridge, St Mary Magdalene (Stour Bridge chapel) Restoration 1867.   5, 9
Cambridge, St Michael. Restoration 1850.   4, 5
Campsall, West Yorkshire, St Mary Magdalene. Restoration
   1873-5.   1, 4, 8, 9
Cannes, France, church (unidentified). New.   1, 9
Canterbury, Kent, St Gregory. New, 1852.   2, 5
Canterbury, Kent, St Margaret. Restoration c 1849-54.   4, 6
Canterbury, Kent, St Martin. Restoration possibly c1845.   1
Canterbury, Kent, St Paul. Restoration c 1856.   5
Canterbury, Kent, Cathedral. Restoration 1860, 1877-80.   1, 3, 4, 5, 7, 8, 9
Capesthorne, Cheshire, Hall. Unexecuted design, 1861.   8, 9
Carshalton, Surrey, fountain. Unexecuted proposal, 1872.
Castle Ashby, Northampton, St Mary Magdalene. Restoration probably
   unexecuted, design c 1858.   5, 9
Caton Hall, lodge (unidentified).   8, 9
Cattistock, Dorset, Sts Peter and Paul. Restoration 1857-8.   4, 9
Cawood, West Yorkshire, All Saints. Restoration unexecuted, 1874.   8, 9
Caythorpe, Lincoln, St Vincent. Restoration 1860.   1, 4, 9
Chantry, Somerset, Holy Trinity. New 1846.   2
Chatham, Kent, St Bartholomew's Hospital Chapel. Restoration 1875-7. 1, 9
Cheddleton, Stafford, St Edward. Restoration 1863-4 with G.G.Scott
   Junior and Robert Edgar.   1, 9
Chepstow, Monmouth, St Mary. Restoration, work removed.   1
Cherry Hinton, Cambridge, St Andrew. Restoration 1875-80.
Chesham, Buckingham, house, 16 High Street. New, 1834.   3
Chesham, Buckingham, St Mary. Restoration 1868-9.   9
Chester, Cheshire, Cathedral. Restoration 1868-75.   1, 3, 4, 5, 7, 9
Chester, Cheshire, St Thomas. New, 1869-72.   1, 4, 9
Chester, Cheshire, St Paul, Boughton. Unexecuted design (?).   9
Chester, Cheshire, Kings School. New - one elevation 1876.   4
Chester, Cheshire, Town Hall. Competition entry, 1864.
Chesterfield, Derby, All Saints. Restoration 1842-3.   1, 3, 4, 5, 9
Chichester, Sussex, Cathedral. Restoration 1861-7, 1872.   1, 3, 4, 5, 9
Chichester, Sussex, cemetery, Jervoise mortuary chapel. New 1876.   1, 7, 9
Childwick Green, Hertford, St Mary's school and chapel. New.   1, 9
Chillenden, Kent, All Saints. Restoration 1871.   1, 9
Chippenham, Wiltshire, St Paul. New, 1854-5.   1, 2, 4, 8, 9
Cholmondeley, Cheshire, St Nicholas. Restoration, unexecuted.

Christchurch, New Zealand, Cathedral. New, 1864-1904.   1, 5, 7, 9
Chudleigh Knighton, Devon, St Paul. New, 1841-2.   2, 4
Chudleigh Knighton, Devon, Pitt House. New, c 1845 (?).
Churchover, Warwick, Holy Trinity. Restoration (?) work removed 1896.   9
Cirencester, Gloucester, Holy Trinity, Watermoor. New, 1847-60 and
    1877-79.   1, 3, 4, 7, 9
Cirencester, Gloucester, St John Baptist. Restoration 1865-7.   1, 4, 5, 8, 9
Clapham, Bedford, St Thomas of Canterbury. Restoration
    1861-2.   1, 2, 4, 8
Clapham, Sussex, St Mary. Restoration 1873-4.   1
Clayworth, Nottingham, St Peter. Restoration 1875 with
    J. O. Scott.   8, 9
Cleobury Mortimer, Shropshire, St Mary. Restoration 1874-5.   1, 4, 7, 9
Clifton, East Yorkshire, Lunatic Asylum. New, 1845.   4
Clifton Hampden, Oxford, bridge. New, 1864.   1
Clifton Hampden, Oxford, parsonage. New, 1843-6.   9
Clifton Hampden, Oxford, St Michael. Restoration 1843-4 and
    (with Buckeridge) 1866-7.   1, 2, 5, 9
Clutton, Somerset, Poor Law Institution. New, 1837.
Coatham, North Yorkshire, Christ Church. Fittings, c 1854.   1, 9
Cobham, Kent, St Mary Magdalene. Restoration 1860-1.   1, 5, 9
Colchester, Essex, Sts Nicholas and Runwald. Restoration
    1874.   1, 2, 4, 7, 8, 9,
Corringham, Essex, St Mary. Restoration 1843-4 (?).
Costock, Nottingham, St Giles. Restoration 1862-3.   4, 9
Coventry, Warwick, St Michael. Restoration 1855-7: ruined.   5, 9
Coventry, Warwick, Holy Trinity. Restoration 1854-7.   1, 5, 8
Coventry, Warwick, St John Baptist. Restoration 1875-8.   1, 4, 7, 9
Cradley, Hereford, St James. Restoration 1867-8.   1, 2, 8, 9
Crewe Green, Cheshire, St Michael. New, 1858.   1, 2, 8, 9
Crondall, Hampshire, All Saints. Restoration 1871.   1, 9
Crosthwaite, Cumberland, St Kentigern. Restoration 1844-5.   4
Crowland, Lincoln, Abbey. West front righted, 1860.   4, 9
Croxton Kerrial, Leicester, St John Evangelist. Restoration 1866-8.   1, 4, 9
Croydon, Surrey, St John Evangelist. Restoration 1859; rebuilt after
    fire 1867-70.   1, 2, 4, 8, 9
Croydon, Surrey, St Peter. New, 1849-51.   1, 4, 5, 9

Danbury, Essex, St John Baptist. Restoration 1866-7: pulpit, 1878.   1, 4, 7, 9
Darlington, Durham, St Cuthbert. Restoration 1862-5.   1, 3, 4, 5, 9
Dawlish, Devon, Luscombe Castle, chapel. New, by 1862.   1, 4, 9
Debenham, Suffolk, St Mary. Reseating (? executed) by 1846.   8
Derby, Derby, St Andrew, Litchurch. New, 1864-6, tower
    1880-1.   1, 2, 4, 5, 7, 9
Derby, Derby, St Andrew parsonage. New, c 1864.   9
Derby, Derby, Poor Law Institution. Competition entry 1838.   4
Denton, Lancashire, Christ Church. New, 1853.   2

Dinton, Buckingham, Vicarage. New, c 1836.
Ditton, Kent, St Peter ad Vincula. Restoration 1860.   4, 9
Doncaster, West Yorkshire, Grammar School and lodge. New, 1868.   1, 4, 9
Doncaster, West Yorkshire, St George. New, 1853-8.   1, 2, 3, 4, 5, 6, 7, 9
Doncaster, West Yorkshire, St James. New, 1858.   1, 2, 3, 5
Doncaster, West Yorkshire, Christ Church, chancel. c 1850.   2, 4
Doncaster, West Yorkshire, Cemetery chapel. 1854, abortive.   4
Donington Wood, Shropshire, St Matthew. New, 1843-50.   1, 2, 4
Dorchester, Oxford, Abbey. Restoration 1858, 1862, 1874.   1, 4, 5, 8, 9
Dorchester, Oxford, churchyard cross. Restoration c 1872.
Dorchester, Oxford, schools. New, c 1871.   1, 4, 9
Dorchester, Oxford, training college. Addition 1877-8.   1, 9
Dorking, Surrey, Pippbrook. Alteration, addition c 1856.   1, 3, 5, 8, 9
Dover, Kent, St Mary in Castro. Restoration 1859-62.   1, 4, 5, 8, 9
Dover, Kent, new church (untraced).   1
Dundee, Angus, St Clement. Tower restored c 1872.   1, 4, 9
Dundee, Angus, St Paul (episcopal). New, 1853-5.   1, 2, 4, 5, 9
Dundee, Angus, Albert Institute. New, 1865-9.   1, 3, 4, 5, 9
Dunkirk, Kent, Christ Church. New, unexecuted, 1839.   6
Dunsany, Co Meath, Castle. New, 1875-8, work abandoned.   1, 4, 7, 9
Duns Tew, Oxford, St Mary Magdalene. Restoration 1861-2.   1, 9
Durham, Durham, Cathedral. Restored tower (with Walton and
    Robson) 1859: choir, 1874-6.   1, 3, 4, 5, 8, 9
Dyserth, Flint, Sts Bridget and Cwyvan. Restoration 1871.   1, 9

Ealing, Middlesex, Christ Church. New, 1850-2.   1, 2, 4, 5, 9
Ealing, Middlesex, parsonage. New.   9
Easby, North Yorkshire, St Agatha. Restoration 1869-70.   1, 4, 9
East Claydon, Buckingham, St Mary. Restoration 1871-2.   1, 4, 8, 9
East Markham, Nottingham, St John Baptist. Restoration.   1, 9
Eastnor, Hereford, St John Baptist. Restoration 1852:
    tomb 1855.   1, 2, 4, 5, 6, 9
Eastnor, Hereford, rectory. New, 1849.   8
East Preston, Sussex, St Mary the Virgin. New aisle, 1869.   9
East Winch, Norfolk, All Saints. Restoration c 1875.   1, 4, 9
East Woodhay, Hampshire, St Martin. Restoration (?).   9
East Woodhay, Hampshire, House. Additions c 1847-55.   1, 8
Eccles, Lancashire, new church (unidentified).   1, 9
Eccleshall, Cheshire, Cross to Bishop Lonsdale. New, 1869.   4, 9
Edensor, Derby, St Peter. New, 1867.   1, 2, 9
Edgcott, Buckingham, St Michael. Restoration 1871-2.   1, 9
Edge Hill, Lancashire, St Stephen. New, 1850-1, demolished c 1881.   1, 4, 9
Edinburgh, Midlothian, St John. Unexecuted, restoration 1865:
    Ramsay monument c 1872.   4, 9
Edinburgh, Midlothian, Cathedral of St Mary. New, 1874-80.   1, 3, 4, 7, 8, 9
Edmonton, Middlesex, Poor Law Institution. New, 1839.
Edvin Loach, Hereford, St Mary. New, c 1859.   1, 9

Ellesmere, Shropshire, St Mary the Virgin. Restoration
  1847-9.   1, 2, 3, 4, 5, 6, 9
Ellesmere, Shropshire, cemetery chapel, house and walls. New, c 1864.
Ellington, Huntingdon, All Saints. Restoration 1863.   1, 4, 9
Ely, Ely, Cathedral. Restoration 1847-78.   1, 3, 4, 5, 7, 8, 9
Englefield, Berkshire, St Mark. Restoration chancel, 1857.   1, 9
Enville, Stafford, St Mary. Restoration 1872-5.   1, 7, 9
Epsom, Surrey, Horton Manor. New (?), c 1871.   1, 7, 9
Eton, Buckingham, College chapel. Stalls, c 1849-51.
Eversholt, Bedford, St John Baptist. Restoration.   1, 9
Exeter, Devon, Cathedral. Restoration 1869-77.   1, 3, 4, 5, 6, 7, 8, 9

Farnborough, Warwick, St Botolph. Restoration 1864-5.   1, 4, 9
Farncombe, Surrey, St John Evangelist. New 1844-7, addition
  c 1860, 1875.   1, 4, 5, 8, 9
Farnham, West Yorkshire, St Oswald. Restoration c 1854.   4
Faversham, Kent, Our Lady of Charity. Tower recased; reredos 1867;
  restoration 1874-5.   1, 2, 4, 8, 9
Feering, Essex, All Saints. Organ case, removed.   9
Findon, Sussex, St John Baptist. Restoration 1867.   1, 4, 9
Flaunden, Hertford, St Mary Magdalene. New, 1838.   3, 9
Flax Bourton, Somerset, Poor Law Institution. New, 1837.
Flaxley, Gloucester, St Mary. New, 1856.   1, 2
Fleet Marston, Buckingham, St Mary the Virgin. Restoration 1868-9.   1, 9
Flixton, Suffolk, Hall. Largely demolished.   1, 9
Forest Gate, Essex, Emmanuel. New, 1850-2.   1, 4, 9
Forest Gate, Essex, schools. New, 1850.   4, 9
Forest Hill, Oxford, St Nicholas the Confessor. Restoration 1852.   5
Frankton, Shropshire, St Andrew. New, 1858, with E. Haycock Junior (?). 1
Frankton, Warwick, St Nicholas. Restoration 1872.   1
Freehay, Stafford, St Chad. New, 1842-3.
Fremington, Devon, St Peter. Restoration 1866-7.   1, 4, 9
Frindsbury, Kent, new church. Unexecuted design, c 1856-61.   8
Frinsted, Kent, St Dunstan. Restoration 1870.
Frogmore, Hertford, Holy Trinity. New, 1841-2.   2
Frome, Somerset, Christ Church. Restoration 1851.   1, 9
Fulney, Lincoln, St Paul. New 1877-80.   1, 2, 7, 8, 9
Fulney, Lincoln, parsonage. New, 1877-80.   1, 2, 7, 9
Fulney, Lincoln, schools. New, 1877-80.   1, 2, 9

Gamston, Nottingham, St Peter. Restoration 1855.   1, 4
Garston, Hertford, All Saints. New, 1853.   1, 2
Geddington, Northampton, St Mary Magdalene. Restoration c 1852.   4
Glasgow, Lanark, University. New, 1867-70: Bute Hall, 1878.   1, 3, 4, 5, 7, 9
Glasgow, Lanark, 13 professors' houses. New, c 1870.   1, 4, 9
Glasgow, Lanark, St Mary (Episcopal). New, 1871-93.   1, 9
Glastonbury, Somerset, St John Baptist. Pulpit, c 1856.   4, 9

Glastonbury, Somerset, St John's schools. New, c 1862.   4, 9
Glasynfryn, Caernarvon, St Elizabeth. New, c 1871.   2, 4
Glenalmond, Perth, College. Hall, 1863 with John Henderson.
Gloucester, Gloucester, Cathedral. Restoration 1854-76, partly with
    Fulljames and Waller.   1, 3, 4, 5, 7, 8, 9
Gloucester, Gloucester, St James. New, 1837-41 with Sampson
    Kempthorne.   1, 9
Gloucester, Gloucester, Poor Law Institution. New.   1
Godalming, Surrey, Sts Peter and Paul. Restoration 1876-81 with Ralph
    Nevill.   1, 4, 7, 8, 9
Godmanchester, Huntingdon, St Mary the Virgin. Restoration
    by 1853.   1, 4
Godstone, Surrey, St Mary's homes. New, 1872.   1, 9
Godstone, Surrey, St Nicholas. Restoration by 1872.   1, 4, 7, 8, 9
Goldsborough, West Yorkshire, St Mary. Restoration 1859.   9
Goudhurst, Kent, parsonage. New, demolished (?).   5
Grahamstown, South Africa, cathedral of Sts Michael and George.
    Additions 1874-8 and 1893.   1, 3, 8, 9
Granborough, Buckingham, St John Baptist. Restoration 1880-1.   8, 9
Grantham, Lincoln, St Wulfran. Restoration 1865-9.   1, 4, 5, 7, 8, 9
Great Bricett, Suffolk, parsonage. New.   1, 9
Great Dunmow, Essex, Poor Law Institution. New, 1838.   3, 9
Great Dunmow, Essex, schools. New, 1866.   4
Great Grimsby, Lincolnshire, St James. Report (?) c 1863.   9
Great Horwood, Buckingham, St James. Restoration c 1874.   1, 6, 8, 9
Great Malvern, Worcester, Priory of St Michael and All Angels.
    Restoration c 1864: Lambert monument 1872.   1, 4, 5, 9
Great Marlow, Buckingham, Holy Trinity. New, 1851-2.   1, 2, 4
Great Milton, Oxford, St Mary. Restoration 1849-50.   4, 5
Great Yarmouth, Norfolk, St Nicholas. Report, c 1863.   4
Green Hammerton, West Yorkshire, St Thomas. New, 1876.   1, 2, 9
Green Hammerton, West Yorkshire, schools. New.   9
Guildford, Surrey, Poor Law Institution. New, 1836-8.   6
Guyhirn, Cambridge, St Mary Magdalene. New, 1877-8.   1, 2, 8, 9

Hales, Stafford, St Mary. New, 1856.   2
Halesowen, Worcester, St John Baptist. Restoration 1873-5;
    reredos, 1878.   1, 4, 8, 9
Halifax, West Yorkshire, All Souls. New, 1856-9.   1, 2, 3, 4, 5, 9
Halifax, West Yorkshire, St John Baptist. Restoration 1875-80.   9
Halifax, West Yorkshire, All Souls vicarage. New, c 1856.   1, 3, 4, 7
Halifax, West Yorkshire, Akroydon. Layout, some houses, 1861—
    continued by W. H. Crossland.   4
Halifax, West Yorkshire, Town Hall. Unexecuted, c 1857.   3, 5, 9
Halstead, Essex, St James Apostle. New, 1844-5.   1, 2, 4
Halstead, Essex, St James Apostle, parsonage. New, c 1844.
Halstead, Essex, St James Apostle, schools. New, c 1844.

Halstead, Essex, Holy Trinity. New, 1843-4.   1, 2, 4
Halton, Cheshire, St Mary the Virgin. New, 1851-2.   1, 2, 4
Ham, Middlesex, The Manor House. Alteration, c 1864.
Hamburg, Germany, Rathaus. Competition entry 1855.   3, 4, 5, 8
Hamburg, Germany, St Nicholas. New, 1845-80.   1, 3, 4, 5, 8, 9
Hampton Lucy, Warwick, St Peter. Apse, c 1857.   1, 5, 9
Hampstead, London, Christ Church. Gallery, 1860.   9
Hanley Swan, Worcester, St Gabriel. New, 1871-3.   1, 2, 4, 9
Hanwell, Middlesex, St Mary. New, 1841.   2, 3, 5, 9
Hardwick, Oxford, St Mary. Restoration 1878-9 with G.G.Scott
   Junior.   1, 7, 9
Harewood, West Yorkshire, All Saints. Restoration by 1863.   1, 4, 9
Harlestone, Northampton, St Andrew. Restoration 1853.   5
Harrow, Middlesex, St Mary. Restoration 1846-9.   1, 3, 5, 9
Harrow, Middlesex, school chapel. New, 1855-6.   1, 5, 9
Harrow, Middlesex, Vaughan library. New, 1861-3.   1, 4, 5, 9
Hartfield, Sussex, St Mary. Report on east window, c 1867.   6
Harting, Sussex, Sts Mary and Gabriel. Survey for restoration 1851.   6
Hartland, Devon, Abbey (house). Alteration 1860s.   1, 9
Hartshead, West Yorkshire, St Peter. Design for restoration 1876.   4, 9
Hartshill, Stafford, Holy Trinity. New, 1840-8, restoration
   1872.   1, 2, 3, 4, 5, 8, 9
Hartshill, Stafford, parsonage. New, c 1840.   5
Hartshill, Stafford, schools. New, c 1840.   5, 9
Hartshill, Stafford, almshouses. New, by 1857.   5
Hatch Beauchamp, Somerset, St John Baptist. Restoration 1867.   1, 9
Hawarden, Flint, St Deiniol. Restoration 1857-61.   1, 4, 5, 9
Hawick, Roxburgh, St Cuthbert. New, 1859.   2, 5
Hawkhurst, Kent, All Saints. New, 1859-61.   1, 2, 4, 5, 9
Hawkstone, Shropshire, chapel. Alteration c 1860.   1, 3
Hayes, Kent, St Mary the Virgin. Restoration c 1856-62.   1, 8
Hayes, Middlesex, St Mary. Restoration 1873.   1, 9
Hayes, Middlesex, schools. New.   1, 9
Hayes, Middlesex, parsonage. New.   9
Haynes, Bedford, St Mary. Tomb canopy, 1863.
Headington, Oxford, St Andrew. Unexecuted restoration 1848.
Headington Quarry, Oxford, Holy Trinity. New, 1848-9.   2, 4, 5
Helmsley, North Yorkshire, Duncombe Park. Alteration 1874-8,
   burned 1879.   7, 9
Helmsley, North Yorkshire, Duncombe Park, Lodges. c 1874.   7
Helmsley, North Yorkshire, Market Cross. New, 1869.   4, 9
Hemington, Somerset, St Mary. Restoration 1859.   4, 6
Hendon, Middlesex, Poor Law Institution. Probably unexecuted, 1839.   6
Henllan, Denbigh, St Sadwrn. Restoration.
Hereford, Hereford, Cathedral. Restoration 1855-63.   1, 3, 4, 5, 7, 9
Hereford, Hereford, Blackfriars Cross. Restoration (?).   9
Heston, Middlesex, St Leonard. Report (?) 1864.   5

Higham, Suffolk St Stephen. New, c 1861.   1, 2, 4, 9
Higham, Suffolk, Rectory. New, c 1861.
Highclere, Hampshire, St Michael and All Angels.
New, 1869-70.   1, 2, 4, 8, 9
Hillesden, Buckingham, All Saints. Restotion 1873-5.   3, 5, 8
Hillesden, Buckingham, vicarage. New, 1870.   1, 6, 8, 9
Hillingdon, Middlesex, St Andrew. New, 1863.   1, 4, 5, 9
Hillingdon, Middlesex, St John Baptist. Restoration 1847-8.   1, 9
Histon, Cambridge, St Andrew. Restoration 1872-5.   1, 4, 9
Hitchin, Hertford, St Mary. Restoration c 1859-65.   1, 9
Hixon, Stafford, St Peter. New, 1848.
Holbeck, West Yorkshire, St John. New, 1847-8.
Demolished.   1, 2, 3, 4, 5, 8, 9
Holborn, London, Kings College Chapel. Alteration by 1864.   1, 3, 4, 5, 9
Holborn, London, Law Courts. Competition entry 1867.   3, 4, 5, 8
Holborn, London, Lincoln's Inn Chapel. Addition 1878-83,
with Samuel Salter.
Holborn, London, Lincoln's Inn new chambers. New Block A, 1873:
Block B, 1876-8 with J. O. Scott.   4, 7, 8, 9
Holborn, Lincoln's Inn library. Addition 1870-2.   4, 9
Holdenby, Northampton, All Saints. Restoration 1867-8.   4, 9
Holme, Nottingham, Survey for restoration c 1851.   6
Holton Beckering, Lincoln, All Saints. Restoration c 1860.
Hornsea, North Yorkshire, St Nicholas. Restoration 1866-7.   1, 4, 9
Holyhead, Anglesey, St Cybi. Restoration 1877-9.   1, 6, 8, 9
Hougham, Lincoln, All Saints. Restoration 1844.   2
Houghton, Hampshire, All Saints. Chancel, restoration 1874.   1, 9
Houghton Conquest, Bedford, All Saints. Restoration 1868-70.   1, 3, 4, 9
Hove, Sussex, St Patrick. Pulpit, 1858.   9
Hulme Walfield, Cheshire, St Michael. New, 1855-6.   2
Huddersfield, West Yorkshire, St Thomas. New, 1858-9.   1, 5, 9
Hull, East Yorkshire, St Mary Lowgate. Restoration 1860-3.   1, 9
Hull, East Yorkshire, Holy Trinity. Restoration 1861, 1865,
1876-8.   1, 4, 5, 8, 9
Hull, East Yorkshire, St Mary Lowgate parsonage. New, c 1860.   1, 9
Hulme, Lancashire, Holy Trinity. New, 1841, demolished 1953.   2, 4, 5
Hundleby, Lincoln, Poor Law Institution. New, 1837.
Huntingdon, Huntingdon, All Saints. Restoration 1861-2.   5
Huntingdon, Huntingdon, St Mary. Restoration.   1
Hythe, Kent, St Leonard. Restoration 1875.   1, 9

Ickleford, Hertford, St Katharine. Restoration 1859.   1, 9
Ilam, Stafford, Holy Cross. Restoration 1855-6.   4, 5
Ilam, Stafford, school. New, 1854.   5
Ilam, Stafford, cottages. New, c 1857.
Islington, London, St Clement, Barnsbury. New, 1864-5.   1, 2, 4, 8, 9
Islington, London, St Matthew. New, 1847-8, addition 1874. Dem. 1, 4, 5, 9

Itchingfield, Sussex, St Nicholas. Restoration c 1866. 1, 4, 9
Iver, Buckingham, St Peter. Restoration 1847-8. 1, 5, 9

Jarrow, Durham, St Paul. Restoration 1865-6. 1, 4, 5, 9
Jedburgh, Selkirk, Abbey. Report (?) 1874. 4

Kelham, Nottingham, Hall. Alterations 1857: new after
fire 1858-62. 1, 4, 5, 8, 9
Kelso, Roxburgh, church. New. 1, 9
Kenley, Surrey, church. Competition assessor, c 1870. 9
Kensington, London, block on Kensington Gore: six unexecuted
designs 1863-5. 3, 5
Kensington, London, Albert Memorial. New, 1864-71. 1, 3, 4, 5, 8, 9
Kensington, London, St Mary Abbots. New, 1870-2 and later. 1, 4, 9
Kettering, Northampton, Poor Law Institution. New, c 1836.
Ketton, Rutland, St Mary. Restoration nave, 1860-2. 1, 5, 9
Kiddington, Oxford, St Nicholas. Restoration apse, 1845.
Kidsgrove, Stafford, St Thomas. Chancel, 1853. 2
Kidwelly, Carmarthen, church. Report (?) 1854. 1, 9
Kilkhampton, Cornwall, St James. Restoration 1858 1, 9
Kilkhampton, Cornwall, parsonage. New, c 1858. 9
Kingsley, Cheshire, St John Evangelist. New, 1849-51. 2, 9
Kings Lynn, Norfolk, St Margaret. Restoration 1863-5. 1, 4, 9
Kings Lynn, Norfolk, St Nicholas. Spire, 1869. 1, 9
Kings Sutton, Northampton, Sts Peter and Paul. Chancel,
restoration 1866. 1, 4, 9
Kinver, Stafford, St Peter. Unexecuted restoration 1878. 7, 9
Kirby Hill, North Yorkshire, All Saints. Restoration 1869-70. 1, 4, 9
Kirby Wiske, North Yorkshire, St John Baptist. East
window, c 1876. 2
Kirkby Moorside, North Yorkshire, All Saints. Restoration
1873-5 1, 4, 7, 9
Kirkstall, West Yorkshire, Abbey. Report, c 1873. 4, 9
Kirtlington, Oxford, St Mary the Virgin. Chancel,
restoration 1877. 1, 8, 9

Ladbroke, Warwick, All Saints. Restoration c 1876. 1, 4, 8, 9
Langton Green, Kent, All Saints. New, 1862-3. 1, 2, 4, 9
Lanhydrock, Cornwall, House. Alteration, addition 1857-64. 9
Latimer, Buckingham, St Mary Magdalene. Addition 1867. 1, 2, 4, 9
Leafield, Oxford, St Michael. New, 1858-60. 1, 2, 4, 9
Leafield, Oxford, vicarage. New. 1, 9
Leamington Hastings, Warwick, All Saints. Unexecuted
restoration c 1877. 7, 9
Ledbury, Hereford, St Michael and All Angels. Font, c 1850-3 (?). 1, 9
Leeds, West Yorkshire, All Souls. New, 1876-80. 1, 2, 3, 7, 8, 9
Leeds, West Yorkshire, St Andrew. New, 1845. 2, 8

Leeds, West Yorkshire, St John. Report 1865.   3, 4, 5, 9
Leeds, West Yorkshire, St Peter. Hook monument, c 1876.   9
Leeds, West Yorkshire, St Andrew's schools. New, c 1845.
Leeds, West Yorkshire, Beckett's Bank, Park Row. New, 1863-7.   1, 3, 4
Leeds, West Yorkshire, Infirmary. New, 1864-7.   1, 4, 5, 9
Leicester, St Andrew. New, 1860-2.   1, 2, 5, 9
Leicester, St John. New, 1853-4.   1, 2, 4
Leicester, St Matthew Apostle. New, 1865.   1, 2, 4, 9
Leicester, St Margaret. Restoration 1864-5.   1, 4, 9
Leicester, St Mary de Castro. Restoration 1860.   1, 4
Leicester, St Saviour. New, 1875-6.   1, 2, 4, 9
Leicester, St Andrew's parsonage. New, c 1861.   9
Leicester, St Saviour's parsonage. New, 1875.   4, 9
Leicester, St Saviour's schools. New, 1875.   4
Leith, Midlothian, St James the Less. New, 1862-6.   1, 2, 4, 9
Leith, Midlothian, parsonage. New, c 1862.   4, 9
Leominster, Hereford, Sts Peter and Paul. Restoration 1864-6,
    1876-8.   1, 4, 7, 8, 9
Lewes, Sussex, Fitzroy memorial library. 1862.   9
Lewisham, London, Christ Church, Lee Park. New, 1853,
    demolished 1944.   1, 2, 4, 9
Lewisham, London, St Margaret. Minor alteration 1870.
Lewisham, London, St Stephen. New, 1863-5.   1, 2, 4, 5, 9
Lichfield, Stafford, Cathedral. Restoration 1855-61, 1877-81,
    Lonsdale memorial, 1872.   1, 3, 4, 5, 7, 8, 9
Lichfield, Stafford, Poor Law Institution. New, 1838.
Lincoln, Cathedral. Pulpit, 1863.   1, 4
Lincoln, St Nicholas. New, 1839-40.   2, 3, 6
Liskeard, Cornwall, Poor Law Institution. New, 1837.
Littlebourne, Kent, Lee Priory (house). Alteration 1860-3, most
    demolished 1954. Stables, c 1865.   1, 5, 9
Little Budworth, Cheshire, Oulton Park. Egerton monument c 1846.
Little Gaddesden, Hertford, Ashridge (house). Alteration (?).   9
Little Horsted, Sussex, St Michael. Restoration 1863.   1, 4, 9
Little Stewkeley, Huntingdon, St Martin. Restoration (?).   1, 9
Liverpool, Lancashire, 'Clevely', Allerton Road. New, mostly
    demolished.   1, 9
Liverpool, Lancashire, College. Competition entry, 1840.
Liverpool, Lancashire, St Mary, West Derby. New, 1853-6.   1, 2, 3, 5, 9
Llandilo, Carmarthen, St Teilo. New, excluding tower, 1848-51.   1, 6
Llanelly, Carmarthen, St Paul. New, 1857.   2
Llangollen, Denbigh, Valle Crucis Abbey. Repair west front, 1872.
Llangurig, Montgomery, St Curig. Restoration 1876-80.   1, 7, 9
Llangernyw, Denbigh, Hafodunus (house). New, 1861-6.   1, 3, 8, 9
Llawr y Bettws, Merioneth, St James the Great. New, 1864.   2, 9
Llywell, Brecon, church. Restoration 1869.   1, 4, 9
London, Grocers' Hall. Competition entry, 1864.   4

London, St Alban, Wood Street. Restoration 1855-6, demolished. 1, 5, 9
London, St Michael, Cornhill. Restoration 1856-60 with W.H.Mason,
  H. and H.J.Williams. 1, 3, 4, 5, 9
London, St Olave, Hart Street. Restoration 1863, work removed. 9
London, St Botolph, Aldersgate. N.G.Scott monument, 1841,
  demolished. 3
Long Buckby, Northampton, St Lawrence. Restoration 1862-3. 1, 4, 5, 9
Long Marston, West Yorkshire, All Saints. Restoration 1869. 1, 4
Long Marston, Hertford, All Saints. Restoration, demolished 1883. 1
Longton, Stafford, Holy Evangelists. New, 1847. 1, 5
Longton, Stafford, Resurrection. New, 1853, addition 1863. 2, 4
Loughborough, Leicester, Poor Law Institution. New, 1837-8,
  demolished 1977. 2, 6
Loughborough, Leicester, All Saints. Restoration 1860-2. 1, 4, 5, 9
Louth, Lincoln, Poor Law Institution. New, 1839. 6
Loversal, West Yorkshire, St Katherine. Restoration 1855-6. 4
Lowdham, Nottingham, St Mary. Restoration. 1, 9
Ludlow, Shropshire, St Lawrence. Restoration 1859-60. 1, 4, 5, 9
Ludlow, Shropshire, St Leonard. New, 1870-1. 1, 2, 4
Lutterworth, Leicester, St Mary the Virgin. Restoration 1867-9. 1, 4, 9
Lutterworth, Leicester, Poor Law Institution. New, 1839-40. 6
Lyndhurst, Hampshire, schools. New, altered. 9

Macclesfield, Cheshire, Poor Law Institution. New, 1843. 3
Malvern Link, Worcester, St Matthias. Addition 1860, probably
  removed. 1, 9
Manchester, Lancashire, Cathedral. Restoration c 1872. 1, 3, 6, 9
Mansfield Woodhouse, Nottingham, St Edward. Restoration
  1847-50. 1, 3, 9
Market Harborough, Leicester, St Dionysius. Restoration c 1860. 1
Marston Moretaine, Bedford, St Mary. Restoration c 1871. 1, 6, 9
Marylebone, London, Gray and Davidson's organ factory.
  Doorway, c 1853, demolished. 4
Melbourne, Derby, Sts Michael and Mary. Restoration 1860. 1, 4, 9
Melbourne, New South Wales, Australia, Hotham monument c 1856. 1, 5
Melton Mowbray, Leicester, St Mary. Restoration c 1871-6. 1, 4, 6, 7, 9
Mere, Wiltshire, Poor Law Institution. New, 1838, demolished.
Middle Claydon, Buckingham, All Saints. Restoration
  by 1870. 1, 4, 6, 8, 9
Middle Claydon, Buckingham, Claydon House. Addition c 1860. , 1
Middleton Cheney, Northampton, All Saints. Restoration 1864-5. 1, 4, 9
Middleton Tyas, North Yorkshire, St Mary. Restoration 1868. 1, 9
Middleton Tyas, North Yorkshire, schools. New (?). 9
Milton Abbas, Dorset, Abbey church. Restoration 1864-5. 4, 5
Milton Abbas, Dorset, Milton Abbey (house). Restoration. 1, 9
Milton, Oxford, Milton Hill House. Alteration, removed. 1, 9
Mirfield, West Yorkshire, St Mary the Virgin. New, 1869-71. 1, 4, 9

Mirfield, West Yorkshire, parsonage. New, c 1869.   1, 9
Mold, Flint, St Mary. Restoration 1865.   5, 7, 9
Moulsford, Berkshire, St John Baptist. New, 1846-7.
Muswellbrook, New South Wales, Australia, St Alban. New, 1863-9.   1, 9

Nailsea, Somerset, Christ Church, New, 1843.   2, 5
Nantwich, Cheshire, St Mary. Restoration 1853-61, chancel seats
   c 1878.   1, 3, 4, 5, 7, 9
Newark, Nottingham, St Mary Magdalene. Restoration 1852-5,
   tower restored 1869.   1, 3, 4, 5, 6, 8, 9
Newcastle upon Tyne, Northumberland, St Nicholas. Restoration
   1867-71, 1872-6.   1, 4, 5, 7, 9
Newcastle upon Tyne, Northumberland, Assize Court.
   Unexecuted 1876.   4, 9
Newcastle under Lyme, Stafford, St Giles. New excluding tower,
   1873-5.   ˙   1, 4, 7, 9
Newcastle under Lyme, Stafford, Poor Law Institution.
   New, 1839, demolished 1938.
Newent, Gloucester, St Mary. Unexecuted, restoration c 1878.   7, 9
New Romney, Kent, St Nicholas. Restoration 1880.   8, 9
New Southgate, Middlesex, St Michael at Bowes. New, 1862-74.   1, 2, 4, 9
New Southgate, Middlesex, St Paul. New, 1873.   1, 2, 8, 9
New Southgate, Middlesex, St Michael's parsonage. New, c 1874.   9
Newton Abbot, Devon, Poor Law Institution. New, 1837, most
   demolished.
Nocton, Lincoln, All Saints. New, 1860-3.   1, 2, 4, 8, 9
Nocton, Lincoln, schools. New, 1869.   1, 9
Norbiton, Surrey, St Peter. New, 1842.   1, 2, 3, 5, 9
Northampton, Asylum chapel. New, 1861-3.   1, 5, 9
Northampton, Asylum. Alteration.   1
Northampton, Poor Law Institution. New, 1836.
Northampton, St Sepulchre. Restoration, addition 1851, 1860-4,
   1866, 1868-9, 1877.   1, 3, 4, 5, 8, 9
Northampton, St Giles. Report by 1853.   5
Northampton, St Peter. Restoration 1850-2.   1, 3, 4, 5
North Aston, Oxford, St Mary. Addition 1866-7.   9
Norton, Radnor, St Andrew. Restoration by 1868.   1, 4
Norton St Philip, Somerset, St Philip. Restoration 1849-50.   1, 2, 4, 9
Norwich, Norfolk, Cathedral. Report.   1, 9
Nottingham, St Mary. Restoration 1845-8, 1865-7.   1, 3, 4, 5, 8, 9
Nottingham, St John Baptist, Lean side. New, 1843-4, demolished.   1, 2

Oakham, Rutland, All Saints. Restoration 1857-8.   1, 5, 9
Odd Rode, Cheshire, All Saints. New, 1863-4.   1, 4
Okeford Fitzpaine, Dorset, St Andrew. Restoration (? executed), 1865.
Okeover, Stafford, All Saints. Restoration 1856-8.   1, 4
Old Malton, North Yorkshire, St Mary. Survey, 1877.   7

Old Windsor, Berkshire, Poor Law Institution. New, 1839.   3, 6
Old Windsor, Berkshire, St Peter, Restoration 1863-4.   1, 4, 5, 9
Olney, Buckingham, Sts Peter and Paul. Restoration 1869, 1873-4,
    1876-7.   1, 4, 7, 9
Orchardleigh, Somerset, St Mary. Restoration 1878-81.   1, 7, 9
Ottershaw, Surrey, Christ Church. New, excluding tower, 1864.   1, 2, 4, 7, 9
Ottershaw, Surrey, Christ Church parsonage. New, c 1864.
Oundle, Northampton, St Peter. Restored 1864.   1, 4, 5, 9
Oundle, Northampton, Poor Law Institution. New, 1836,
    demolished 1976.
Owston, West Yorkshire, All Saints. Restoration 1873.   1, 4, 9
Oxford, Merton College hall. Restoration 1872.   1, 4, 8, 9
Oxford, New College chapel. Restoration 1877-80.   1, 7, 8, 9
Oxford, New College hall. Roof renewed, 1865.
Oxford, New College, new rooms, Holywell Street. 1872-5.   4, 9
Oxford, All Souls College chapel. Restoration 1873.   8, 9
Oxford, University College library. New, 1860-1.   4, 5, 9
Oxford, University College chapel. Restoration 1862.   4
Oxford, Exeter College chapel. New, 1857-9.   1, 3, 4, 5, 9
Oxford, Exeter College library. New, 1856-7.   5
Oxford, Exeter College, Rector's house. New, 1857-8.   1, 5
Oxford, Exeter College, Broad St range. New, 1855-6.   5
Oxford, Magdalen College, President's room. Restoration 1856.   1, 5
Oxford, Magdalen College, new buildings. Unexecuted, c 1878.   7
Oxford, St Mary the Virgin. Restored 1856-7, exterior 1862-4.   4, 5, 9
Oxford, St Mary Magdalene. Restoration 1841-2.   1, 3, 4
Oxford, Martyrs' Memorial. New, 1841-3.   1, 3, 9
Oxford, Christ Church Cathedral. Restoration 1870-2, tower,
    unexecuted, 1874, furnishings 1874-6.   1, 3, 4, 8, 9
Oxford, Radcliffe Infirmary. Addition 1869-71, with C. Buckeridge.   4, 9
Oxford, Bodleian Library. Alteration c 1877.   9

Padbury, Buckingham, St Mary the Virgin. Restoration 1881-2.   7, 9
Patrixbourne, Kent, St Mary. Restoration 1857.   1, 9
Patshull, Stafford, St Mary. Restoration, perhaps unexecuted.   1, 9
Pattingham, Stafford, St Chad. Restoration 1865. Fittings 1878.   1, 4, 7, 9
Penkhull, Stafford, St Thomas Apostle. New, 1842.   1
Penmaenmawr, Caernarvon, church. Dean of Ripon's monument.   9
Penpont, Brecon, church. New, 1854.   1, 9
Penshurst, Kent, St John Baptist. Restoration 1854-8.   1, 9
Pentrefoelas, Denbigh, church. New, 1857.   1, 2, 9
Penzance, Cornwall, Poor Law Institution. New, 1838.
Pershore, Worcester, Abbey of the Holy Cross. Restoration 1861-4,
    decorations 1867.   1, 4, 5, 9
Peterborough, Northampton, Training College. New, 1856-64.   1, 5, 9
Peterborough, Northampton, Cathedral. Restoration 1855-60.   1, 3, 5, 9
Peterborough, Northampton, Deanery. Restoration c 1875.

Peterborough, Northampton, schools. New.   1, 9
Peterstow, Hereford, St Peter. Restoration 1865-6.   1, 5, 9
Pitminster, Somerset, Sts Mary and Andrew. Restoration 1869.   9
Plymouth, Devon, St Andrew. Restoration 1874-5, ruined.   1, 4, 9
Pockley, North Yorkshire, St John Baptist. New, 1870.
Polebrook, Northampton, All Saints. Restoration.   1, 9
Portsmouth, Hampshire, All Saints. Restored chancel, 1876-7.   1, 7, 9
Prestbury, Cheshire, St Peter. Restoration 1881-8.   7, 8, 9
Preston, Lancashire, Town Hall. New, 1862-7, demolished.   3, 4, 5, 9
Preston, Lancashire, markets. New, possibly unexecuted.   4, 5, 9
Preston, Lancashire, Emmanuel. Unexecuted design c 1861-9.   8

Queenhill, Worcester, St Nicholas. Tower, restoration c 1855.   1

Raithby by Spilsby, Lincoln, Holy Trinity. Restoration 1873.
Ramsgate, Kent, Christ Church. New, 1846-8.   4
Ranmore, Surrey, St Barnabas. New, 1859.   1, 2, 3, 9
Ranmore, Surrey, schools. New, 1859, addition 1874.   7
Ranmore, Surrey, vicarage. New, c 1859.
Raunds, Northampton, St Mary. Restoration 1873-4.   1, 4, 9
Reading, Berkshire, gaol. New, 1842-4.   .   1, 3, 4, 9
Reading, Berkshire, Abbey gateway. Rebuilt after collapse 1861.   1, 9
Redruth, Cornwall, Poor Law Institution. New, 1838.
Reigate, Surrey, St Mary Magdalene. Report 1873.   4
Rhuddlan, Flint, St Mary. Restoration 1868.   1, 8, 9
Rhyl, Flint, St Thomas. New, 1860, spire, 1874.   1, 2, 8, 9
Richmond, Surrey, St Matthias. New, 1856-8, later additions.   1, 4, 5, 7, 9
Richmond, North Yorkshire, St Mary. Restoration 1859-60.   1, 9
Ridgmont, Bedford, All Saints. New, 1855.   1, 2, 4, 5
Rievaulx, North Yorkshire, Abbey. Restoration, unexecuted,
   c 1877.   6, 8, 9
Ripon, West Yorkshire, Cathedral. Restoration 1862-72.   1, 3, 4, 5, 9
Rochester, Kent, Cathedral. Restoration 1871-4.   1, 3, 4, 8, 9
Rotherham, West Yorkshire, All Saints. Restoration 1873-5,
   reredos, 1876.   1, 4, 9
Rottingdean, Sussex, St Margaret. Restoration 1856.
Roxeth, Middlesex, Christ Church. New, 1862, south aisle, 1866.   1, 9
Rugby, Warwick, Holy Trinity. New, 1852-3.   ‧ 1, 2, 4, 5
Rugby, Warwick, School laboratory. New, 1852.   1
Rugby, Warwick, School master's houses. New (?).   9
Ruislip, Middlesex, St Martin. Restoration 1870.   1, 9
Rushden, Northampton, Poor Law Institution. New, 1839 (?).   6
Ryde, Isle of Wight, All Saints. New, 1869-72.   1, 2, 4, 8, 9
St Albans, Hertford, dispensary. New, unidentified.   1, 9
St Albans, Hertford, fountain. Unexecuted (?).   6, 9
St Albans, Hertford, clock tower. Restoration 1867.   1, 4, 9
St Albans, Hertford, St Michael. Restoration 1866.   1, 3, 4, 9

St Albans, Hertford, Abbey. Restoration 1871-80.   1, 3, 4, 5, 6, 7, 8, 9
St Albans, Hertford, Abbey gateway. Restoration.   4, 5, 9
St Asaph, Flint, Cathedral. Restored chancel, 1866-9,
  reredos, 1871.   1, 3 4, 9
St Asaph, Flint, Sts Kentigern and Asaph. Restoration c 1872.   1, 4, 9
St Austell, Cornwall, Poor Law Institution. New. Demolished.   6
St Blazey, Cornwall. St Blaze. Restoration 1839.   6
St Columb Major, Cornwall, Poor Law Institution. New, 1838.   6
St David's, Pembroke, Cathedral. Restoration 1864-76.   1, 3, 4, 5, 8, 9
St Hilary, Glamorgan, St Hilary. Restoration c 1861-2.   1, 4, 8, 9
St John's, Newfoundland, Cathedral. New, 1847 on.   1, 3, 4, 5, 8, 9
St Lawrence, Isle of Wight, St Lawrence. New, 1878.   1, 2, 7, 9
St Mellons, Glamorgan, church. Restoration 1859.
St Neots, Huntingdon, St Mary. Newton monument.   9
St Pancras, London. St Pancras Station. New, 1866-76.   3, 4, 5, 8, 9
Salhouse, Norfolk, All Saints. Restoration 1881.   8, 9
Salisbury, Wiltshire, Cathedral. Restoration 1865-71, nave interior
  1877-9.   1, 3, 4, 5, 7, 8, 9
Salisbury, Wiltshire, Canon Swayne's house. Restoration.   4, 9
Salisbury, Wiltshire, St Edmund. Restoration 1866-7.   1, 4, 9
Sandbach, Cheshire, St Mary. Restoration 1847-9.   1, 5, 9
Sandbach, Cheshire, Grammar School. New, 1849.   5
Sandbach, Cheshire, Public building. New, 1857.   1, 5
Sandbach Heath, Cheshire, St John Evangelist. New, 1861.   2, 5
Sandwich, Kent, St Bartholomew's Hospital chapel. Restoration
  1877, 1883, 1887.   1, 7, 8, 9
Sarratt, Hertford, Holy Cross. Restoration 1866.   1, 4, 9
Savernake, Wiltshire, cottage hospital. New, 1871-2.   1, 4, 9
Sawbridgeworth, Hertford, St Mary the Great. Restoration c 1867.   1, 4, 9
Saxby All Saints, Lincoln, All Saints. New, excluding tower 1845-9.   1, 2, 9
Seal, Kent, St Peter. Restoration 1855 (?).   1
Seedley, Lancashire, St Luke. New, 1865, addition 1875.
Selby, West Yorkshire, Abbey. Restoration 1872-4, burned 1906.   1, 4, 9
Sewerby, East Yorkshire, St John Evangelist. New, 1847-8.   2, 3, 4, 5, 8
Sewerby, East Yorkshire, school. New, 1850.
Shackleford, Surrey, St Mary. New, 1865.   9
Shaftesbury, Dorset, Holy Trinity. New, 1842. Demolished.   2, 3, 4, 8
Shalstone, Buckingham, St Edward Confessor. Restoration 1861-2.   1, 2, 9
Shanghai, China, Holy Trinity Cathedral. New, 1868-9.   1, 4, 9
Shapwick, Somerset, St Mary. Restoration 1860-1.   1, 4, 9
Sheffield, West Yorkshire, Sts Peter and Paul. Report (?) c 1877.   4
Shellingford, Berkshire, St Faith. Repairs, 1852.
Sherbourne, Warwick, All Saints. New, 1862-4.   1, 2, 4, 5, 9
Shifnal, Shropshire, St Andrew. Restoration 1871-9.   1, 7, 8, 9
Shilton, Warwick, St Andrew. Restoration 1865.   1, 9
Shinfield, Berkshire, St Mary. Restoration 1855-6.
Shippon, Berkshire, St Mary Magdalene. New, 1855.

Shirley, Surrey, St John Evangelist. New, 1856.	1, 2, 8
Shrewsbury, Shropshire, Shelton Lunatic Asylum. New, 1843.	8
Skendleby, Lincoln, Sts Peter and Paul. Restoration 1875 (?).	
Skirbeck, Lincoln, St Nicholas. Restoration 1869-75.	4, 7, 8, 9
Skirbeck, Lincoln, Holy Trinity. New, 1846-8.	2, 4, 5, 8
Smeeth, Kent, Weston house (unidentified). New.	1, 9
Southampton, Hampshire, St Denys. New, 1868.	1, 2, 4, 8, 9
Southampton, Hampshire, Portswood schools. New, c 1866.	4, 9
Southgate, Middlesex, Christ Church. New, 1861-2.	1, 9
Southwark, London, Blackfriars Almshouses (unidentified).	1, 9
South Weald, Essex, St Peter. Screen, c 1877.	1, 7, 8, 9
Spalding, Lincoln, St Peter. New, 1875-6.	1, 2, 7, 9
Spalding, Lincoln, Sts Mary and Nicholas. Restoration 1867-74.	1, 5, 8, 9
Spratton, Northampton, St Andrew. Restoration 1847.	4, 5
Sprotborough, West Yorkshire, St Mary. Restoration.	1
Stafford, Stafford, St Mary. Restoration 1842-5.	1, 3, 4, 5, 9
Stafford, Stafford, St Chad. Restoration 1873-5.	1, 4, 8, 9
Stafford, Stafford, St Mary's schools. New, 1856.	9
Stafford, Stafford, St Mary Castlechurch. Restoration 1844, 1898, 1912.	1, 2, 5, 8
Standon, Stafford, All Saints. Restoration 1846-7 (?).	
Staveley, Derby, St John Baptist. Restoration 1868.	1, 4, 9
Staveley, Derby, Hall. Alteration (?).	1, 9
Steeple Claydon, Buckingham, St Michael. Restoration chancel c 1875.	1, 9
Stoke Newington, London, St Mary. New, 1855-8.	1, 4, 5, 9
Stoke Newington, London, St Mary's parsonage. New, c 1855.	9
Stoke Talmage, Oxford, St Mary Magdalene. Restoration 1861.	9
Stoneleigh, Warwick, St John Baptist. New, 1842-4.	2, 4, 8
Stourport, Worcester, St Michael, Mitton. New, 1879-1910, incomplete.	2, 4, 9
Stowford, Devon, St John. Restoration 1874.	1, 9
Streatham, London, schools (unidentified). New.	1, 9
Stretton, Cheshire, St Matthew. New, excluding chancel, 1870.	1, 2, 9
Stroud, Gloucester, St Lawrence. Reredos, 1872.	4, 9
Sudeley, Gloucester, Castle. Restoration part, unexecuted, 1854: possibly later work, lost.	1, 8, 9
Sudeley, Gloucester, Castle chapel. Restoration 1861.	1, 4
Swallowcliffe, Wiltshire, St Peter. New, 1842-3.	2
Swindon, Wiltshire, St Mark. New, 1845-6.	1, 2, 5, 8, 9
Swindon, Wiltshire, St Mark's parsonage. New, c 1846.	5
Swindon, Wiltshire, St Mark's schools and houses. New, c 1846.	5, 9
Swindon, Wiltshire, Christ Church. New, 1850-51.	1, 2, 4, 8, 9
Sydney, New South Wales, Australia, St Andrew's Cathedral. Chancel decoration, c 1868.	9
Tadcaster, West Yorkshire, St Mary. Survey, 1875.	4, 9
Tamworth, Stafford, St Editha. Restoration 1851, 1868-71.	1, 4

Tandridge, Surrey, St Peter. Scott tomb, 1872. Restoration 1875.   1, 4, 9
Taplow, Buckingham, St Nicholas. Restoration 1864-5.   1, 4, 8, 9
Taunton, Somerset, St John Baptist. New, 1860-3.   4, 5, 9
Taunton, Somerset, St Mary Magdalen. Restored tower, 1859-62
   with Benjamin Ferrey.   1, 4, 9
Tavistock, Devon, Poor Law Institution. New, 1837.
Tavistock, Devon, St Peter. Restoration 1867-8.   1, 4, 9
Tedstone Delamere, Hereford, St James. Restoration 1856-7.   1, 2, 9
Teffont Evias, Wiltshire, rectory. Rebuilt 1842.
Temple Balsall, Warwickshire, St Mary. Restoration 1849.   1, 9
Tewkesbury, Gloucester, Abbey. Restoration 1874-9.   1, 3, 4, 5, 7, 8, 9
Theddingworth, Northampton, All Saints. Restoration 1858.   5, 9
Thriplow, Cambridge, St George. Restoration 1877.   1, 7
Timsbury, Somerset, St Mary. Restoration 1851-2: survey 1878.   2, 4, 7, 9
Tiverton, Devon, Poor Law Institution. New, 1836.
Tonbridge, Kent, Sts Peter and Paul. Restored chancel 1856
   (? executed).   1, 5
Totnes, Devon, St Mary. Restoration 1868-74.   1, 4, 9
Totnes, Devon, Poor Law Institution. New, 1836.
Towcester, Northampton, Poor Law Institution. New, 1836.
Trefnant, Denbigh, Holy Trinity. New, 1855.   1, 4, 9
Trefnant, Denbigh, parsonage. New, c 1855.   9
Trefnant, Denbigh, schools. New, c 1855.   9
Trofarth, Denbigh, St John. New, 1873.   2
Truro, Cornwall, Polwhele house. Addition c 1870.   9
Turnham Green, Middlesex, Christ Church. New, 1841-3.   1, 2, 3, 5, 9
Turvey, Bedford, All Saints. Restoration 1852-4.   1
Tuxford, Nottingham, St Nicholas. Restoration.   1
Tydd St Giles, Cambridge, St Giles. Restoration.   1, 9
Tydd St Giles, Cambridge, rectory. New, 1868.
Tydweiliog, Caernarvon, St Cwyvan. New, 1850.   2, 5
Tysoe, Warwick, Schools. New, 1856. Demolished.
Tysoe, Warwick, Assumption. Restoration 1854.   1, 5

Underriver, Kent, St Margaret. New, c 1867.   1, 2, 4, 9
Upton, Huntingdon, St Margaret. Restoration 1871.   1, 8, 9
Uckfield, Sussex, Holy Cross (?). Restoration, no details,
   possibly unexecuted.   1, 9
Upton Bishop, Hereford, St John Baptist. Restoration 1862.   1, 4, 9
Uttoxeter, Stafford, Poor Law Institution. New, 1839 (?).   6

Wakefield, West Yorkshire, All Saints. Restoration 1858-9, 1860,
   1865-9, 1872-4.   1, 5, 9
Wakefield, West Yorkshire, asylum chapel. New.   1, 9
Wakefield, West Yorkshire, bridge chapel. Restoration
   c 1847.   1, 3, 4, 5, 8, 9
Wakefield, West Yorkshire, St Andrew. New, 1846.   2, 8

Wall, Stafford, St John. Design 1839, possibly unexecuted.   6
Wallasey, Cheshire, St James. New, 1854-6.   1, 2, 5, 9
Waltham on the Wolds, Leicester, St Mary Magdalene.
Restoration 1850.   5, 8
Walton, Warwick, Hall. New, c 1858-62, 1875.   1, 3, 4, 7, 9
Walton, Buckingham, St Michael. Restoration 1860.   4
Wanstead, Essex, Christ Church. New, 1861, 1867.   1, 2, 9
Wanstead, Essex, Infant Orphan Asylum. 1841-3.   1, 3, 4, 8
Wappenham, Northampton, Schools. New, c 1862.   4, 5
Wappenham, Northampton, vicarage. New, 1833.   3
Wappenham, Northampton, house. New, c 1835.
Warmington, Northampton, St Mary the Blessed Virgin.
Restoration 1876-7.   1, 4, 7, 8, 9
Washingborough, Lincoln, St John Evangelist. Restoration 1859, 1861-2,
with Goddard.   4
Wasperton, Warwick, St John Baptist. Restoration 1843.   5
Watford, Hertford, St Mary. Restoration unexecuted, 1869.   4, 8
Weaste, Lancashire, St Luke. New, 1864-5.   1, 2, 4, 8, 9
Weaste, Lancashire, St Luke's parsonage. New, c 1865.   4
Weeton, West Yorkshire, St Barnabas. New, 1852.   3, 4
Weeton, West Yorkshire, parsonage. New, c 1852.   4
Welford on Avon, Warwick, St Peter. Restoration 1866-7.   9
Wellingborough, Northampton, All Hallows. Restoration 1850,
chancel: 1860-1 with E.F.Law.   4
Wellington, Berkshire, College chapel. New, 1861-3.   1, 3, 4, 5, 8, 9
Wells, Somerset, Lunatic asylum. New, 1845.   4, 8
Wells, Somerset, Cathedral. **Report on West Front, with Ferrey, 1869.**   4, 9
Welton, East Yorkshire, St Helen. Restoration 1862-3.   1, 4, 9
Welshampton, Shropshire, St Michael. New, 1863.   1, 2, 4, 9
Wembley, Middlesex, St John Evangelist. New, 1845 and later.   1, 5, 9
Wembley, Middlesex, parsonage. New, 1846.
Westcott, Surrey, Holy Trinity. New, 1851, alteration 1871.   1, 2, 9
West Felton, Shropshire, St Michael. Restoration chancel 1848: Kenyon
monument 1851.
West Ham, Essex, All Saints. Restoration 1847-9 with George Dyson,
reredos 1866.   1, 4, 9
West Meon, Hampshire, St John Evangelist. New, excluding
tower, 1845-6.   1, 4, 5
Westminster, London, Abbey. **Restoration, repairs and fittings,**
1848-78.   1, 3, 4, 5, 8, 9
Westminster, London, Chapter House. Restoration 1864-5.   3, 4, 5, 9
Westminster, London, Army and Navy Club, Pall Mall. Unexecuted
competition entry, 1847.   4, 5
Westminster, London, Broad Sanctuary houses. New 1852-4.   1, 3, 4, 9
Westminster, London Bayliff's Hospice, Dean's Yard. Alteration c 1856.   8
Westminster, London, 'Campo Santo'. Unexecuted memorial cloister.   8
Westminster, London, Deanery. Restoration.   8

Westminster, London, Dean's Yard houses (1, 3 and 3a). New, 1862.   1, 9
Westminster, London, Receiver General's House, Dean's Yard.
New, 1872.   1, 4, 8
Westminster, London, Government offices, Whitehall. New.
(4 unexecuted schemes) 1862-75.   1, 3, 4, 5, 8, 9
Westminster, London, Grosvenor Place, three houses. New.   1, 9
Westminster, London, Tothill Street Schools. New, Demolished.   9
Westminster, London, St Andrew. New, 1854-5, demolished c 1955.   1, 2, 5
Westminster, London, St Margaret. Restoration 1877-8.   1, 3 4, 7, 8, 9
Westminster, London, St Matthew. New, 1849-50.   1, 2, 4, 5, 8, 9
Westminster, London, Crimea monument, Broad Sanctuary.
New 1858.   1, 4, 5, 9
Weston on Trent, Stafford, St Andrew. Addition north aisle, 1860.   1, 4, 9
Weston on Trent, Stafford, parsonage. New, 1858.   1
Weston, Lincoln, St Mary. Restoration 1860.   1, 9
Weston Turville, Buckingham, rectory. New, 1838.   8
Whitby, North Yorkshire, Seamen's houses. New, 1842.
Whitnash, Warwick, St Margaret. Restored chancel 1855, south
aisle 1867, nave 1880.   5, 9
Whittlesey, Ely, St Mary. Restoration 1861-2.   1, 4, 9
Whixley, West Yorkshire, Ascension. Restoration 1861-2.   1, 4, 9
Wilburton, Cambridge, St Peter. Restoration c 1868.   1, 9
Williton, Somerset, Poor Law Institution. New, 1836.   8
Wimbledon, Surrey, St Mary. Restoration 1843, chancel
rebuilt 1860.   1, 2, 5, 9
Winchcombe, Gloucester, Almshouses. New, 1865.   1, 9
Winchcombe, Gloucester, school. New, 1868.   9
Winchester, Hampshire, Cathedral. Restored chancel,
Wilberforce monument 1875.   3, 4, 8, 9
Winchester, Hampshire, city cross. Restoration 1865.   1, 4, 5, 9
Windsor, Berkshire, Castle, St George's Chapel. Restoration
1863.   1, 4, 5, 8, 9
Windsor, Berkshire, Castle, Albert Memorial or Wolsey
Chapel. Restoration 1861-75.   1, 3, 4, 9
Windsor, Berkshire, Castle, Horseshoe Cloisters. Restoration
1871.   1, 9
Wing, Buckingham, All Saints. Restoration 1848-50.   3, 5
Winterton, Lincoln, All Saints. Restoration 1867-73 (?).   1, 7, 8, 9
Winslow, Buckingham, Poor Law Institution. New, 1835.   1, 8
Wirksworth, Derby, St Mary. Restoration 1870-2.   1, 4, 8, 9
Wisbech, Ely, Clarkson monument. New, 1880-2.   4, 7, 9
Wisbech, Ely, Sts Peter and Paul. Restoration with W. Bassett
Smith.
Woking, Surrey, St John Baptist. New, 1842, additions.   1, 2, 5, 9
Wolsingham, Durham, Sts Mary and Stephen. Restoration c 1848.   2, 4
Wolverton, Buckingham, St Mary the Virgin. New, 1864,
north aisle 1867.   1, 9

Wolverton, Buckingham, St Mary's vicarage. New (?).

Woodbastwick, Norfolk, Sts Fabian and Sebastian. Restoration
1877-81.   1, 7

Wood Green, Middlesex, St Michael and All Angels. New,
1843-4, totally rebuilt.   1, 4, 5

Wolland, Dorset, New 1855-6.   1, 2, 6

Woolton, Lancashire, Hall. Porch c 1865 (?).   9

Woolwich, London, Dockyard chapel. New, 1858-9, moved
bodily to Rochester Way as St Barnabas, 1933.   1, 5, 9

Worcester, Worcester, Cathedral. Restoration 1863-4, 1868.
1874 with A. E. Perkins.   1, 3, 4, 5, 9

Worcester, Worcester, Guildhall. Restoration 1876-80 with
Rowe.   1, 4, 7, 9

Worcester, Worcester, Mr Southall's House. New.   1, 9

Worsley, Lancashire, St Mark. New, 1844-6, tomb 1860.   1, 2, 3, 5, 9

Yarpole, Hereford, St Leonard. Restoration 1863-4.   1, 4, 9

Yiewsley, Middlesex. St Matthew. New, 1859.   1, 2, 9

York, East Yorkshire, Minster. Mason and Dixon monument
1860: desk 1861.   5

Zeals, Wiltshire, St Martin. New, 1845-6 (unexecuted design
1842).   1, 4, 5

Barrack School Chapels for HM Government. No details.   9

Baths and washhouses for the labouring poor. Competition
entry c 1845.   4

Model labourers' cottages. 1848, (?) unexecuted.   5

The following ninety-six items appear in the list in *The Builder*,
xxxvi, 360, but are not otherwise known as works or reports by
Scott. There is in addition a number of unidentified monuments.

Churches (new or restored)

Abergavenny, Adel, Algarkirk, Aldworth, Acton, Bowen (?), Bebington, Brance-
peth, Broughton Gifford, Boxmoor, Buckley, Cornway (?), Churchover, Cavers-
wall, Chetwode, Cossington, Cottingham, Chester (Holy Trinity), Dacre, Dud-
ley, Dedham, Dowlais, Erwarton, Filleigh, Fulham, Gosforth, Godshill, Gawcott,
Gazeley, Hereford (St Peter), Hereford (All Saints), Hessle (?), Heanor, Hungar-
ton, Horstead, Icklesham, Kirk Hammerton, Little Waltham, Latton; Llanidloes,
Lydford, Lugwardine, London (St Margaret, Lothbury), London (St Sepulchre),
Llandough, Laughton en le Morthen, Merthyr Tydfil, Pembroke, Petworth,
Stepney, Stratford on Avon (Holy Cross), Southampton (St Peter), Silverstone, St
Ives, Swainswick (?), St Albans (St Stephen), Skipton, Shipton, Streatham,
Trenthall, Twickenham, Twisleton, Upnor, Worcester (new), Woodbastwick,
Warlingham, Wye, Wingrave, Wingham, Wilmerton (?), Worldham, Westmin-
ster (St Peter), Woolverstone, West Walcot, Ylvsley (new) (?), York (Holy
Trinity).

Other works

Ardrossan schools, Burton Abbotts schools (?), Cambridge (University College Chapel) (?), **Colchester Castle, Croydon almshouses, Dundee (Albert Fountain)**, Edinburgh theological college, Holdenby House, Hull (fountain), Kingston Grange, Luton Hoo, Oxford Convocation house, Oxford (Worcester College), **Oxford (Magdalen College Chapel), Stafford asylum, Scott's Hall, Sir Francis** Scott's lodge, bridge and boathouse, Trevellyn Vean, Westminster House, Yarm (mansion at).

Appendix 3
Barnstaple Church

General specification of works required to be done in the Proposed Restoration of Barnstaple Church

Remove all the Pews, Galleries, and other modern fittings.

Take up all the floors; previously to which a correct plan must be made of all Monumental Slabs. The Slabs to be carefully preserved for the purpose of being relaid as nearly as possible in their original positions, or where directed.

The south wall and roof of the south aisle of the nave to be carefully taken down.

This aisle to be made wider according to the accompanying plan; the new roof to be made of clean deal with oak wall plates; the design to be like that of the north aisle.

Take down a portion of the north wall of the north aisle of nave, and build a new second north aisle; the roof to be like the new roof for south aisle, to have stone stairs for approach to the gallery.

The arcades of the nave, chancel, and transept, which have been destroyed, to be restored in box ground stone, according to the plan.

The plaster to be removed from the ceilings of all the roofs, and the woodwork to be carefully cleansed, and substantially restored in all respects according to the original design as regards both material and construction. The wall plates must be for the most part new, and also a great portion of the panelling.

The slates, laths, and boarding to be taken off all the roof; the defective timbers repaired with English oak. The gutters to be reformed and relaid with new lead. The roofs to be boarded on the back of the rafters with deal, to be wrought in all cases where there is no under panelling. Asphalte felting and slating laths to be fixed on the back of the boarding, and then all the roofs to be reslated with good slates of the sort already used, making use of all the old sound slates. The stack pipes to be renewed where defective.

All the internal ancient stone dressings to windows and door-ways, responds, etc. to be carefully cleaned from all whitewash and other extraneous substances, and the natural clean surface of the stone exposed to view.

The white wall-paint, etc. to be taken off by scraping and chemical means, and on no account are the ancient surfaces of the stones to be retooled. Plaster to be removed from the walls, and the walls to be re-plastered, excepting where there are ancient paintings; in such cases the paintings must be carefully preserved.

All defective, mutilated, and unsubstantial stone dressings and walling to be carefully restored in stone, and set in cement, the stone to be like the stone of the original work. Insert several bond stones to strengthen the walls, and also several strong iron ties.

The spire timbers to be very carefully and substantially repaired and strengthened with English oak; new wall plates will be required, and a considerable quantity of wrought iron ties. The external lead work to be carefully repaired and made weatherproof.

The bell floor and frames to be repaired and strengthened. A new ringers' floor, and stairs to it to be substituted for those which are there at present.

The external stone dressings and walls to be carefully and substantially repaired where defective; all defective pointing to be made good. The ground on the north side of the Church to be lowered 6 in. below the level of the floors internally. The foundations of the walls, where defective, to be underpinned with hard thin stones set in cement, and a proper and complete system of drainage to be made.

The whole area within the Church to be covered with a 6 in layer of good concrete.

The top of the concrete under the wooden floors to be at least 18 in. below the joists, and ventilators to be fixed in the external walls to ventilate these spaces. A layer of smith's ashes to be spread over the concrete under the wooden floors, and a 2 in. layer of sand over the concrete to receive the stone or tile pavement.

Brick or stone dwarf walls to be built to receive the floor joists.

The wooden floors to have oak sleepers and joists, and to be laid with $1\frac{1}{4}$ in. wrought deal battens, grooved and tongued with hoop iron; English oak cills to grip the floors into which the ends of the deals are to be fixed.

The floors of the passages and other portions not occupied by fixed seats to be laid with the old monumental stones, and the best plain black and red Minton's or Godwin's 4 in. tiles bedded in Portland cement. The steps to be of rubbed hard stone, making use of the old steps as far as they may be found good and applicable.

The new seats to be constructed of the best wainscot oak, and the gallery of the new second north aisle of English oak, excepting the floor-boards of the latter, which are to be of deal.

The Pulpit, Chancel, Stalls, Prayer Desk, and Altar Table, to be also of oak, according to designs which will be given.

˙The new windows to be glazed with hard quarry lights, with strong lead and glass, and the glazing of the other windows repaired and proper ventilators to be introduced where necessary.

Generally, all the works to be done in the best manner, with the best materials, and no material or workmanship to be omitted necessarily connected with the proper execution of all the works.

Appendix 4
Assistants and Pupils

This list of ninety-two names cannot be complete, but enumerates those for which there is evidence.

	Lived	In Scott's office	
Herbert J. Austin		-1868	To practice with Paley
Charles Bailey			
Arthur Baker	1841-96	1864-78	To practice. Obituary *Jnl RIBA*, 3s, iv, 360
John W. Barker		1866-78	
Alfred Bell		1849	Later stained glass designer
A. Bickerdike			
Joseph M. Bignell		1878	To J. O. Scott
Jabez Bignell		1862	
John Bignold		1858	
E. Birchall			
George Frederick Bodley	1827-1907	1845-56	To practice. Fawcett (ed), *Seven Victorian Architects*
Boyce		1839	
W. Boyle			
Broughton			
Charles Buckeridge	1833-73	1856-7	To practice
John Burlison	c 1810-68	1841-68	Died. Ob. *The Builder*, xxvi, 911
James Burlison	c 1839-	1860-72	
Butters ·		1878	
A. W. H. Burder			
Burleigh		1839	
Somers Clarke	1841-1926	1865	To practice
J. R. Clayton		1863-9	

	Lived	In Scott's office	
Richard Coad		1847-64	To practice
W. Conradi		1870-6	
H. E. B. Coe	1826-85	1844-47	To practice. Ob. *The Builder*, xlix, 876
W. H. Crossland			To practice by 1858
Robert Edgar	c 1838-73	1859-62 and 1870-2	
Enright		1839	
Ensch		1839	
W. B. Fassnidge		1877	
C. J. Ferguson		1864	To practice with Cory
C. Hodgson Fowler	1840-1910	1856-60	To practice. Ob. *The Builder*, cxix, 794
G. E. Fuller			
Thomas Garner	1839-1906	1856-61	To practice
F. Garrard			
George Edwin Gwilt		1842	
W. J. Gillett			
Albert Hartshorne			
H. B. Hofland			To practice by 1858
Edward Hughes			
C. Hynam		1840s	
James Thomas Irvine	c 1825-1900	1854-78	To J. L. Pearson. Ob. *The Builder*, lxxviii, 593
Thomas Graham Jackson	1835-1924	1858-61	To practice. Jackson (ed), *Recollections of Thomas Graham Jackson*
Robert James Johnson	c 1831-92	1849-58	To practice. Ob. *The Builder*, lxii, 343, 353
William Jolley			
Frederick E. Jones		1868-78	
Charles Rt. Baker King	1838-1916	1859-78	To J. O. Scott. Ob. *The Builder*, cxi, 354, 385
R. Lamprell		1840s	
Lea		1839	
John Swanwick Lee	1828-83	1878	
John T. Micklethwaite	1843-1906	1862-9	To practice
W. H. Monkton		1877-8	

	Lived	In Scott's Office	
John Medland		1868-78	To J.O.Scott
Wm. Bonython Moffatt	c 1812-87	1835-46	Partner. To practice on own. Ob. *The Builder*, lii, 829
Benjamin W. Mountfort	1824-98	1841-6	To New Zealand
Edwin Nash	1814-84		Ob. *The Builder*, xlvii, 619
Geo. Newenham			
John Newton		1858	
Wm. J. Niven		1877	
John Norton		1870-8	
Edward (?) O'Brien		1853-8	
C.W.Orford		1840s	
E.F.Osborne			
E.Oliver		1840s	
J.M.Peddie			
Perkins		1878	
A. Kemp Potter			
C.E.Powell			
T.J.Ricauti	- c 1846 (?)	1839	Colvin, H.M., *Biog. Dict. Eng. Archts.*, 1954, 495
F.J.Robinson	c 1833-91		Ob. *The Builder*, lxii, 364
Edward Robert Robson	1835-1917	1854-9	To practice. *The Architectural Review*, cxxii, 393
R.Rowden			
Edward Rumsey		1840s	To New Zealand
George Gilbert Scott Junior	1839-97	1858-63	To practice
John Oldrid Scott	1842-1913	1858-78	Continued practice
C.J.Stafford			
John James Stevenson	1831-1908	1858-60	To practice
George Henry Stokes	c 1827-74	1843-7	To Sir Joseph Paxton
George Edmund Street	1824-81	1844-9	To practice. Street, *Memoir of G. E. Street, RA*
W.Strugnell		1878	

	Lived	In Scott's Office	
Edward Shears		1868	
Arthur B. Thompson		1867	
M. Thompson	-1878	1846-8	Ob. *Jnl. RIBA*, 1878, 6
George D. Tinling			Took holy orders 1868
Charles F. Tonge			
Hugh Thackeray Turner		1878	To J. O. Scott
Henry Walker			
Ward		1842-6	
W. S. Weatherley	1854-1922	1870-8	To J. O. Scott
William White	1825-1900	1845-7	To practice
George Wood		1870-8	
John Drayton Wyatt	1820-91	1841-67	To practice

Appendix 5
Clerks of Works

Ashbee		J. M. Johnston	1855
Bindley	1869	Kaberry	1873-8
Blackie	1870	Charles R. Baker King	1867
Charles Buckeridge	1856-62	Thomas Leigh	1867
James Burlison	1872-81	Little	1870-8
H. Cane	1867	E. G. S. Luscombe	1876
John T. Chapple		Marshall	1851-62
1826-87	1866-78	Merrick	1863
Chick or Cheaike	1862-6	Morgan	1867-78
Clark	1873-6	Mortimer	1842-5
G. Clarke	1853-4	Prosser	1878
J. B. Clear	1864-6	Henry Pulman	1867
George S. Cleverley	1853-8	H. Roome	1860-78
W. Conradi	1864	A. Roome	1871-8
William Cook	1865-71	Ruddle	1866-7
W. M. Cooper	1863-9	John Saville	1866-78
Dalby	1861-2	John Sheffield	1866-78
Darkin	1862-4	Shepherd	1856-7
Forrest	1874	Sissons	1862-3
James Frater	1868-75	H. R. Snelgrove	1871-8
Godfrey	1878	Nathaniel W. Vickers	1874-5
Charles Edwin Gwilt	1842-5	Willis˘	1875
George Hannaford	1870-8	Wills	1868
Hutchins	1864-6	James Yeoman	1864-75
James Thomas Irvine			
c 1825-1900	1854-73		

Index

The appendices on pages 205-227 and 232-236 are in alphabetical order and have not been included in the Index. The italic references are to photographic illustrations.

Abergwili, Carm., ch.   26, 27, *24, 25*
Abraham, H.R.   152
Aconbury, Heref., ch.   193
Akroyd, Edward   59, 71, 74, 75, 141, 172
Albert, Prince Consort   14, 56, 102, 117
Albourne, Sx., ch.   *72*
Alderney, C.I., St Anne   41, 58, 60, *34*
Alford, Lincs.,   3
Allen, Bruce   55, 141
Allport, James   150
Alnwick, Northd., cas.   70
Ambleside, Westd., ch.   20
Amersham, Bucks., P.L.I.   *8*
Amesbury, Wilts., P.L.I.   8
Amiens, cath.   48
Anderson, R.   168
Angell, Samuel   194
Anstey, Warks., ch.   82
Architectural Association   33, 40, 142
Architectural Museum   55-6, 85, 119, 141, 198
Armstead, H.H.   119, 121, 141, 191, 195
Arthington, W. Yorks., Ho.   194
Ascot, Berks., hospital   103
Ashbee, —   100
Ashby de la Zouch, Leics., Loudoun Meml.   169
Ashby Folville, Leics., ch.   111
Ashbourne, Derby, ch.   163
Ashley, Northants, bldgs.   128, 147, 149
Aston Sandford, Bucks.,   1
Atherstone, Warwick, ch.   131
Atkinson, J.B. & W.   *9*
Austin, George & H.G.   173
Aylesbury, Bucks., ch.   44-5, 47, 98, 190, 196, *38*

Baird, John   154
Baker, Arthur   182, 200
Baliol, John   1
Bangor, Carn., Cath.   65, 90, 137-8, 198
Barker, John W.   200
Barlow, W.H.   150
Barnes, Surrey, ch.   29, 189
Barnet, Herts., Christ Ch. 39:   pars. 39, *32*
Barnsbury, London, St Clement   115
Barnstaple, Devon, ch.   131-2
Barry, Sir Chas.   6, 22, 74, 81, 87, 153, 194:
   Chas. Jr. & R.R. Banks 74-5, 78-9, 151, 181:
   E.M.   117, 149-53, 194, 198
Barton, Admiral   69

Bath, Som., Abbey   90-2, 195:   Partis Coll. Chap.
   60:   St Andrew 143-4
Battlefield, Salop., ch.   103
Bayeux   98
Beanland, J. & W.   192, 196
Beckenham, Kent, Kelsey Pk.   116
Bedborough, A.   197
Beeston, Notts., ch.   29
Belfast, N.I., Cath.   191
Bell, John   119, 121
Bellamy, T.   74, 141
Benson, E.W.   117, 197
Bentley, John F.   193
Bentham, Jeremy, 'Panopticon'   9
Berlin, Parliament Ho.   149, 155, *128*
Bestwood, Notts., Ho.   72
Betley, Staffs., ch.   29, 188
Beverley, E. Yorks., Minster   5, 83-4
'Bible, The, with Explanatory Notes'   1
Bickersteth, Edw.H. 109, 193:   Robert 94
Bideford, Devon, P.L.I.   11
Bideford on Avon, Warwick   2
Bignall, Jabez 196, 200:   John 200
Bignold, John   87
Billings, James   138
Bilton in Ainsty, W.Yorks., ch.   130, 160
Birkinshaw, J.C.   195
Birmingham, Warwick, sch.   6:   St Mark 19, 20, 188
Bladwell, —   92
Blakesley, Northants, pars.   15
Bledlow, Bucks., ch.   166
Blomfield, A.W. 90-1, 172, 196-7:   Sir Reginald 81
Blore, Edward   13, 21, 29, 48, 50-1, 55, 67, 72, 74, 92, 136, 187
Bloxham, Oxon., ch.   39
Bodelwyddan, Denbigh, ch.   57
Bodley, Geo.F. 33-4, 87, 94, 140, 187, 191, 193, 196:   family 127, 189
Boiserè, Sulpice   36
Boitrel d'Hazeville   74
Bombay, University   *130*
Boston, Lincs. 3, 13:   St Botolph 29, 32, 189
Boxgrove, Sx., Priory   134, 160, 198
Boyce, —   33
Boys, H.Cowell   198
Bradfield, Berks., St Andrew 20, 42, 60, 62, *35, 36*:
   Sts Simon & Jude 190:   P.L.I. 190:
   sch. 42-3, 103, 190
Bradford, W. Yorks., Town Hall   71
Bradford on Avon, Wilts., ch.   180
Brandon, David   152, 198
Bratoft, Lincs.   1
Brecon, Priory   90, 92, 97, 196, *84*
Brereton, Staffs., ch.   166

Bressey, J. 114
Brettingham, Matthew, Sr. 167: R.F. 186
Bridlington, E. Yorks., Christ Ch. 19, 20, 188
Brighton, Sx. 3: college 53: baths 149, 194, *121*
Brill, Charles 149
Brindley, Wm., see Farmer & Brindley
Bristol, Cath. 64-5: St James 103: St Mary Redcliffe 147
Britton, John 13
Brock, — 195
Bromborough, Ches., St Barnabas 57
Brooks, James 187
Brunel, I.K. 194
Brydon, J. 82
Buckingham, ch. 130, 135, 179, *108*: gaol 187
Buccleuch, Duke of 52, 194
Buckeridge, Chas. 34, 103, 147, 189, 195
Buckland, Dr. (Dean) 16, 50-1, 187
Buckler, J.C. 84, 140-1
Buckley, Rev. W.C. 110
Burcot, Oxon., chapel 149
Burges, William 51, 68, 88, 141, 152, 161, 198
Burleigh, — 33
Burlison, James 87: John 33, 67, 86-7, 189
Burn, William 74, 79, 194
Burne-Jones, Edward 42, 85, 110, 115
Bury St Edmunds, Suffolk, St James 96-7, 196
Busbridge, Sy., ch. 142-3, 167
Bushby, — 196
Butterfield, William 28, 55-6, 96-7, 109, 116, 125, 191
Butters, — 200
Buxton, C. 74, 80

Cadeby, W. Yorks., ch. 193
Caernarvon, Lord 172
Calais 34, 52
Camberwell, London, Camden Cha. 60, *51*: St Giles 21, 23, 58, *18, 19, 20, 21*: Collegiate Sch. 6
Cambridge Camden Society, see Ecclesiological Society
Cambridge, Cemetery Chapel 60: Pembroke Coll. 184: St Mary the Great 84: St Michael 45-6: Trinity Coll. 45-6: University 2, 3, 94
Camden, Marquis 97
Cameron, — 35
Canterbury, Kent, Cath. 47, 65, 177-9
Capesthorne, Ches., Hall 74
Cardigan, Lord 168
Carlisle, Cumbd., Cath. 32, 64
Caroë, M. 198: W.D. 196
Carpenter, Richard C. 98
Carroll, Lewis (pseud.) 198
Carshalton, Sy., fountain 173
Castlechurch, Staffs., ch. 29, 111
Cattistock, Dorset, ch. 84-5
Cawdor, Earl 52
Chadwick, Edward 7: Dr. 123
Chambers, Sir Wm. 4, 185
Chantry, Som., ch. 39
Chapple, J.T. 134, 171-2, 189, 200
Cheddleton, Staffs., ch. & cross 103
Chesham, Bucks., ho. 6, *2*
Chesham, Lord 136
Chester, Cath. 43, 65, 89-91, 128, 177-8, *77, 78, 79*: Kings sch. 91: St John 91: St Thomas 143
Chesterfield, Derby, All Sts. 29, 31, 179, 189, *26*
Chetwode, Bucks., ch. 3, 39, 45
Chichester, Sx., Cath. 65, 93-4, 115, 196, *80, 81*

Chick (Cheaike), W. 34, 112, 189, 193
Christchurch, N.Z., Cath. 116
Christian, Ewan 90, 159, 161-2, 167, 172, 198
Chudleigh Knighton, Devon, Pitt Ho. 15: St Paul 19, 20, *17*
Church Missionary Society 2, 185
Cirencester, Glos., Holy Trinity 39-40, 190: St John Baptist 130, 141
'Clapham Sect' 2, 43
Clarendon, Lord 117
Clarke, Joseph 198: Somers, Sr. 55: Jr. 87, 145, 149-50
Clayton, J.R. 120, 191
Clayton & Bell 96, 101-2, 120, 130, 143, 160, 195
Clear, J.B. 98, 196
Cleobury Mortimer, Salop., ch. 165
Cleveland, Duke of 106
Cleverley, J.S. 193
Clifton, E. Yorks., asylum 14, *9*
Clifton Hampden, Oxon., bridge 124: ch. 29, 32-3, 189: pars. 15
Clutton, Henry 56, 88
Coad, Richard 87, 120, 189
Cockburn, Sir Alex. 152
Cockerell, C.R. 59, 79: F.P. 79, 149
Coe, Henry E. 74-5, 78, 87, 189
Colchester, Essex, St Nicholas 168
Cole, (Sir) Henry 56, 119
Collins, John 104: & Cullis 96-7, 176
Cologne Cath. 36, 59
Coningham, — 76
Conradi, W. 154
'Conservation of ancient architectural monuments and remains, On the' 112-13, 179
Continental travels, Scott's 34-7, 48, 54-5, 123, 158
Cornish, Robert 169
Corringham, Essex, ch. 29
Cotterill, Bishop 161
Cottingham, Lewis N. & Nockalls J. 42, 50-1, 55, 64-5, 98, 171-2, 190-1
Coventry, Warks., Holy Trinity 83: St John Baptist 165: St Michael 83
Cowper, Earl 172: Mr. 152-3: William 185
Cox, — 23-4, 47
Cradley, Herefs., Ch. 129-30
Cranstoun, James 96
Crowthwaite, Cumbd., ch. 29, 33, 189
Crossland, W.H. 71, 87
Crowland, Lincs., Abbey 83-4
Cubitt, William 117
Cundy, Samuel 51, 191
Cunningham, Rev. J.W. 2, 43: Peter 136
Curzon, Henry 188

Danbury, Essex, ch. 130, 165
Darbishire, H.A. 149
Darkin, — 196
Darlington, Durham, St Cuthbert 98, 106
Dawkes, Samuel W. 109
Dawlish, Devon, Luscombe 116
Deane (& Woodward) 74, 152
Dearman, Justice 183
Debenham, Suffolk, ch. 29, 189
de Grey, Earl 55-6
Denison, see Grimthorpe
Dent, Mrs 127
Derby, P.L.I. 12: St Andrew 143-4
Derby, Lord 78, 117, 180
Derick, John M. 40
Devey, George 147
Dinton, Bucks., vic. 15, 194

Donaldson, Prof. T. L. 78-9
Doncaster, W. Yorks., Christ Ch. 60, 193:
  cemy. cha. 64: St George 63-4, 163, 192-3, *57,
  58*: St James 64, 193
Donington Wood, Salop., ch. 27, 188
Dorchester, Oxon., Abbey 46, 96
Dorking, Sy., Pippbrook 70-1, 194
Dove Bros. 145
Dover, Kent, St Mary 108-9
Drumlanrig, Cas. 155
'Dublin Review' 22
Dufferin, Lord 54
Dunblane, Cath. 116, 147, 163
Duncombe, N. Yorks., Park 168
Dundee, Angus, Albert Inst. 149, 154-5, *126*:
  Old Town ch. 58: St Paul 58, 131
Dunkirk, Kent, ch. 20, 181
Durham, Cath. 65, 177
Dwyer, — 74
Dyserth, Flint, ch. 166

Ealing, Mddx., Christ Ch. 39
Earlswood, Surrey, Asylum 38
Earp, Thomas 138
Eastlake, Sir Chas. 117, 120: Chas. L. 158
Eastnor, Herefs., ch. 62, *52*: rec. 61-2
Ecclesiological Society 22-4, 31-2, 37, 40, 43-4,
  48, 57-8, 97, 99
'Ecclesiologist,' The' 22-4, 37, 40, 46, 48, 50, 84,
  102, 114, 123
Edensor, Derby, ch. 143
Edinburgh, Cath. 158, 161-3: St Giles 163
Edmeston, James, Sr. 4-6
Edvin Loach, Herefs., ch. 114, 197, *95*
Elcho, Lord 75, 78, 80
Eleanor Crosses 5, 15, 118, 169
Elgin, Cath. 163
Ellesmere, Salop., ch. 43, 98, 190: cemy. 190
Ellesmere, Earl of 29
Ely, Cambs., Cath. 47-50, 65, 91, 170, 191, *39,
  40, 41, 42*
Emberton, Bucks. 1
Englefield, Berks., ch. *73*
Enright, — 33
Ensch, — 33
Essex, James 47-9, 191, *39*
Eton, Berks., Coll. cha. 117
Evans (of Ellaston) 193
Eversley, Lord 194
Exeter, Devon, Cath. 65, 169-70, *134*
Exhibition, 1851 37, 51, 70: Paris 1855 37, 137:
  1862 66, 193. See also Royal Academy

'Faithful Restoration of our Ancient Churches'
  47, 179, 191
Farmer & Brindley 99, 101, 130, 163, 173, 192
Farnborough, Warks., ch. 165
Farncombe, Sy., ch. 24-5, 39, 166-7
Farnham, W. Yorks., ch. 62
Fassnidge, W. B., & — 116
Faversham, Kent, ch. 165
Feild, Bishop 40
Ferguson, C. J. 189
Fergusson, J. 79, 153
Ferrey, Benjamin 54, 65, 83, 168, 178, 192
Feversham, Earl 167-8
Fitzroy, Henry 124
Flaunden, Bucks., ch. 16-18, 136
Fleet Marston, Bucks., ch. *107*
Flint 17, 26, 42, 59, 62, 82, 188
Florence, Or San Michele 118
Foley, John H. 119-21

Forest Hill, Oxon., ch. 62
Forman, W. H. 70
Foulston, John 166
Fowke, Capt. 119
Fowler, Charles 5: Charles H. 87, 172, 174, 187:
  James 103
Frampton, Lincs., ch. 115
Frater, James 195
Freehay, Staffs., ch. 25
Freeman, Archdeacon 170
Frogmore, Herts., ch. 19, 187
Fulljames, Thomas 100
Fulney, Lincs., ch. etc. 160, 199
Fussell, — 39

Garlick, — 198
Garling, Henry B. 74, 79, 80, 152, 189
Garner, Thomas 87
Gawcott, Bucks. 2, 3, 5
Gawsworth, Ches., ch. 192
Geflowski, Edward 131, 190
Gibbs, Geo. H. 26: Henry H. 33
Gibson, John 57, 152
Gilbert, family 2: Bishop 93: Nathaniel 2,
  185
Glasgow, St Mary 20, 143: University 149,
  153-4, *127*
Glastonbury, Som., Abbott's Kitchen 154:
  schs. 103
Glasynfryn, Carns., ch. 142
'Gleanings from Westminster Abbey' 51, *111,
  113*
Glenalmond Coll., Perth 103, 196
Gloucester, Cath. 61, 65, 100-2, 191: All Saints
  160, *129*: St James 17
Godalming, Sy., ch. 167, 199
Goddard, Henry 103
Godfrey, — 200
Godstone, Sy., almshouses 147, *119*: ch. 132,
  134, *104*: Rooks-nest 127, 155, 158, 198
Godwin, George 153
Graeme, Yarburgh 40
Grahamstown, S. Africa, Cath. 162
Grantham, Lincs., St Wulfran 130, 134-5
Great Dunmow, Essex, P. L. I. 12, 13, 186, *6*
Great Malvern, Worcs., Priory 61
Great Marlow, Bucks., All Saints 198
Great Milton, Oxon., ch. 46, 191
Great Northern Railway 64
Great Western Railway 26
Great Yarmouth, Suffolk, ch. 103
Green, A. H. 57
Green Hammerton, W. Yorks., ch. & sch. 159,
  160
Greenstead Green, Essex, ch. 25, 188: sch. & ho.
  188
Grey, Gen. Chas. 118, 197
Grimthorpe, Lord 63-4, 124, 136, 153, 169, 171,
  192-4
Grissell & Peto 5
Guest, Sir Josiah 13
Guildford, Surrey, P. L. I. *5*
Gwilt, Edwin 32

Habershon, Edward 74
Haddon, G. C. 61
Haden, — 195
Halesowen, Staffs., ch. 165
Halifax, W. Yorks., All Souls 59, 146, 192, *49, 50*:
  vic. 71: St John Baptist 164: Town Hall
  71, 74
Halstead, Essex, Holy Trinity 26-7

Ham, Sy., The Manor Ho. 127-8, 158, 180
Hamburg, Nikolaikirche 34-7, 60, 67, *31*:
    Rathaus 71, *61*
Hamilton, Bishop 89
Hampstead, London, Christ Ch. 109-10:
    Grove Ho. 69
Hampton Lucy, Warks., ch. 60, *54*
Hanley Swan, Worcs., ch. 143
Hannaford, George 200
Hanwell, Mddx., ch. 19, 187-8
Hardman, John 99, 106
Hardwick, P.C., Sr. 117: Jr. 151
Hardwick, Oxon., ch. 164
Hardy, Thomas 156-7
Harewood, Lord 52, 103, 192
Harmondsworth, Mddx., barn 190
Harrison, J.P. 96: Thomas 89
Harrow, Mddx., liby. 71, 80, *37, 63*: sch. chap.
    59, 190, *37*: St Mary 2, 20, 43, 190, *37*
Hartshill, Staffs., ch. 21, 187-8
Haswell, — 195
Hawarden, Flint, ch. 98
Hawkhurst, Kent, All Saints 114-15, *90, 91, 92*
Hawkstone, Salop., chapel 60
Haycock, Edw., Jr. 197
Hayward, Jas. 170: P.B. 170
Headington, Oxon., ch. 140
Heckington, Lincs., ch. 59, 177
Henderson, John 103
Henllan, Denbigh, ch. 57
Hereford, Cath. 64-6, 89, 191, 193, *59*
Heston, Mddx., ch. 141
Higginson, Edmund 114, 197
Higham, Suffolk, ch. & rec. 114
Highclere, Hants., ch. 143
Highnam, Glos., Ch. 191
Hildesden, Bucks., ch. 3, 164, 179: vic. 164
Hillingdon, Mddx., barn 190: St Andrew 116
Hills, Gordon M. 144
Hine, Thos.C. 149
Hiorn, William 135, 190
Histon, Cambs., ch. 168
Hixon, Staffs., ch. 39
Hoare, Henry & Peter 116
Hofland, H.B. 74-5, 78
Holborn, London, Kings Coll. Cha. 60:
    Law Courts 149, 151-3, 198, *125*: Lincolns Inn
    169, *132*
Holyrood Abbey 163
Homerton 4
Honeyman, John 154
Hook, Dean 93, 161, 165, 196
Hope, A.J.B.Beresford 69, 75-7, 141, 152, 173,
    177-8, 181, 194
Horne, Melville 185
Hougham, Lincs., ch. 29
Hudson, Octavius 89, 193
Hull, E. Yorks. 5: Holy Trinity 106:
    St Mary 2, 106
Hulme, Lancs., Holy Trinity 19, 20
Hunt, Holman 50: — 80
Huntingdon, Hunts., ch. 106
Hurst, William 60
Hussey, R.C. 89-90, 195
Hynam, C. 189

Ilam, Staffs, bldgs. at 62-3: Dwg. Socy. 192
Inglesham, Wilts., ch. 176
Irvine, James T. 57, 87, 182-3, 196, 200
Islington, London, St Clement 115: St Matthew
    39, 40

Jackson, Thomas G. 81, 85-6, 93, 126, 192, 195-7
James & Price 97
Jarrow, Durham, ch. 106, 114, 177
Jebb, John 89
Jedburgh, Abbey 163, 168
Jeffreys, Rev. H.A. & Miss 114
Johnson, John 188
Jones (drawing master) 3: Owen 149: — 200

Kaberry, — 200
Keating, Justice 170
Kelham, Notts., Hall 72-3, 81, 147
Kelk, John 119, 121-2
Kelso, Abbey 163
Kemble, Rev. Charles 92
Kempe, C.E. 163
Kempthorne, Sampson 6, 7, 9, 10, 17, 186
Kenley, Sy., ch. 103
Kennedy, Henry 137
Kensington, London, Albert Mem. 1, 117-22,
    155-6, 197, *101*: Courtfield Ho. 180-1:
    Kensington Gore bldgs. 118-19: St Mary
    Abbots 143-7, *118*
Kerr, Robert 74
Kettlethorpe, W. Yorks., Hall 47
Ketton, Rutland, ch. 108, 197
Kiddington, Oxon., ch. 60
King, Bishop 91-2: Chas.R.Baker 87, 106, 200:
    Samuel 3-5, 16, 127, 136
Kings Langley, Herts., Priory 5
Kings Lynn, Norfolk, St Margaret 167
Kirkby Moorside, N. Yorks. 168
Kirkstall, W. Yorks., Abbey 168
Kirtlington, Oxon., ch. 168

Lamb, Edward B. 58, 110
Lambeth, London 86: Waterloo Rd. 50-1:
    Palace 115: St Agnes 184
Lamprell, R. 189
Latimer, Bucks. 3: ch. 136, 186, *116*
Law, Edmund F. 103, 147
Lawlor, John 120
Layard, Sir Austin 120-1
Lea, — 33
Leafield, Oxon., ch. 82, 146, 166, *69*
Leaver, — 160
Lechmere, Sir Edmund 175
'Lectures on the Rise and Development of
    Medieval Architecture' 95, 183
Ledbury, Herefs., ch. 62, 81
Lee, & Dewsbury 12: John S. 200
Leeds, W. Yorks., All Souls 161: bank 124:
    Infirmary 122-4, 197, *102*: St Andrew 27-8:
    St John 132-3, 179, *105*: St Peter 165
Leicester, St John 59: St Mary 108:
    St Matthew 143: St Saviour 160
Leigh, Lord 24
Leith, Midlothian, St James & pars. 115-16, 114,
    147, *99, 100*
le Mesurier, John 41
Leominster, Herefs., ch. 104-7: 196
Leopold, King of the Belgians 14
Lessels, — 161
l'Estrange, Henry 50, 191
Lethaby, W.R. 86
Le Vau, — 81
Lewes, Sx., Fitzroy Liby. 124, 154, 198
Lewis, Thomas F. 186
Lewisham, London, St Stephen 143-4
Leytonstone, London, chapel 4
Lichfield, Staffs. 5: Cath. 21, 55, 64-7, 99,
    193-4, *60*

Liddell, H.G. 138, 140, 198
Lincoln, Cath. 55, 65, 140, 191, *115*: St Nicholas 17, *13*
Little, — 189
Little Horsted, Sx., ch. 111
Littlemore, Oxon., ch. 187
Liverpool, Lancs., Cath. 184: coll. 13
Llandaff, Glam., Cath. 64, 179
Llangurig, Montg., ch. 164-5
Lloyd, — 149
Lockwood (& Mawson) 149, 152, 198
London & Middlesex Archaeological Society 67
London, Fishmongers' Hall 6, *3*: Grocers' Hall 124, 198: National Provincial Bank 152: Offices, Lothbury 55: Public Record Office 137: Royal Exchange 13, 75: St Alban, Wood St. 84, 195, *74*: St Andrew, Holborn 191: St Michael, Cornhill 84, 109, 195: St Olave, Hart St. 195: St Paul's Cath. 64, 77, 91
Longton, Staffs., Holy Evangelists 188, 192: Resurrection 56, 192, *46*
Loughborough, Leics., ch. 108
Louth, Lincs., ch. 6
Loversal, W. Yorks., ch. 193
Lower, M.A. 111
Lucknow, India, Cath. 20
Ludlow, Salop., St Lawrence 87, 104, 196: St Leonard .142, *116*
Lutterworth, Warks., ch. 130
Lutyens, (Sir) Edwin 143
Lynam, C. 124, 192
Lynch, see Scott

McCann, — 61
MacDowell, Patrick 120
MacFarlane, Rev. 96
Maddox, George 4, 5
Maddingley, Cambs., Hall 168
Maids Moreton, Bucks., ch. 3
Mainwaring family 57, 190, 192
Manchester, Albert Mem. 118: Cath. 145, 169: Town Hall 151
Manners, G.P. 92: Lord John 75-8, 153, 181
Mansfield Woodhouse, Notts., ch. 190
Market Harborough, Leics., ch. 106
Marochetti, Baron Carlo 119-21
Marshall, Wm.C. 120: — 196
Mason, W.H. 195
Massie, Rev. Edward 192
Maxwell, Sir William S. 152
Medland, John 200
Melbourne, Vic., Cath. 116
Melton Mowbray, Leics., ch. 60, 106, 192, 196
Merrick, — 103
Micklethwaite, John T. 87, 132, 145
Middleton Cheney, Oxon., ch. 110
Minton, Herbert 21, 113, 187: Rev. Thomas W. 20
Mirfield, W. Yorks., ch. 143, *117*
Mitford, Miss 3, 62: A.B.F. 181
Moffatt, William B. 4, 6, 8, 9, 12-16, 20, 21, 24, 28, 31, 33, 34, 36-9, 41, 186-90
Mold, Flint, ch. 60
Monkton, W.H. 200
Moore, L.T. 189: Temple L. 184, 189
Mordaunt, Sir Charles 72
Morgan, — 200
Moriarty, — 86
Morris, William 83, 110, 112, 114, 115, 130, 155, 172, 174-6, 179-80
Mortimer, — 189
Moulsford, Berks., ch. 39

Mountfort, Benjamin W. 33, 116
Murray, John 69, 111, 183
Muswellbrook, N.S.W., Australia, ch. 114, *93*, *94*

Nailsea, Som., ch. 25
Nantwich, Ches., ch. 43, 61, 89, 192
Nash, John 86, 99, 116
Neale, John M. 22, 172
Nesfield, W.E. 149
Nevill, Ralph 199
New Romney, Kent, ch. 164
New Southgate, Mddx., St Michael 159-60: St Paul 160
Newark, Notts., ch. 60, 135, *53*
Newcastle on Tyne, Northd., Assize Court 169: St Nicholas 159-60
Newcastle under Lyme, Staffs., St Giles 160-1
Newman, John H. 21-2, 78, 187
Newton, Charles 121: John 185
Nicholls, George 186
Nichols & Lynam 124
Nicholson, Sir Charles 82: Peter 4, 185: Thomas 105
Nightingale, Florence 123
Norbiton, Sy., St Peter 19, 20, 26
Norfolk, Duke of 93
North Aston, Oxon. 131
North Staffordshire Infy. 134
Northampton, St Peter 60-1, 108, 192: St Sepulchre 108-9, 196-7
Norton, Radnor, ch. 135, *109*
Norton, Hon. George 47: — 200
Nottingham, St John Baptist 27: St Mary 41-2, 98, 190
Norwich, Norfolk, Cath. 65

Oakham, Rutland, ch. 83
Oldfield, Edward 23
Oldrid, Caroline see Scott: Euphemia (Scott) 3, 127: John Henry 3, 32
Oliver, E. 189
Olney, Bucks., ch. 165
Orcagna 118
Orchardleigh, Som., ch. 164, 199
Orford, C.W. 189
Osborn, — 195
Osborne, I.O.W., Ho. 136
Ottershaw, Sy., ch. 57, 116: pars. 116
Oundle, Northants., ch. 108
Ouvry, Frederic 181
Overend & Gurney 150
Oxford Archaeological Socy. 32, 46, 64: Movement 21-2
Oxford, Cath. 65, 138-41, 145: Exeter Coll. 83-4, 116, *70*, *71*: Martyrs' Meml. 15-16, 23, 50, 69, *12*: Merton Coll. 140: New Coll. 140, 169, *138*: Radcliffe Infy. 147: St Mary Magdalen 16-17, 187: St Mary the Virgin 84, 140, 147, 195

Padua 54
Padworth, Berks., ch. 42
Paisley, Abbey 147, 163
Palmer, Sir Roundell 152
Palmerston, Viscount 75-80, 119
Paris, Louvre 80-1: Sainte-Chapelle 67, 83, 117
Parker, John H. 62, 158
Parnell & Smith 53
Parry, T.Gambier 50, 100, 191
Parsons, — 103, 192
Patteson, Bishop 170

Pavings, John 158, 180-2
Paxton, Sir Joseph 34
Peacock, Dean 48-9
Pearson, John L. 67, 182, 191, 193-4: & Son 112
Peddie & Kinnear 161
Pendell Co., Sy. 194
Penkhull, Staffs., St Thomas 19, 20, 187
Pennethorne, James 75, 80, 117, 137
Penshurst, Kent, ch. 62
Penson, R. Kyrke 104
Perkin, William B. 124
Perkins, A.E. 99: — 200
Perry, J. 167
Pershore, Worcs., Abbey 94, 96, *83*
'Personal & Professional Recollections' 126, 156, 176, 183, 187
Peterborough, Northants., Cath. 5, 64-5, 67, 87, 191: Training Sch. 71, 194
Peterstow, Herefs., ch. 193
Petit, Rev. J.L. 141, 178
Peto, Samuel M. 5
Philip, John B. 50, 119, 121, 155, 191, 193, 195
Phillpotts, Archdeacon 170
Phipson, R.M. 114
Pinner, Mddx., ch. 20
Place, G.G. 32, 193
Plymouth, Devon, St Andrew 166, 199
Pollard, — 98
Polwhele, Cwl., Ho. 194
Polychrome 56-7
Poor Law Institutions 6-13, 85, 186
Pope & Bindon 103
Porden, William 149
Potter, — 160
Pownall, George 152, 194
Pratt, — 23
'Present State of Christian Architecture' 22
Preston, Lancs., liby. 124: markets 124: Town Hall 124, *103*
Pritchard, John 74, 103, 179
Pritchett, S.T. 106
Prosser, — 200
Prussia, Crown Princess of 118, 155
Public Baths & Wash-houses 13
Pugin, A.C. 192: Augustus W.N. 15, 20-3, 29, 65, 69, 144, 153, 189
Pultenay, Rev. Richard 147
Pusey, Edward B. 21
Pywell, W. 187

Queenhill, Worcs., ch. 62

Ramsgate, Kent, Christ Ch. 39: St Augustine 39: ho. 69
Ranmore, Sy., ch. 55, 82, 115
Rattee & Kett 192
Reading, Berks., gaol 14
Redfern, James 100-1, 119, 155
Redgrave, Richard 181
Redpath, — 64, 193
Reed, Dr. Andrew 13
'Remarks on Secular and Domestic Architecture' 68-70
Ricauti, T.J. 33
Richmond, Sy., St Matthias 82, 195
Rickman, Thomas 60
Rievaulx, N. Yorks., Abbey 168
Ripon, N. Yorks., Cath. 94-5, *82*
Ripon, Lord 156
Roberts, David 194: Henry 5-6
Robson, Edward R. 87, 173-4
Rochead, — 74

Rochester, Kent, Cath. 65, 172, *135*
Roddis, — 100
Rome, St Peter 155
Roome, H. and A. 200
Ross, Alex. 161
Rossetti, D.G. 115
Royal Academy 3, 6, 14, 37, 40, 48, 57-8, 66-7, 71, 74, 79, 80, 87, 95, 121, 124, 142, 158, 181, 183, 191, 193
Royal Commission on Historical Monuments 51, 196
(Royal) Institute of British Architects 53, 55, 68, 78-9, 87, 112, 113, 158, 177, 181
Rubens workshop 87
Ruddle & Thompson 193
Rugby, Warks., Holy Trinity 58, 117
Rumsey, Edward 189: Henry 6
Rushforth & Luck 187
Ruskin, John 23, 54, 55, 60, 113, 159, 173, 179
Russell, Jesse Watts 31, 62
Ryde, I.O.W., All Saints 20, 143, 147
Rylands, Miss 115

St Albans, Herts., Abbey 171-2, 177-9: Gorhambury 136: St Michael 135-6, 179
St Asaph, Flint, Cath. 65, 138, *114*
St Austell, Cwl,, P.L.I. 14
St Blazey, Cwl., ch. 14, 15, 187, *11*
St David, Pemb., Cath. 65, 97-8, 179, *85*, *86*
St Hilary, Glam., ch. 111, *89*
St John, Newfoundland, Cath. 40-1, 190, *33*
St John's Wood, Avenue Rd., ho. 34
St Lawrence, I.O.W., ch. 160
St Pancras, London, model dwellings 38: station 1, 124, 149-52, 155, 183, *122*, *123*, *124*
Salisbury, Wilts., Cath. 65, 88-9, 98, 115, 127, 135, 163, 170, 195, *75*, *76*
Salter, Samuel 169: Stephen 33, 37, 115
Salviati, — 191, 196
Salvin, Anthony, Sr. 72, 74, 81: Jr. 54
Sandbach, Ches., ch. 43, 89, 190
Sang, Frederick 150
Sarratt, Herts., ch. 128, 133-4, *106*
Savernake, Wilts., hosp. 147-8, *120*
Saville, John 103, 200
Sawbridgeworth, Essex, ch. 131
Scarborough, E. Yorks., St Martin 193
Scholefield, Rev. Prof. 46
Schopenhauer, Artur 35
Scott, Adrian Gilbert 184: Albert Henry 34, 127: Alwyne 127, 158, 184: Benjamin 2: Caroline (Oldrid) 5, 13, 34, 38, 123, 126-7, 155-6: Charles M.O. 173, 182: Dukinfield H. 158, 182-4: Euphemia (Lynch) 2, 127: Euphemia, see Oldrid: Sir Francis 54: George Gilbert Jr. 13, 85, 93-4, 103, 120, 143, 164, 180-4, 187, 190, 199: Giles Gilbert 183-4, 190: Jane (Kell) 2: John (1701-77) 1: John (1779-1834) 2, 5, 185: John (1809-65) 106, 127, 197: John (1809-86) 3, 35, 160: John Oldrid 13, 40-2, 59, 60, 85, 89, 91, 103, 116, 126-7, 137, 143, 145, 151, 155, 158, 161, 163, 169, 172, 173, 180-3, 190-5, 198-9: Mary Ann (Stevens) 180, 190: Mary Jane 127: Melville Horne 3, 144: Nathaniel G. 3: Richard G. 184: Robert 198: Samuel King 3, 127, 189: Thomas (1747-1821) 1-2, 185: Thomas (1780-1835) 2-3, 6-7: Thomas (1807-80) 3: William L. 3, 40, 182
Sedding, J.D. 172
Seddon, J.P. 74, 152, 179
Seedley, Lancs., ch. 143

Selby, W. Yorks., Abbey 5, 172-3
Semper, Gottfried 36
Sewerby, E. Yorks., ch. 40
Shackleford, Sy., ch. 143-5, 167
Shaftesbury, Dorset, Holy Trinity 19, 20, 187-8, *14, 15*
Shalstone, Bucks., ch. 55, 111-12
Shaw, John, Sr. 198: Jr. 117, 152: R. Norman 81, 117, 132, 149, 179
Sheffield, John 200
Shellard, E. H. 38
Sherborne, Dorset, Abbey 98
Sherbourne, Warks., ch. 115, *96, 97*
Shere, Sy., ch. 179
Shields, F. W. 88, 121
Shinfield, Berks. 3: ch. 42, 62, *55, 56*
Shippon, Berks., ch. 57
Shrewsbury, Salop., asylum 14
Sinclair, Archdeacon 144
Skidmore, James 66, 83, 89, 99, 120, 130, 141, 149, 155, 160, 192, 193, 195
Skirbeck, Lincs., ch. 27, 188
Slater, William 93-4, 193
Sleaford, Lincs., ch. 13
Smirke, Sir Robert 5, 101: Sydney 58, 66, 79, 117, 193
Smith, George 86: S. Pountney 103: — 35: — 112
Snelgrove, H. R. 200
Soane, Sir John 6
Society for the Protection of Ancient Buildings 175, 194
Society of Antiquaries 87, 181
Sorby, Thomas C. 149-50
South Weald, Essex, ch. 165
Southampton, Hants., St Denys 142-3
Southey, Robert 33
Southgate, Mddx., Christ Ch. 115
Spalding, Lincs., St Peter 199
Speechley, — 116
Spring Gardens Sketching Club 141-2
Stafford 3: St Mary 29, 31-2, 98, *27, 28, 29:* St Chad 167
Stanger, James 189
Stanhope, Lord 194
Stanley, Arthur (Dean) 52, 137, 141, 181: Lord 75-6
Stephen, James 2
Stephenson, Robert 51
Stevens, Thomas 20-1, 31, 42-3, 188, 190
Stevenson, J. J. 87, 176-9
Stirling, — 75, 194
Stoke Goldington, Bucks. 1
Stoke Newington, London, St Mary 58-9
Stoke Talmage, Bucks., ch. 110, *88*
Stokes, George H. 34
Stone: Alabaster 99, 102: Ancaster 114, 169: Bargate 143: Bath 14, 59, 142, 146, 199: Bolsover Moor 16: Blyth Marsh 161: Caen 23, 41, 47: Cefn 43: Chilmark 88: Granite 41, 117, 120, 149: Grinshill 43: Headington 84: Hornton 110: Kentish Rag 23, 59, 116, 144, 146: Mansfield Woodhouse 16, 42: Marble 59, 71, 84, 146: Milton 169: Minden 37: Portland 136, 149: red sandstone 43, 89: Roche Abbey 16: Runcorn sandstone 90: Sneaton 14, 23: Steetley 63: York 5
Stourport, Worcs., St Michael 161, 199
Stowe, Bucks. 3
Stowford, Devon, ch. 164
Strack, — 36

Street, George E. 35, 40, 55, 74, 81, 86, 87, 110, 125, 151-3, 159, 161, 172, 177, 181, 189, 193, 198
Stroud, Glos., ch. 131
Stuart & Revett 4, 185
Sudbury, Suffolk, ch. 58
Sudeley Castle, Glos. 127
Sutherland, Duke of 188
Sutton Coldfield, Warks., ch. 196
Sutton, St Mary, Lincs., ch. 39
Swallowcliffe, Wilts., ch. 26, 27
Swindon, Wilts., Christ Ch. 59: St Mark 26-8, 33, 40, 63, 64, 166
Sydney, N. S. W., Parliament Ho. 154

Tadcaster, W. Yorks., ch. 165
Tandridge, Sy., ch. 156, 165
Tattersall, George 53
Taunton, Som., assize hall 38: St Mary 83
Tavistock, Devon, P. L. I. *4*
Teale, — 193
Tedstone Wafre, Herefs., ch. 197
Teffont Evias, Wilts., rec.. 15
Temple, Bishop 170
Teulon, Samuel S. 56, 60, 72, 74, 114, 165
Tewkesbury, Glos., Abbey 175-6, 191, *136, 137*
Theed, William 102, 119
Thirlwall, Connop, Bishop 26, 97, 99
Thompson, Gen. 76: — 193, 195
Thomson, Dr. Allan 180
Thoresby, Lincs., Ho. 72, 81
Thorneycroft, Thomas 120
Thornton, Henry 2: William 83
Thorpe, Edmund 159
Thynne, Lord John 51
Tidmarsh, Berks., ch. 42
Tiles: see stone Godwin's 112, 130, 146-7, 160, 192: Maw's 149: Minton's 21, 96, 113, 130: roofing, Broseley 130, 142
Tinglewick, Bucks., ch. 3
Tite, Sir William 13, 75, 78, 117, 152-3
Tiverton, Devon, P. L. I. 12, 13
Tonge, Charles F. 200
'Tractarians' 21, 187
Traherne, Rev. J. M. & Mrs. 111
Trefnant, Denbigh, ch. 57, 82, 192, *47, 48*
Trench, R. Chenevix 52
Triqueti, Baron H. de 196
Trubshaw, Thomas 166
Truefitt, George 53
Turner, H. Thackeray 180, 200
Turnham Green, Mddx., ch. 19, 23, 83, 187, 188, 194, *16*
Tydd St Giles, Cambs. 3

Underriver, Kent, ch. 142
Underwood, A. J. 187
Upton Bishop, Herefs., ch. 112, 193
Uttoxeter, Derby, P. L. I. 20

Venice, Scott in 54
Venn, John 2
Verona, S. Fermo 60
Victoria, Queen 117-22, 145, 156
Vincent, Dean 137
Viollet-le-Duc, Eugene 67-8
Voysey family 186
Vulliamy, Lewis 172

Wailes, William 191, 192
Wakefield, W. Yorks., bridge cha. 46-7: St Andrew 47
Walker, Misses B. & M. 161

Wall, Staffs., ch. 15, 187
Waller, F.S. 100-2
Wallis, — 141
Walsingham, Alan de 48-9
Walters, Edward 149-50
Walton, Warks., Hall 72-4, *67*
Walton, — 173
Wanstead, Essex, asylum 13-14, 186: ch. 114
Wappenham, Northants., ho. 15: rec. 6
Warmington, Northants., ch. 115
Warwick, Cas. 155
Washingborough, Lincs., ch. 103
Wasperton, Warks., ch. 29, 198-9
Waterhouse, Alfred 151-3, 198
Weatherley, W.S. 95, 179, 183, 200
Webb, Sir Aston 59, 190: Benjamin 22:
    Philip 110, 175, 190
Weekes, Henry 120
Weeton, W. Yorks., ch. 58, 192
Wellington College, Berks. 117, 197
Wells, Som., asylum 14: Cath. 65
Welshampton, Salop., ch. 57, 192
Wembley, Mddx., ch. 24, 25, 188
West Derby, Lancs., ch. 58
West Meon, Hants., ch. 26-7
Westminster, London, Abbey & Chapter Ho. 3,
    50-2, 76-7, 87, 134, 136-7, 141, 181, 191, 194, *43,
    44, 45, 112, 113*: Army & Navy Club 52:
    Broad Sanctuary hos. 150: Carlton Chambers
    (offices) 6, 8, 13: Dean's Yard hos. 77:
    Government Offices 74-82, 151, 155, 194-5, *68*:
    Houses of Parliament 22, 77: Hungerford
    Market 5, 185: Lock Hospital 1: National
    Gallery 151-2: New Scotland Yard 81:
    Park Lane, ho. 38: St Andrew 58: 20, later
    31, Spring Gardens (house, offices) 13, 34, 85-7,
    186
Weston Turville, Bucks., rec. 15
Weston Underwood, Bucks. 1-2
Westwood Heath, Warks., ch. 24, 25
Whichcord, John, Sr. 187
Whitby, E. Yorks., almshouses 15
White, William 57, 134, 172

Whitehall, ho. 74
Whitland Abbey slates 146
Wilberforce, Samuel, Bishop 44, 47, 117, 140:
    William 2
Wilkinson, George 187
Willement, Thomas 104
Williams, Herbert & H.J. 195
Williamson, Dr. 96
Willis, Prof. 48, 66
Wimbledon, Sy., St Mary 27, 188
Winchester, Hants., Cath. 65, 169: City Cross
    140: St Cross 109
Windsor, Berks., Castle 102, 196: P.L.I. 9, *7*
Wing, Bucks., ch. 47, 191
Wirksworth, Derby, ch. 130
Wisbech, Cambs. 3: Clarkson Mont. 169, *133*
Witham, Essex, window 189
Withers, Robert J. 111
Woking, Surrey, St John 25, 188, *22*
Wood, George 171, 200: John 179: & Sons
    98
Wood Green, Mddx., St Michael 24, 25, 188
Woodyer, Henry 191
Woolland, Dorset, ch. 57-8, 67, 192
Woolwich, London, chapel 83, 194
Worcester, Cath. 65, 99-100, 196, *87*
Worsley, Lancs., ch. 27, 29, 30, 190
Worthington, Thomas 118
Wren, Sir Christopher 84: Jane 98
Wyatt, Digby 75, 80, 81, 117, 151, 152: G. 191:
    James 65-7, 88-9, 140: Jeffrey 87: John D.
    33, 67, 71, 87, 127, 141, 196, 197, *40, 50*: Lewis
    137: T.H. 151

Yankalilla, S. Australia, ch. 195
Yarpole, Herefs., ch. 112
Yiewsley, Mddx., ch. 57, 82
York, Minster 5, 58, 65
Ypres, Belgium, public buildings 37, 71

Zeals, Wilts., ch. & sch. 25, 188, *23*
Zwirner, — 36